Advance Praise for *Sav*

Joy

Some of it)!
Best
always!
Holly

2/2019

pg. 25 ✳

"Having visited these remarkable dunes, I'm all the more taken by the exciting story of their conservation. On a troubled planet, it is stories like this that provide deep and abiding hope. This is a lovely book."
—Bill McKibben, author of *Deep Economy*

"A heartwarming story of hope and preservation that will inspire all communities to follow their heart in preserving those places that mean so much. Heather Shumaker brings a fresh new voice to the importance of conservation. For those who were part of the journey, you'll cherish this memoir of our experience; and for those who are new to this amazing conservation accomplishment, I encourage you to sit down with this great read, for you'll be inspired to never give up and to pursue what is most important to you."
—Helen Taylor, Michigan State Director, The Nature Conservancy

"*Saving Arcadia* is a wonderful book about an epic effort to preserve a large area of pristine dunes on Lake Michigan and highly productive adjoining farm land. The way in which a couple tiny communities came together over a period of years, raising funds at suppers and bake sales and joining with visionary philanthropists in a dramatic race against commercial development is told in this riveting account. As the drama unfolded, at times the race seemed lost, only to be rescued in a 'Perils of Pauline' fashion by long hours of work, passionate presentation, by seeming miracle or sheer luck. Heather Shumaker's love affair with Arcadia and the people of the region suffuses each page and produces a compelling story, often heart-stopping and always heartwarming. *Saving Arcadia* is a beautifully told tale, full of hope for our future."
—U.S. Senator Carl Levin (retired)

"Heather Shumaker tells the story of the saving of Arcadia Dunes with passion and clarity and with the authority of one who was there from the beginning. I highly recommend this book to everyone who cares not just about the Great Lakes and their freshwater dunes but about the importance of preserving land and water for the well-being of all living things."
—Jerry Dennis, author of *The Living Great Lakes*

"*Saving Arcadia* is the untold chronicle of thousands of people committing thousands of selfless acts, backlit by the sweep of dune, the rush of blue water. *Saving Arcadia* is an essential portrait of the most rewarding work there is: saving the land we love and telling its story even as the land changes us. This history of one of our most beautiful and quintessential places will sit alongside Roger Tory Peterson and *A Sand County Almanac* and should be read by their enthusiasts as well as businesspeople and others working to create social and environmental change. By saving Arcadia, a way of life is preserved, too."

—Doug Stanton, *New York Times* bestselling author
and co-founder of the National Writers Series in Traverse City

"What better, in the 'no place of cyberspace,' to discover than Heather Shumaker's nonfiction account of land reclamation and preservation. *Saving Arcadia* did for me what reading John Muir, Wendell Berry, and Annie Dillard always does: It buoyed my spirits, and made me want to plant a copy of this wonderful book in the hands of every reader I know."

—Jack Driscoll, author of *The Goat Fish and the Lover's Knot*
(Wayne State University Press, 2017)

"In a world where so often Goliath wins, Heather Shumaker tells a David and Goliath tale that will startle, frighten, and delight you in both its threat and its humanity. At stake? The stunning tract of land known as the Arcadia Dunes, including its miles of Lake Michigan shoreline, forests, open land, orchards, and rare flora and fauna. Heather Shumaker takes us on a dune ride of astonishing tension to resolution that is both hopeful and real. The writing is clean and the story utterly absorbing."

—Anne-Marie Oomen, author of *Love, Sex and 4-H*
(Wayne State University Press, 2015),
winner of the Next Generation Indie Award
(in the category of memoir)

"This is a book of national significance. It is a story of a monumental accomplishment in conservation, but it's much more than that. Heather Shumaker's graceful prose and storytelling skill make it entertaining, unforgettable reading. *Saving Arcadia* makes you care about individual people, a great place, and a rich legacy for our descendants."

—Dave Dempsey, co-author of *The Great Lake Sturgeon*
(2014 Michigan Notable Book award winner)

Saving Arcadia

SAVING ARCADIA

A STORY OF CONSERVATION AND COMMUNITY IN THE GREAT LAKES

Heather Shumaker

A Painted Turtle book
Detroit, Michigan

ISBN 978-0-8143-4204-6 (paperback)
ISBN 978-0-8143-4205-3 (e-book)
Library of Congress Control Number: 2016959427

Painted Turtle Books is an imprint of Wayne State University Press

Wayne State University Press
Leonard N. Simons Building
4809 Woodward Avenue
Detroit, Michigan 48201-1309

Visit us online at wsupress.wayne.edu

To my father,

who introduced me to wilderness

Contents

Part III. Coastal Campaign: 2003–2005

Part IV. More Beginnings: 2005–2009

Author's Note

Arcadia's story is a universal story: the simple act of a stranger coming to town. I suppose in Arcadia's case, there was a series of strangers. First Derks, then Glen, then me. Derks arrived at Arcadia Dunes in 1969, the year I was born, and he set off a cascade of events that impacted thousands of people in the Great Lakes. Years later I arrived to work for Glen and his nonprofit, the Grand Traverse Regional Land Conservancy.

This is a work of creative nonfiction. It tells the story of real people with the flair of fiction. As Coastal Program director for the Conservancy, I lived through most of the events depicted in the book. Glen Chown was my boss and colleague for eight years, and we worked side by side during the Coastal Campaign.

When Glen first asked me to write this book, I demurred. "I'm too close to the subject," I told him. "Let's wait for a year or two." A year or two slipped by and, to my alarm, so did my memory. I groped to recall the smallest thing.

My memory was jolted by reading diaries, journal entries, and letters from 1998 to 2010, along with personal interviews. I interviewed more than fifty people intimately involved in the project, from farmers and neighbors to donors, staff, and board members. I tracked down former colleagues who had left the Conservancy and moved on to other jobs or out of state. I retraced my path, drove the road to Watervale, hiked the dunes, and swung on porch swings. My research included land project file notes, memos of phone calls, emails, newspaper articles, land deeds, meeting minutes, and weather reports. The Conservancy's archives of photographs sparked countless details and memories—what clothes we wore at the governor's announcement, who stood next to whom, and what the walls looked like. As I revisited old scenes, my own memories unwound and revealed themselves.

For events I did not personally witness, I portrayed scenes based on research and extensive personal interviews with those who were there. A note on quotes. When a remark is enclosed with quotation marks, it is based on one of three sources: (1) my memory of scenes I witnessed, (2) the memory of another person who witnessed the event, based on personal interviews, or (3) dialogue recorded on video or in written documents such as newspaper reports, file notes, and individual journals. A quote in italics represents a person's thoughts, as told to me in personal interviews. A few times short bits of dialogue are included without quote marks or italics. These words are intended to convey the gist of what was said, but not the precise wording.

The book also includes a few scenes that are imagined, based on probable realities of known events. I was not on the plane with Bill Mc-Cormick, but I know he flew out of Manistee's airport in a small charter plane, I know his development plans for the dunes, and I imagine he looked out of the window. I will alert you within the text when these scenes occur. It is not my intention to mislead in any way.

Those who know Arcadia Dunes firsthand will recognize that many people were omitted from this story. Five thousand people contributed to saving Arcadia. In an attempt to embrace them all, my first draft included so many names that the story grew cluttered and confusing. Nor was every key person who played a part in the events willing or able to participate in the book project. For these reasons, and to protect privacy, some names and characters in the story have been changed. The book also uses a composite character: two people in real life appear as one character in the book. Thank you for respecting others' privacy, and I hope those who were left out for the sake of readability will understand.

In the same way, chronology has been altered in a few cases to promote story flow and readability. Exact dates were used to the greatest extent possible, based on diaries, memos, and newspaper articles, but a handful of scenes occur slightly out of chronological order.

At first I avoided inserting myself into the story as anything more than a minor character. I was desperate to give credit where credit was due, and I knew firsthand how many, many folks played significant roles in the complex community-wide work of saving Arcadia. But a story demands a guide, so I became the guide for this story.

Finally, since much of this book is based on memory, it also contains the faults of memory. Memory plays tricks, alters details, and reinvents itself. When I asked five people to describe the same scene, I heard five different perspectives. This book represents a synthesis of life memory.

What is the true story? It is true that people loved a great sand dune. It is true that families loved their orchards. Together they saved Arcadia. And that story is worth telling.

Those dunes are to the Midwest
what the Grand Canyon is to Arizona
and the Yosemite to California.
They constitute a signature of time and eternity.
Once lost, the loss would be irrevocable.

—Carl Sandburg

Prologue
1998

This is what you shall do:
Love the earth and sun and the animals.

—Walt Whitman

Traverse City, Michigan
January 1998

The day I arrived in Traverse City I carried nothing except the clothes on my back. It was blizzard weather. My luggage was stranded in a Chicago snowstorm and it was unlikely we'd be reunited before 10 a.m. tomorrow. Cherry Capital was by far the smallest airport I'd ever seen. Back then it had the flavor of a Greyhound bus depot. Not the big bus terminals you find in a major city, but a remote outpost, the kind that smells of damp floor mats and 1950s suitcases hauled up from the basement.

The day before in Madison, Wisconsin, my college roommate had helped me choose an outfit for my first post-graduation interview. "You've got to look professional," Ellen said, matching skirt, top, and jacket, "with just a touch of nature." She pinned a metal lizard brooch on my lapel. Luckily, I'd decided to wear my interview jacket instead of packing it. I could feel the lump of the brooch through my coat and it gave me courage. Ellen was a PhD student immersed in international land conservation projects in East Africa. If I got this job, I'd be saving habitat right here at home. My home: the Midwest, the Heartland, the Great Lakes.

Well, not quite my home. The Midwest has many faces. Although I was born and raised a midwesterner, I knew no one in Michigan. I mispronounced Traverse City (forget its French roots; locals say, *Tra-verse*), I didn't like small towns, and I didn't know or care much about farms. My hometown was Columbus, Ohio, a city of a million; I was a university-town girl through and through. It was the wild places that brought me north: lakes, loons, and acres of forestland. I was out to save the world.

In my case, the first step in saving the world was a visit to the open-all-night Meijer store where, at 11 p.m., I bought a new set of interview clothes, down to shoes and stockings. A snowstorm stealing my clothes wouldn't stop me.

I'd grown up with a fierce love of wilderness side by side with a gnawing, growing fear about pollution and species extinction. For years I'd felt too young, too ignorant, and too unimportant to do anything about it. That wasn't true anymore. I was twenty-eight and armed with a master's degree in land resources. The job listing said, "Land Protection Specialist." The very title tantalized me.

A day later I was back in the bus stop–sized airport, staring at a row of colorful Cherry Festival posters hanging in frames along the back wall. The interview had been a success, and now I observed my surroundings with different eyes. If they hired me, would I like my new home? I stared at the watercolors of cherry blossoms. I'd have to get used to life in northern Michigan. People had been farming this land and raising cherries here for more than a hundred years. Each poster marked the years back in time: 1997 . . . 1996 . . . 1982 . . . 1970 . . .

Without my realizing it, my fate was edging closer to lives tucked away in Arcadia. I got the job and moved to northern Michigan during the course of the next month. But only over time did I learn Arcadia's story and understand its multiple storylines: of cherry farmers planting trees near the Great Lakes coast, of plants and animals eking out life on a massive sand dune, of generations of families loving a place called Baldy.

Arcadia's story began before I ever set foot in Michigan. A story I became part of, though not at first. The full story has its roots in the geologic past and in times before western settlement and statehood, but this particular story begins in 1969, the year I was born.

Part I

Beginnings
1969–1989

1 Dry Hill

The rights of posterity are more important
than the desires of the present.

—Frederick Law Olmsted, designer of Belle Isle Park,
Detroit, and Central Park, New York

Blaine Township, Benzie County, Michigan
September 2009

"What did he look like?"

So far no one had been able to tell me. This man who changed so
many lives was like a specter hovering faceless over Arcadia. Or at least
that's how I imagined him. Of course, it had been nearly forty years since
the stranger had arrived, a city man with a list of properties to buy. "He
had money," people said. "He was a straw man for Consumers." But no
one could describe him.

I shouldn't have been surprised. Forty years is long enough to narrow
or obliterate memory. Most of the landowners who'd met the man in
person had been called by the Good Lord, as people around here liked
to say. The cherry and apple farmers near Arcadia still carried the same
family names—Evans, Orr, Putney, Smeltzer—but it was largely the
next generation farming now. These forty- and fifty-year-olds had been
children when the stranger arrived.

Derks. His name was Gerald Derks, and he came alone, criss-crossing
the same back roads I'd been driving. The dirt potholes on Matzinger
Road had probably been there when he bumped along in whatever 1960s
car he was steering. His car had undoubtedly turned at the white-spired
church at Putney Corners and his gears, like mine, had protested as he'd
topped the ridge to Dry Hill. I knew the roads he'd traveled, even though
the houses along them were gone.

He came for the forest as well as the farms, for the high dunes and the sugar sand beaches. Back then the Arcadia land was divided into 115 private parcels of land: some wild and wind-sculpted dunes with deep forest ridges, others ordered into neat blocks of tart cherries, Northern Spies or Idareds, the trees spaced tractor-width apart. Up here were the best fruit sites: orchards perched at high elevations and close to Lake Michigan, sites that could dodge the killer late-spring frosts. But Derks's orders did not concern frosts or good fruit sites. He was eyeing a block of real estate stretching two miles north to south and six miles inland from the lake. Wild land or tamed—he had instructions to get it all.

In those days Arcadia was still wiping the sleep out of its eyes. Downstate, Detroit and Flint bustled with the sweat and steel of auto-building boom times, but up north there wasn't a single traffic light in Benzie County. Life inched along at the pace of the land and seasons. Orchard families charted the year by prunings, plantings, harvests, and snow plowings. Vacationers also flocked north and, to them, the north country existed in a state of perpetual summer.

It was summer now. Forty years since Derks showed up. I'd been invited into dozens of homes to learn the story, but until I met Elaine the view remained muddy.

"Those shoes!" she cried.

"You remember Derks's shoes?"

"Very classy shoes. I couldn't stop looking at them. Handsome! I thought. He wore the best-looking dress shoes I'd ever seen. Right on my back doorstep."

Elaine Putney beamed at me. She leaned forward, nodding her head of brown permed hair and brushing her elbow against the vinyl tablecloth. We were in her kitchen, a farm kitchen decorated with wedding pictures, an aerial photo of the farm, and apple ornaments of every variety. This branch of Putneys raised beef, cherries, and apples, but Elaine loved the apples best, and adored being called the Apple Lady. She gave orchard tours to schoolkids every fall, admonishing them: "Apples don't come from a plastic bag!" Apple magnets covered her fridge, apple knick-knacks hung from the walls, and the kitchen tablecloth was an apple pattern. Elaine was about sixty, a grandmother of five who shuffled when she walked, but back in Derks's day she'd been a young farm wife of nineteen.

As Elaine talked, I realized this is what I'd been longing to hear. What it had felt like on that bleak winter day, the day the stranger arrived in Arcadia. With Elaine as my guide, Derks sprang to life. I could see him as he slowed on Taylor Road and turned into a gravel drive flanked by six mature sugar maple trees. I could see him cut the ignition as he parked by the well house, then place a polished dress shoe on the tractor-rutted driveway. I watched as he made his way past the tractor shed, past the barn and granary, and knocked on the Putneys' kitchen door.

Blaine Township, Benzie County, Michigan Winter 1969–1970

Elaine Putney heard the knock above the sound of the wringer washer's electric motor. It was winter and washday. Each winter she moved her Maytag indoors from the back shed to the farmhouse kitchen, and after a little rearranging of the table and chairs, there it sat, a seasonal inhabitant. Upstairs she strung her clotheslines in the spare room for the jeans and aprons to dry. Downstairs she and Dave stepped around the white washing machine until April thawed the world and water could flow once more through the backyard taps.

Dave was ten years older and she'd married him two weeks after her high school graduation. Elaine was heavyset, her brown hair styled in a pixie cut: "pixie dixie," she called it. She dressed in farm clothes: T-shirt, jeans, an apron. For orchard jobs she wore men's work boots; inside she wore tennis shoes or Hush Puppies. When she smiled, she showed a space between her teeth wide enough to slip two quarters tipped on edge.

Today she had her arms in the rinse tub, sleeves rolled up, her hair slightly swaying as she kneaded and wrung. A hose stretched from the wringer washer to the sink, and next to her slumped a pile of work shirts, sweatshirts, and baby outfits waiting for her to squeeze them through the black-and-white wringer three times each. The smell of bacon lingered in the air, mixed with the aroma of eggs, pancakes, and black coffee. She glanced toward the dining room, where one-year-old Brian peered back at her through the wooden slats of his playpen.

The Putneys were in the fruit business. Elaine's girlhood farm had raised hay and cattle, but Dave's family were cherry farmers, and he farmed with his mother and two brothers up on Arcadia's Dry Hill. He'd courted Elaine despite the fact her family always served him tuna noodle casserole, a meal he hated. He swallowed the casserole and asked Elaine to marry him in March of her senior year. That same day, Dave signed the papers to buy his first tract of prime fruit land: eighty acres near his family's home farm. "This is a really big day for me," he told the attorneys at the closing. "I signed my life for this piece of property and I asked my girlfriend to marry me." Three months later they married, and Elaine left her family's cattle business to settle into a life of orchard farming at the old farmhouse on Taylor Road.

It was a two-story house with grey siding surrounded by six grand sugar maples. The house itself had been cobbled together over time, with new rooms added here and there, and a woodshed connected to the mainframe to become the kitchen. Elaine loved her first home as a married woman. The house had spare rooms, but Dave and Elaine both came from big families—ten kids each—and were looking forward to children. A year after their marriage, Brian was born. Dave took to calling Elaine "Mother" and she called him "Dad."

The knock came mid-morning. Coming! Elaine wiped her wet hands on her apron, glanced at the baby to assure herself he was fine, and answered the door.

Out on her back step stood the classiest man she had ever seen. He wore a suit jacket and tie knotted under a crisp collar. He was about six feet tall, with brown hair and a fine shave. Shiny dress shoes peeked out below his pant cuffs, looking out of place on a kitchen stoop accustomed to farm boots. Elaine's eyes were so busy sizing up his clothes she barely registered his face.

"Hello, Mrs. Putney? I'm Gerald Derks, from the Viking Land Company."

Elaine said nothing. If he wanted to buy their land, he was wasting his time. They weren't selling. That land was everything to Dave. He owned two eighty-acre parcels now and had recently planted more than 6,000 new tart cherry trees.

"Is your husband home?" Derks went on.

"He's at work." Elaine looked down. *Those shoes!* She couldn't take her eyes off the high polish of those shoes.

"I'd like to talk to him," Derks said. "I'd like to make a generous offer on your land."

"We're not interested in selling."

That was that, thought Elaine, back to my wash, but she watched his face change from its polite smile to shock. His eyes had roamed to the wringer washer behind her, with its hose drooping toward the sink and the array of clothes and rinse tubs. "What are you doing?" he asked, dumbfounded.

"I'm doing my laundry," replied Elaine.

"You know, you could do this differently," Derks said. "There are other types of washing machines these days."

Elaine stared back at him. Of course she knew. But Dave said the well couldn't handle a regular washer; it took too much water. So she had the wringer washer for now. It was just the way things were. Lots of folks had them, and besides, hers was electric, not a hand-crank model.

"I'll come back again sometime when your husband's here," Derks said, handing her a card with his name and "Viking Land Company" printed on it. He turned to go, then looked back at the wash again. "Things could be a lot easier for you," he said. "Money can make things a lot easier."

A blast of December air swept into the kitchen as she shut the door.

When Dave came home for lunch, Elaine told him about their visitor. The wringer washer squatted dormant in its corner, and the kitchen now smelled like country gravy and potatoes. Elaine was new at being a farm wife, but she knew leftovers from supper made a good midday meal.

Steam wafted above the vinyl tablecloth as Dave dug into his lunch and listened to Elaine's agitated story. "We're not letting that man in the house again!" she said. "You should have heard what he had to say to me about my wash!"

Elaine watched her husband's reaction. He wasn't thinking about the wash. Dave sat hunched at the kitchen table fingering the Viking Land card. "We're not going to sell," he said. "This is our land. It's my life."

She sighed with relief. She knew he'd say that. Dave's family had been farming here since the 1800s and they wanted to expand, not sell. Yet they both also knew that they hadn't seen the last of Derks.

There was talk in the community about this man. He was likely the same one who'd talked to dairy farmer Carl Green on Taylor Road and the Phelps family around the corner on Butwell. The township had buzzed with the news when both families had decided to sell. Of course, the two families were connected, the wives were sisters, but still—so sudden. Big money, people said, real riches, enough to buy a new home and take your children on vacation out to Yellowstone National Park.

Elaine let her mind drift to what that kind of money could bring, and then snapped back to the image of the block of young trees Dave had planted last year, just before Brian was born. A new generation of trees to match a new generation of Putneys. Dave had chosen this fruit site carefully and planned to work the land until the Lord called his name. They weren't selling. Not now, not ever.

Meanwhile, Gerald Derks was still in the neighborhood. His car continued to crawl about Dry Hill. The man was persistent; he didn't seem to hear the word no. He knocked on Bug Evans's door. He talked to Gene Orr of Twin Orr-chards. He made a deal with Glen Stone and signed papers with Joe Smeltzer, both orchard families. He bought woodland from Pete and Iva Rodriguez. Elaine and Dave watched as sales spread from Taylor Road to around the corner on Butwell Road and beyond.

A few miles over, Derks was also working his way west to the dune land. He purchased dunes from the Lukens and quietly bought out Bob Lucas, a man who owned another swath of Lake Michigan's coast. Lucas had envisioned a subdivision on the high dunes and concocted a cable-car run down to the lakeshore below, but the land mostly stood empty: wild land with a few dirt roads.

If this part of northern Michigan had been inland farmland, Derks would never have bothered. But this land was unique. It lay near the Lake Michigan coast, and for a two-mile stretch the coastline contained a prize—a towering bluff rising 335 feet above the water. Old Baldy, some called it. The North Bluff. The Blowout. The Sugar Bowl. Here sand had blown for centuries to perch on top of a massive glacial moraine, giving the sand dune its awe-inspiring height. Here wind scooped and sculpted the landscape daily, creating habitat for rare plants like the Pitcher's thistle, which thrived in a shifting landscape. Land like this was so unusual that the U.S. government had created Sleeping Bear Dunes National Lakeshore a few miles north.

To men like Derks, however, the main benefit of the dune was its height. The nearby farm acreage could provide space to store 27 billion gallons of water. Old Baldy could drop that water and send it plunging down more than 300 feet into Lake Michigan—to generate power for thousands upon thousands of Midwest homes.

Blaine Land Buying Creates Mystery
Benzie County Patriot, Frankfort, Michigan, December 25, 1969

How much longer will Benzie County's Dry Hill remain dry? About two months ago, land owners in this part of the county began to receive offers for their holdings much in excess of anything offered before. To date the Viking Land Company has acquired several hundred acres of Lake Michigan frontage and inland property. The higher than average market prices being offered indicate that the property is badly wanted and presumably in a solid block.

The entire project and the mystery surrounding it closely resemble what took place just south of Ludington four or five years ago when buyers began purchasing property there for an unknown client which turned out to be Consumers Power Co. A strong possibility exists that a Pumped Storage Power Plant is planned for the Dry Hill area just north of Arcadia.

The neighborhood buzzed with speculation. Viking Land was obviously a front. But who was the rich client behind them? It must be Consumers Power. The Arcadia farm sales mirrored land-buying patterns in Ludington, all bought using a straw man like Derks, all carefully consolidating acres into one big block. Dry Hill had the same high ground as Ludington, which lay fifty miles south. If rumors were true, thousands of acres of good timber and fruit land were doomed to be flooded. Consumers would pump Lake Michigan water up the dune at night, hold it in a reservoir, and release the water downhill during the day. Electricity from these new hydropower turbines would give the company a boost of energy during peak hours. If it were to be anything like Ludington's reservoir, Arcadia's flooded area would be big. The Ludington plant was supposed to be the largest hydroelectric pumped storage system in the world.

It had to be something big. Derks was certainly offering good money. To everyone who sold, that is.

The Putney family remained a holdout. Together branches of the Putney family owned sizeable holdings in the center of Dry Hill, so Derks kept after them. He became a regular visitor to the Putney farmstead. Elaine had got used to seeing his shiny shoes on her doorstep. "Is your husband home?"

"No, he's at work," Elaine would say, then shut her mouth tightly. She never let on that she knew exactly which field Dave was pruning that day. But she could hold him off for only so long. Orchard work was slow in the winter, and dusk fell fast. Some days when the pruning was done, Derks did catch Dave at home. "I'm not selling," Dave told him. When Derks persisted, Dave invoked his family. "We farm together," Dave told him. "I'm not selling out from under my family."

Each time he and his shoes left, Elaine would hold Brian's plump cheek close to hers, praying Derks would leave her family alone.

Mother Putney still owned the original Putney farmstead. The Putney family had settled the area and established a farm on Dry Hill in 1865 and, like many longtime orchard families, their roots stretched deep into the community. It was a Putney great-uncle who had given the land for the Blaine Christian Church at Putney Corners. For nearly a century, orchard families had baptized their babies and mourned their losses there. Across on the north side of Putney Corners another Putney great-uncle had owned a general store. Youngsters trotted down to buy penny candy—spiral striped peppermint and cinnamon sticks, Mary Janes and Tootsie Rolls. The general store was gone, but Putney brothers, uncles, and cousins still owned and farmed the surrounding land, including Dave, two brothers, Frank and Ken, and their mother, Mildred.

A mile north from Dave and Elaine, Dave's brother Ken and his wife, Charlotte, lived in a two-story gable house built in the 1800s. The walls were lath and plaster. Someone had added grey siding during World War II but, according to Charlotte, the wind still blew through. Like Elaine, Charlotte delighted in her house, and Ken loved the land. They owned 120 acres surrounding their home, plus 80 acres west of Putney Road.

As a boy, Ken had dreamed of owning this exact stretch of land. He knew it would be a prime location, with good soil, elevation, and air drainage. When it came to growing fruit, high elevation with good airflow was imperative. The low spots with still air could be frost pockets, fatal for orchard blossoms. This land had exactly the right combination. Ken was thrilled when he bought the land from the Williams family at the age of twenty-six. Soon he and Charlotte were throwing every ounce of energy into farming the Dry Hill orchards and raising four daughters.

The Putneys would not sell. By now they knew for certain that Derks and his Viking Land Company represented the public utility Consumers Power. They also knew that the land they carefully tended was slated to be underwater or on the banks of the reservoir if Consumers' plans went through. But not if they didn't sell. When Derks made the rounds to each branch of the Putney family, he got the same blunt refusal.

Derks needed this family's land. Together, the Putneys controlled more than 400 acres, acreage critical to the pumped storage plans. If the lure of big money wouldn't budge them, he would have to try another tactic.

One bitter January night in 1970, Derks gathered the Putney clan together at Dave and Elaine's house on Taylor Road. Mother Putney, Ken, and Frank were there. They talked about the land, about the price Derks could offer. There would be no rush to move out. Derks could offer five-year leases. All the families could remain in their homes and keep farming orchards and cutting timber for several years. What Derks said next scared Elaine so much she remembered every word forty years later: "You can hole up all you want, but it's going to happen. As a utility, we can use eminent domain to condemn your property. We will have this land."

Dave and Elaine went to bed sick at heart at the thought they'd be forced to sell the land. Ken and Charlotte returned home to Putney Corners. Though it was late, he and Charlotte revved up their snowmobiles and rendezvoused with their friends the Smeltzers. The young couples raced across Dry Hill, sandwiched between the black night sky above and the sweep of white snow below. When they stopped at the Smeltzers' house to warm up, Ken did something he never did. He got drunk. He drank for his farm he'd have to sell. He drank for giving up his boyhood dream. He drank for the uncertain future.

Three months later, in April 1970, Consumers Power bought hundreds of acres of Putney land. By October, Consumers owned the last Putney holdings on Dry Hill.

Consumers Power Acknowledges Purchase of 4,100 Acres Here for Pumped Storage

Benzie County Patriot, Frankfort, Michigan, January 14, 1971

During the past 12 months land buying has gone on at a rapid pace and what started out as a closely kept secret began to become public knowledge, but it was not until Thursday, January 7th at the annual meeting of the Benzie Soil District that Consumers Power Co. publicly acknowledged that it had acquired 4,100 acres of land in Benzie and Manistee counties.

Dave looked at the young trees he had just planted on Dry Hill. There they stood, thin sapling branches poking up, more than 6,000 tart cherry trees, barely two years in the ground. Cherry trees couldn't turn a profit for ten years, and with a five-year lease, the numbers didn't add up. He could do better with a cash crop of corn. Dave fired up the brush hog and crushed his young cherry trees, toppling row after row.

2 Interlude

Leave it as it is. The ages have been at work
on it and man can only mar it.

—Theodore Roosevelt

Jackson, Michigan
2003

That might have been the end, of course. If the story of Arcadia had gone the usual way, Elaine's children might have grown up and moved on, remembering only a reservoir on the land that straddled Benzie and Manistee counties. The landscape would have vanished, flattened and flooded into something else. As for me, I might have driven by decades later, avoiding the land as an eyesore.

But something strange happened in Arcadia during the years I was growing up. The land changed hands, families moved out, but the end didn't come. Instead there was a pause. Time went by. Then more time. The land was left to itself. And left to itself, the land began to change hearts.

I pieced together the next part of the story from studying reams of land deeds at the title company, consulting newspaper accounts, and sorting through dusty boxes of files at the CMS headquarters in Jackson. CMS, now the parent company of Consumers Power, still kept records of all the land deeds Derks negotiated on Dry Hill. A CMS employee trundled the records up to me on a dolly and tipped a stack of boxes on the floor. Decades of dust coated the cardboard, and a plume of it whuffed in the air as the boxes landed. "Enjoy!" he said, and strode away.

I cracked open the first box and peered inside. There was Derks's angular, slanted scrawl on the signature line. There it was again, on deed after deed. I dug deeper and found nestled among the deeds a collection of letters written on crinkled stationery in blue ballpoint pen. "Please may we take our freezer," one said. "We want to remove our pets from the pet cemetery on the property," read another. I could picture young farm wives like Elaine composing these letters at their kitchen tables. First they would have stood silently on their Dry Hill properties, trying to picture what it would look like underwater. Then they would have hurried inside to write a note, trying to save what they couldn't bear to leave behind.

How do you disengage from a landscape? Once a human life settles into the seasons on a piece of the planet, that life is linked to the land. Hearts are obstinate that way. After all, you can dig up a pet skeleton or trundle out a freezer, but you can't take what matters.

The land itself won't budge.

Benzie and Manistee Counties, Michigan 1970s–1980s

Gerald Derks was doing well. In addition to 4,100 acres, Consumers soon owned about twenty farmhouses, now empty of people. Still the company acquired more land. Month by month, Consumers amassed the missing pieces needed for its giant reservoir.

Derks (or the money backing him) was persuasive. No land was officially condemned; in the eyes of the law all owners were willing sellers. Some owners were eager to strike a deal. Other families sold after repeated visits, lured by promises or threats. But still they all sold, one after another. It could be that the prices he offered—$400 an acre, $750 an acre, *more than $1,000 an acre*—had never been seen before for land like this in Benzie County. It could be that owners, like the Putneys, felt the weight of the spoken or unspoken threat: we *will* have your land. It was almost as if folks could feel the pressure of billions of gallons of water already bearing down.

Downstate, Consumers Power engineers drafted maps of reservoirs and calculated turbine speeds for the new Arcadia Pumped Storage site. Up north, deeds exchanged hands at the county courthouses for two years until the entire Dry Hill landscape—nine square miles, or nearly 6,000 acres—was registered in the name of Consumers Power. It was only a handful of parcels in 1969, then more and more through 1970 into 1971 . . . Per-Clin Orchards, Finch, Finney, Lemley, Smeltzer. Slowly Arcadia's Dry Hill emptied of people.

The transferred land parcels contained a slice of Michigan's history. To examine the deed records of Dry Hill is to read of the heartache of earlier farmers who attempted to farm the sandy soil after the timber boom loggers left. With soil stripped of its forest cover and much of its nutrient layer, crops repeatedly failed. By the 1920s and 1930s, many farmers slipped on property tax payments, and the state government reclaimed the land, later selling it to new buyers. Other deeds bear the marks of deep racism. The deed of the main sand dune, Baldy itself, plus a mile of coastline, was scarred with these words when the land changed hands in 1950: "The use, ownership and occupancy of said premises shall be restricted to those of the Christian faith and of the Caucasian Race."

Dave and Elaine left their grey-sided farmhouse on Taylor Road and built a new place on acreage they bought to the east. Ken and Charlotte resettled their family half a mile farther north on Putney Road, next to the old Putney millpond. They salvaged doors and light fixtures from the old farmhouse, partly to save money and partly to bring some familiar piece of home.

Excavators came next, demolishing the Putneys' houses along with all the others. Bulldozers rumbled in and pushed over the homes, barns, and granaries. They leveled Dry Hill's empty one-room schoolhouse. They flattened sheds and any left-behind clotheslines and mailboxes. On Taylor Road, the grey siding crumpled and the old spot where the Maytag sat vanished. Some debris got hauled away, but much of it was buried on-site. The crews scraped the earth flat with the backside of a bulldozer's blade, erasing each home.

When the demolition crews had finished, all that remained to show that houses had once stood there were a few botanical clues. Patches of daffodils poked up spring after spring, and remnant shade trees remained, marking what once had been a drive.

Meanwhile, the coastal dunes and forest played out their age-old rhythms, unsuspecting. Hardly any life could survive in the sand, but some unique beings had discovered a way and claimed this niche as their own. Odd species such as the fascicled broomrape lived here, a pallid pinkish-brown plant only four inches high that lacked chlorophyll so it stole nutrients from other plants' roots. Some were as drab as the Pitcher's thistle with its silvery leaves, or the ash-colored Lake Huron locust, a grasshopper no bigger than a human thumbnail. These plants and animals had adapted to the shifting sand and would die without this habitat. But being rare and endangered would not save them. It was 1970, and protective laws like the Endangered Species Act were still three years off.

Each spring, migrating songbirds followed the coast, gaining shelter and gulping bugs in the forests next to Old Baldy. Each summer, dune flowers added drops of color: yellow clumps of hairy puccoon, blue harebells, and deep orange wood lilies. Each fall, monarch butterflies traced the coastline en route to Mexico. Each season, the land drew closer to planned obliteration.

But the floodwaters didn't come. The monarchs flew, the Pitcher's thistle bloomed and dropped its seeds, but the new owners of the land appeared to lose interest. "No trespassing" signs fell off their rickety nails. Locked gates tilted off their hinges. Nearly twenty years passed since Gerald Derks first came knocking, and Consumers Power, once so eager for the land, remained silent. The land stood waiting.

Down in Ludington and east in Midland, though, events were taking place that impacted the Arcadia dunes. Hydropower from Arcadia was meant to work in tandem with Consumers Power's soon-to-be-completed nuclear power plant in Midland. But construction problems plagued that project, including buildings that cracked and sank. When Three Mile Island's nuclear accident occurred in 1979, Consumers struggled to meet new government safety requirements for Midland. Five years later, the Midland plant was eighty-five percent complete, but Consumers decided to scrap the project. The $4 billion Midland mistake left the company teetering on the edge of bankruptcy. At that point, Consumers Power brought in Bill McCormick to fix their troubles. As new CEO, he steered the company away from bankruptcy, and created CMS Energy Corporation, which folded the Consumers Power utility under its wings.

Down the coast in Ludington, Arcadia's sister site—the Ludington Pumped Storage Plant—opened in 1973. Consumers Power and Detroit Edison partnered on the plant. The water went up to the reservoir fine, but engineers overlooked a vital part of lake water: the fish. Millions of perch, trout, alewives, and salmon got sucked up and killed by the turbine blades. The air around Ludington reeked with the stench of foul fish. Fish corpses floated on Lake Michigan's surface and beached on the shoreline. Ludington's fish kill was massive, attracting the wrath of the Federal Energy Regulatory Commission, Michigan attorney general Frank Kelley, the Sierra Club, Michigan United Conservation Clubs and others. They filed a lawsuit.

The ensuing legal fight dragged on for years. In 1994, Michigan imposed on Consumers Power the largest environmental damage settlement in state history. Consumers endured the negative spotlight and installed fish filters. Together with Detroit Edison, Consumers Power paid a $172 million penalty for the fish kill and gave the state of Michigan sixty miles of waterfront property. It was clear that Consumers had enough to handle without adding a new pumped storage plant at Arcadia. Plans for flooding Arcadia halted.

But something still tied Consumers to Arcadia. All the land Consumers agreed to transfer to the state as part of the lawsuit settlement was coastline. The giveaway list even included land near Arcadia along the Manistee River. But not Arcadia. Despite its two miles of Lake Michigan coastline, Arcadia stayed the property of Consumers.

You might say the land sat vacant over those twenty years, but of course it wasn't vacant, simply stripped of buildings. Besides the dune and forest species, people were there, too. People dodged around gates and created footpaths and mountain biking tracks through the woods. Locals from the village of Arcadia hiked into the dune forest with their kids and dogs, scouting for mushrooms. Farmers tended the leased orchards and fields, but they also began to teach their children to shake cherries on that land. Week after week, season after season.

Campers from the Lutheran summer camp in Arcadia trekked north to the Blowout, where they held vespers services high above the lake with a wooden cross they shouldered up the dune. They traversed the ridge tops and gazed at the vastness around them. From the opposite side of the dune, summer guests at Watervale resort climbed the forested backside of the dune to Old Baldy, then raced down to the lake in a near free-fall, dropping the 300 feet in a wild, hair-flying run.

Spring morel mushroom hunts, summer beach walks, fall deer hunts, winter snowmobile rides. The seasons cycled through a generation at Old Baldy, aka the North Bluff, aka the Blowout, aka Dry Hill, aka the Consumers Power Land, as the land itself seeped into the soul of locals and summer visitors.

To each family Arcadia became a private paradise. Six thousand acres to play in with an absent, distant landlord who was easy to forget. Who owned the land? The people did. The name on the deed didn't matter.

During those long idle years, something indeed happened. Something that Consumers Power did not realize and could not see. The community embraced the land. Thousands of people learned to love Arcadia.

3 Innkeepers

> One cannot live if he does not belong anywhere.
>
> —German saying

Watervale, Benzie County, Michigan
Spring 1998

"You'll see." There was something in Carl's voice as he spoke, as if he were about to reveal something extraordinary.

These were the early days after I got hired, and self-appointed guides like Carl were eager to show me around Benzie County. I nodded, a bit surprised. Carl Freeman was a dragonfly expert and a watercolor painter who ambled through the marshes and forests with binoculars looped over his shoulder and a sketchbook or spotting scope in his hand. Carl was the kind of person who wore green and brown and melded with the trees. He cultivated a long, scraggly beard that seemed lichen-like to me, since I was fond of lichen. He reminded me of John Muir. That's why I was surprised to hear this tone of reverence in his voice. He was about to show me a lakeside resort. I didn't much care for lakeside resorts—typically overblown development displacing shoreline habitat—but Carl was a man who paid attention to blue flag iris and identified dragonfly species, a man I was willing to trust.

Watervale's chief charm lies in its row of two-story Victorian cottages lined up like ladies in pale lavender, pink, and green dresses and bonnets: Cecelia, Johanna, Mary Ellen, and more. The cottages, set back from the shore, come in all shapes and sizes. Some, like the Barbara, are not much bigger than a cozy room with fireplace. Others are grand, like the Margaret. Watervale is an oasis of peace. When you enter its realm, time suspends and the world seems ageless. Life moves at the pace of wicker porch swings. Watervale's nearest neighbor is also ageless: Old Baldy, the sand dune itself.

Carl introduced me to Dori, Watervale's proprietress. During that first visit I registered the Victorian staircases, creaky inn doors, and alluring smell of baking bread. I didn't notice the lobby curtains. Years later as I sat by the fireplace, snug in Dori's winter quarters in the Johanna cottage, she told me about the drapes. The day the strangers came. For Elaine, it was Derks's shoes, but for Dori, it was chintz drapes.

Benzie County, Michigan
Spring 1988

It was tree-planting time. The northern Michigan spring was about to leap from the brown, matted earth to the glory of pink-tipped cherry and apple blossoms. But first came mud season, which lasted two months. When the weight of three feet of snow finally lifted, the earth below emerged squashed, dark, and muddy. Strands of withered grass pressed into the soil. Here and there lay lumps of dog, coyote, and fox scat, or dark pebbles of deer and rabbit droppings, the winter's accumulation suddenly exposed. The soil seemed naked, caught in that groggy, in-between moment of just awakening. The earth had thrown back its thick, white bedclothes of snow and was staggering under the bright sunlight, too stunned yet to go on and pull on its clothes, the green leaves of summer.

It was tree-planting time, but on the Consumers Power property, no one was planting trees. The orchards stood locked in time, the trunks and branches thickening. Twenty or thirty years is the lifespan of a productive fruit tree, but some of the orchard trees on Taylor and Joyfield roads were pushing forty or fifty. Time was beginning to choke the Dry Hill orchards.

Consumers Power seemed to have forgotten the Arcadia land. Corporate urgency had disappeared along with Derks, who'd vanished downstate years before, and at times orchard farmers could almost forget they didn't own the Dry Hill land. They carried on business as usual: pruning, spraying, picking apples, and shaking cherries, the same families tending the same fields year after year. The original farm leases had been renewed in a series of long-term leases. Their babies grew up to become extra hands driving the tractor and stretching canvas on the cherry shaker. In 1986, Brian Putney headed off to college to study horticulture, planning to return to the family cattle and orchard business. Yes, at times people could almost forget that Consumers owned the land. But not at tree-planting time.

Tree planting was the time of long-range thinking, the time for investing in the earth and making plans that extended a generation ahead. An orchard depended on new trees being planted, but who could plant trees with a five-year lease?

Then, after long years of waiting, fear crept back over Arcadia. Helicopters hovered and rumors flew. It's the Japanese. It's a big downstate developer. It's Consumers. Now they want a resort. They want to dredge out the Herring Lakes and harbor luxury yachts at the foot of Dry Hill.

Consumers Power was stirring to life. The company sent a new "Derks" to Arcadia, a man named Robert Eva. Eva systematically ended the long-term farm leases and replaced them with one-year license agreements. Now, instead of being able to plan five years at a time, farmers faced annual uncertainty.

Short-term, year-to-year planning changed the landscape. Field after field turned into cornscapes as orchardists bulldozed their cherry trees and planted quick cash crops. Christmas tree farmers also abandoned their crop, and soon Dry Hill sprouted overgrown Scotch pine stands, the trees interlocking their branches and growing fifteen feet tall. A few, like Dave Putney, kept nursing their aging fruit trees. But the yearly licenses hung like a shadow over them. Dave waited to prune the branches until Consumers Power accepted his rent check for the coming year.

It was becoming clear that Consumers Power had new plans. Despite the flurry of paperwork involved in negotiating new farm licenses, the true focus of Consumers' new plans lay west of the farmland. West toward the Lake Michigan coastline. West four miles, winding down a tree-shaded dirt lane, to a spot perched beside two lakes: Watervale.

In 1988, quiet, quirky Watervale became the utility's next target. It lay along the shores of a gentle inland lake called Lower Herring. A spit of sand separated Watervale from Lake Michigan's great waters where schooners used to dock and haul timber down the lake to Chicago. Its choice position between these two lakes had caught Consumers Power's eye. Watervale: rich in shoreline, next to Consumers Power–owned land, a secluded family resort with aging owners.

Watervale existed in an ageless world of its own. Victorian buildings defying time. A world ensconced by lakes, dunes, and forest. On this spring day in the late 1980s, Dori Turner stood in the lobby of the Watervale Inn, pressing draperies for the lobby windows. She ran her iron over the chintz folds. It was a floral print her mother had sewn: a pale teal background with green leaves and pink and bronze flowers. Dori's mother, Vera, and her Aunt Emma were also in the lobby, running down the long checklist of preseason chores. In May, Watervale was always a hive of spring-cleaning. Summer guests would begin to arrive in two weeks and they expected a well-ordered vacation paradise. That meant multiple claw-footed bathtubs to scrub, Pullman blankets to air out, rowboat oars to find, and wicker swings to hang from the broad porches. The inn plus fifteen cottages must be cleaned from top to bottom. When the plumber turned on the water, they'd discover several leaky sinks. Then there was painting to do, lamp repairs, broken windowpanes to fix, and inevitably a skunk to chase out from under a cottage.

Each year it was a scramble to set the place to rights. Watervale's summer staff would arrive soon, the cooks, college-kid waitresses, and dishwashers, plus local hands to clean the cottages weekly and keep pace with bins of laundry. Laundry. Until last year or so, all guest towels and bathmats had gone through Watervale's wringer washer, then hauled to the town Laundromat to dry.

Today it was cool. Spring crept in gradually in northern Michigan, and although it was May, the leaves remained mere nubs on the branches. Dori's mother wore a neatly pressed McMullen cotton dress, but Dori herself wore jeans, a long-sleeved shirt, and a sweater. Her face was framed with round-rimmed glasses, and her brown hair, shorter than shoulder length, was streaked with grey. Dori was in her fifties, the youngster in this family-run resort. With her father dead and her mother and that generation getting older, it was Dori who shouldered the brunt of the work these days. Now she tackled the pile of draperies before her, folds of pink, teal, and bronze spilling down the ironing board to the floor, when the inn door opened and three strangers walked in.

They were all men, wearing dark suits and leather dress shoes. The first man looked about, and his eyes rested on Vera in her cotton dress and grey hair cut short in a wavy bob. He smiled and extended his hand. "Mrs. Noble?" he said. "I'm Tom Davis. We're from Consumers Power."

Dori set the iron down and watched her mother. "Yes?" said Vera.

"We'd like to talk to you about buying your property here."

"Oh," said Vera. "I really don't think we're interested in selling."

Dori's uncle Freddy walked into the lobby. He sized up the three strangers and the three Watervale women standing with lists and drapes in their hands.

"These gentlemen would like to buy Watervale," said Vera.

"No," said Uncle Freddy in astonishment. "No!"

The force of his answer cut the interview short. The inn door scraped closed behind the Consumers Power men, leaving the family speechless in the lobby.

"Well," said Vera, after a time. "There's important things to do, like getting the kitchen cleaned for the season."

Vera Kraft Noble's family had owned Watervale for generations. Watervale had been founded with grand ideas back in 1892 during peak timber days. Leo Hale established a logging company and "the pretty little town of Watervale" around his lumber mill. His company town boasted a post office, telegraph office, butcher shop, and general store along with a narrow gauge railroad to haul wood out to the schooner pier. He built clapboard cottages for married loggers and a large boardinghouse with slanted eves to house single laborers. For a short time, Watervale cut, sawed, and shipped logs to Chicago. But the great financial panic of 1893 caught Leo Hale the very next year. His newly launched logging company went bankrupt, Watervale went into foreclosure, and the buildings sat abandoned.

That's where Oscar Kraft found them. An ophthalmologist from Chicago, Oscar stumbled upon the logging ghost town in 1917. Since Hale's time, sand had swirled around the deserted cottages. Some cottages hung lopsided, tilted off the cedar stumps Hale had set down as a foundation. Yet the original Victorian structures were still sound. Oscar bought the property. He propped up the cottages, tilting some back into place with a team of horses, and shook out the cobwebs. He painted the three-story boardinghouse green and white, named each cottage after Chicago friends and family, and set about prettying the place up, transforming the onetime company mill town into a summer resort. Years later each cottage acquired its own distinct shade: yellow for the Ursula, pink for the Johanna, lavender for the Cecelia, and celery green for the Mary Ellen. Where the narrow gauge rail line had once hauled logs, families strolled along the lakeside.

Watervale thrived under Oscar's care. He had no children himself, but he welcomed friends and family to stay at his oasis. It was only natural that Watervale should stay in the family. He installed his cousin as Watervale's first manager. Then in 1960, Oscar's niece Vera Kraft Noble and her husband, Vernon, took over and ran the Watervale resort with its inn and fifteen cottages. Twenty-eight years later, as Vera and Vernon began to find the Watervale property hard to manage, they knew it was time to shift leadership to the next generation. They called on their daughter, Dori.

Dori had moved to Minnesota but worked summers at Watervale. Now she was back home full-time and took up the family mantle. Watervale guests marveled at the serenity, the paper birch trees by the inn porch, the tidy cottages with braided rugs and old-fashioned enamel sinks. But to Dori and her family, Watervale was much more. It was early hours kneading bread dough in the kitchen, it was scraping plates while the guests meandered to the beach. When guests were gone, it was snug winters by the Johanna's fireplace, and storytelling about the logging days. It was hikes to Baldy. Watervale was simply everything: it was home.

Watervale was home to the summer guests, too. Families forged deep links to Watervale over generations of summers, even though most came up only for a week or two a year. Watervale did not advertise, and had no need to. The same families—from Detroit, Cincinnati, Cleveland, Milwaukee, and Chicago—returned year after year, booking their favorite week to seek the peace of Watervale. In time they brought their children, their grandchildren, and even their great-grandchildren, every year digging their hearts a little more deeply into the dune sand.

Consumers Power was patient. Its executives knew that a family-run resort is not an easy business. Dori's father had moved into a nursing home and then died in 1985, leaving her mother to struggle on without him. The inn and cottages were showing their age. Every cottage needed new paint plus a major overhaul for new wiring and plumbing. Times were tough. The resort scraped by at the edge of the dune as tenuously as dune plants clung to the sand. Each year there was just enough money to pay for cottage upkeep, food, staff, and property taxes. The family sighed with relief each time Watervale squeaked by for another season.

This was the situation when the three Consumers Power men visited. Soon after, Consumers Power came back again, this time with a written offer in hand for $3 million. "It's a generous offer, Mrs. Noble. We hope you will consider it."

It was a different man this time. His name instantly forgotten: Blankenship? From someplace downstate, perhaps Grand Rapids. "Take a look at it—once you sign, you get $300,000. Then even if we don't buy it, you get to keep the $300,000 free and clear."

"But this is what we do," said Vera. "If we sell, what would we *do?* Where would we *go?*"

"You could do anything you wanted to," said Blankenship. "You could go anyplace you wanted to go."

Vera looked down at the hundred-year-old maple floor, then out at the lake shimmering beyond the inn's window. "But this is where I want to be," she said.

Consumers Mum on Plan for 5,800 Acres
Traverse City Record-Eagle, June 18, 1988

Frankfort—Consumers Power Co. is trying to buy property near its 5,800-acre holdings on the Benzie-Manistee county line—possibly to sell in one block or to develop into a massive resort.

Paul Knopick, chief spokesman for the utility, declined comment on "anything we may or may not be doing there."

Watervale friends and family gathered at Uncle Oscar's cottage. This was a different Uncle Oscar, the original family patriarch having died long ago. What with offers from Consumers Power real estate men, shortened farm leases, and helicopter sightings, the rumor mill had been abuzz all summer. Even if Dori's family didn't buckle under and sell Watervale, their oasis could be ruined by a massive development next door. It was time to pool their ideas together. The conversation up at the Kraft cottage went something like this: It's going to be a golf course, an airstrip, the site of a luxury hotel. I bet the Japanese are behind this. The Japanese are loaded with money and they like golf. No, Consumers is going to build an upscale resort. Haven't you seen the survey crews on M-22? They're going to move the highway to put in an airstrip. We should get a biologist up here. If they just see how many rare plants there are, the government won't let them build on the dune. They want a deepwater harbor. They're going to push out Watervale and build a new resort on top of it. We've got to stop them. We'll form a new society: the Watervale Preservation Society.

"If they open a resort, they'd need a beer and wine license for that," said Dori.

The rest of them looked at her.

"There's only one beer and wine license available in Blaine Township," continued Dori.

"If we get the license first . . ." someone said.

"That's how we'll stop them," said Dori.

From the height of his private plane, Consumers Power board chair Bill McCormick could not hear their conversation. The Manistee airport was rapidly receding; soon he would be flying over the Arcadia property.

The Manistee Blacker Airport was kept busy with flights to Arcadia that spring. According to the airport manager, the rural airport launched several helicopters and at least one chartered plane, all headed to Arcadia. The passenger lists included Bill McCormick and an executive from an Atlanta-based hotel chain.

I wasn't up in the plane with him, but I've circled the Arcadia land by twin-prop engine, and I imagine this is how the scene unfolded. There he is, leaning forward, picturing luxury homes nestled among the trees. Up ahead along the wooded coast is the spot he had selected. What the property needs, he thinks, is a harbor. It would be simple to dredge a deepwater harbor on Lower Herring Lake to connect to Lake Michigan. They'd need an airstrip, too. Puddle-jumping from Manistee is too much hassle. The plane banks, displaying the full glory of the dune. A golf course would be perfect there, he thinks—look at it, a natural sand trap.

Down on the ground, a botanist from the Cranbrook Institute hiked the hills and inventoried the wild species. The Watervale folks had hired him as part of their strategy to save the land. Jim marveled as he recorded rare plants like fascicled broomrape, and noted seven majestic American chestnuts that had escaped the chestnut blight. He marked healthy patches of the threatened Pitcher's thistle on the dunes, noting, "This may be the densest population, more than Nordhouse Dunes Wilderness Area which has the largest population in the world." Soon a copy of his findings hung under a plexiglass cover next to a homemade map at the trailhead to Old Baldy.

The Watervale neighbors organized. Dori and her cousin, Steve Kraft, teamed up with another Watervale neighbor, Dean Luedders. Dean and his wife lived at the base of the Baldy trailhead. Dean worked as an investment manager and Steve was an economics professor, though Dean kidded him about his shaggy beard and 1972 hippie-era van. Dean drew up paperwork to incorporate the nascent Watervale Preservation Society. Dori was named president.

Instead of Consumers Power buying Watervale, perhaps Watervale could buy land from Consumers. They decided to tap funds from the Michigan Natural Resources Trust Fund to buy as much of the Consumers property as they could. At the very least, perhaps they could gain a buffer around Watervale. The Trust Fund awarded $12 million a year for natural areas around the state. The money came from oil revenue from state-leased mineral rights. Dean's sister had chaired the first Trust Fund board and the Natural Resources Commission, and had good contacts there. It was just possible that the state might be willing to fund the land purchase—if Consumers agreed to sell.

Dori was wary of the Trust Fund grant at first. If the state owned the land, more people would be coming to Baldy. Dean tried to reason with her. "Change is coming to Watervale," he said. "Better a state-run nature preserve than a nuclear plant or condo development."

Dean slid a page of the Preservation Society's letterhead through the page guides of his electric typewriter. He typed out a letter to the head of the Nature Conservancy in Michigan asking for help in negotiating with Consumers Power. "Dear Mr. Woiwode, Nice to chat with you. . . . If Consumers Power / CMS should see merit in a wholly eleemosynary act, by gift, that would, of course, be a pleasing development. . . . Please do let me know how I, or we, might amplify. Cordially, Dean R. Luedders."

A month later, Dean called Consumers Power directly. Dick Erhardt answered the phone, instantly recognizing the name Luedders, as if he'd been studying ownership maps of the area. "You're a landowner, aren't you?" he said.

"Yes," said Dean. "It's a difficult name to forget once you've seen its Teutonic form."

"What about the Krafts?" Erhardt asked.

"There's a lot of them out there."

When Dean proposed buying the Arcadia property with state funds, Erhardt showed no interest. "No, there's no reason to talk of disposing of the property now," he said. "We're just sitting on it. It's in the CEO's hands."

"CEO?" asked Dean. "You mean McCormick?"

If Bill McCormick were personally interested in the Arcadia land, that could spell bad news. As soon as they could, Dean, Steve, and Steve's father, Oscar, met Erhardt and his colleague face-to-face in Consumer Power's office downstate in Jackson. They made little headway. No, Consumers did not want to sell the dunes and forest. But Erhardt appeared *greatly* interested in one topic: did Watervale have historical designation?

Dean and the Krafts drove home that afternoon with a new mission: slap as many protective historic designations on Watervale as possible.

Soon after, their efforts to get a state grant came to an abrupt end. The Michigan Department of Natural Resources sent Dean a curt letter in August 1989. No willing seller, they said. No Trust Fund money. Dean sighed and jotted a note to Dori and the others on the letter's margins: "So they've held on to it in its pristine state for 20+ years now. Shall we trust to 'luck' that it'll so remain for another 20?"

But Consumers Power was moving faster than that. Less than a month later, the newspapers blazed this headline:

Consumers Sells 5,700 Acres to Sister Company
Traverse City Record-Eagle, September 24, 1989

Traverse City—Consumers Power Co. has sold a 5,700-acre plot of land in southern Benzie and northern Manistee counties to a sister company for more than $7.7 million, county records show.

The purchaser, CMS Arcadia Land Management Co., like Consumers Power, is a subsidiary company of CMS Energy Corp. The main effect of the transaction, company officials say, is that it gives CMS Energy more options and removes the property from regulation by the state Public Service Commission.

"This transfers the property from the utility side of the company to the non-utility side," said Eric O. Fornell, chairman of the Arcadia company. . . . "We have no plans for the property now, but clearly it's a beautiful piece of land and it has a lot of possibilities," he said.

At Watervale, the Preservation Society examined the news printed in the *Record-Eagle* and the *Benzie County Record Patriot.* So Consumers had transferred the Arcadia land to a real estate holding company. That move certainly cleared the path for a new major resort development. No wonder Consumers had not been interested in selling to Watervale neighbors. Several farmers had also tried to buy back acreage in the last year, but except for Evans Brothers Orchards, which acquired some acres at the far eastern fringe, Consumers would not deal. In fact, Consumers Power had just bought 100 acres on Herring Road to add to the Arcadia block.

Undaunted, Dori pursued her own preservation plan, and before long Watervale was the triumphant holder of Blaine Township's single liquor license.

"You did what?" said Dori's friend Reg Bird when he heard.

Dori explained her strategy. Reg chuckled. "Well, now you can serve wine at weddings," he said.

Dori looked deflated.

"Look, you need something stronger than that," said Reg. "You need to lock up your shoreline. With a conservation easement you can place your land under permanent restriction. No buildings, no dredging."

"How do we do that?" asked Dori.

Reg told her about plans in the works to set up a new land trust, a conservancy for the Grand Traverse region. The land trust could draft the conservation easement and guard the restrictions.

"Sign us up," said Dori. "And quickly. As the man who pumped the septic tanks said: 'What are you going to do when they add a few more zeros to that offer?'"

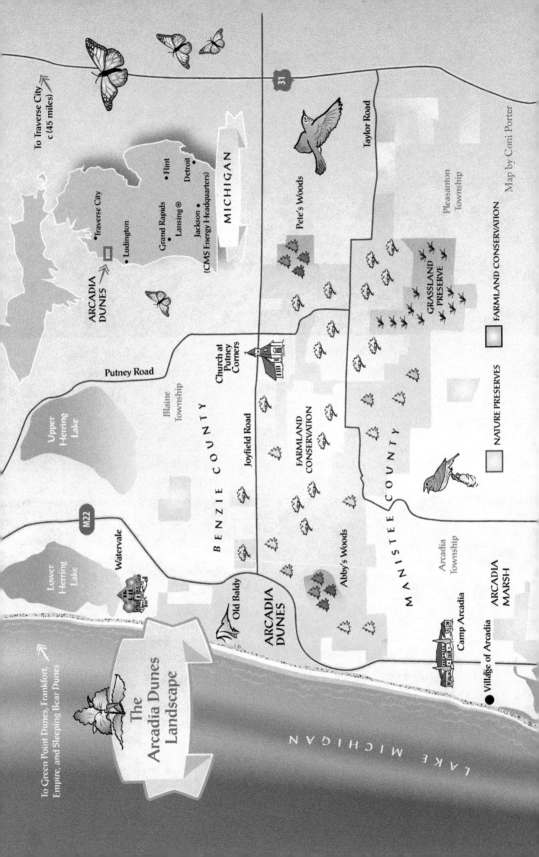

The Arcadia Dunes Landscape

To Green Point Dunes, Frankfort,
Empire, and Sleeping Bear Dunes

To Traverse City
c (45 miles)

MICHIGAN

Traverse City
Ludington
Grand Rapids
Lansing
Flint
Jackson
Detroit
(CMS Energy Headquarters)

ARCADIA DUNES

31

Putney Road

Blaine Township

BENZIE COUNTY

Upper Herring Lake

Lower Herring Lake

M22

Watervale

Old Baldy

ARCADIA DUNES

Church at Putney Corners

Joyfield Road

FARMLAND CONSERVATION

Abby's Woods

Pete's Woods

Taylor Road

Pleasanton Township

GRASSLAND PRESERVE

MANISTEE COUNTY

Arcadia Township

Camp Arcadia

Village of Arcadia

ARCADIA MARSH

LAKE MICHIGAN

FARMLAND CONSERVATION

NATURE PRESERVES

Map by Coni Porter

The majesty of the Arcadia Dunes coast showing Old Baldy, the heart of the nature preserve, where Bill McCormick planned to build a dune golf course. The perched dune plunges more than 300 feet down to Lake Michigan. (Photo by Jim Lindner Photography)

The beach at Arcadia Dunes looking north toward Watervale and Green Point Dunes. (Photo by Michael D-L Jordan / DLP)

Unbroken acres of hemlock, black cherry, beech and maple forest grow on the forested dune. (Photo by Paula Dreeszen)

High up on Old Baldy, the wind sculpts sandy blowouts on the constantly shifting dune landscape. (Photo by Christine Arvidson)

The Grassland Preserve at Arcadia Dunes on a misty morning. (Photo by Angie Lucas)

Apple and cherry trees blossom along Joyfield Rd. in Arcadia Dunes' farmland conservation area. Arcadia Dunes is part of Michigan's "Fruitbelt" – land ideal for growing fruit. Tart cherries, sweet cherries, apples and wine grapes are a large part of the agricultural economy. (Photo by Heather Shumaker)

The "Sound of Music" view from Green Point Dunes Natural Area shows the full sweep of Arcadia Dunes and protected coastline. Watervale sits at the southern tip of Lower Herring Lake. (Photo by Drew Smith)

The black-and-white warbler, a migratory species that builds its nest on the ground and thrives in unfragmented forest. (Photo by John Ester)

A grasshopper sparrow finds a home at the Grassland Preserve. Grasshopper sparrow populations are in steep decline across the country, mostly due to habitat loss and degradation, but annual bird counts show that Grasshopper sparrows are thriving at Arcadia. (Photo by Carl Freeman)

Pitcher's thistle, a federally threatened species, lives only on Great Lakes sand dunes and depends on shifting sands. Here Pitcher's thistle grows on Old Baldy. (Photo by Paula Dreeszen)

Fascicled broomrape on Arcadia Dunes. A threatened species, this rare, parasitic plant steals nutrients from other plants. (Photo by Paula Dreeszen)

Dune flowers bloom each summer atop Old Baldy. From left to right: hairy puccoon, harebell, and wood lily. (Photos by Paula Dreeszen)

Part II

Dune Giants
1991–2003

4 Trailblazing

The greatest use of a life is to spend it for
something that will outlast it.

—William James

Madison, Wisconsin
1997

If someone had told me that I would need calculus to save life on earth, I would have sat up and paid attention in high school.

The wind was blowing the sweet scent of lake water off Lake Mendota, the scent of freshwater with a mix of leopard frogs and cattails. I often came down to the lakeside to study, and today I was studying the graduate school course catalogue. My eyes zeroed in on the prerequisites for conservation biology.

Conservation biology is the science of how to save nature from extinction. It's a practical, do-something-about-it branch of biology. Instead of recording habitat loss or species population decline, conservation biology strives to take action. It's an ambitious field, partly because there are so many parts to save—not just species but the genes they contain, the habitats they live in, and the planetary ecosystems they're part of.

My trouble was I'd never seen the connection between my interests and math before. Later that afternoon, a professor handed me a textbook, telling me I could join the conservation biology class only if I did a summer self-study of statistics. "Oh, and you'll need calculus, too."

I soon found out why. Understanding how to save wild species involves charting their population fluctuations. When a species is endangered, it doesn't just mean there are too few individuals, it means their genetic health is at risk. Wild populations need to maintain a broad gene pool to stay robust, and even thousands of a single species aren't enough.

That same semester, across campus, another of my professors passed around a bag of pretzel rods. This was a class on landownership, and he used the pretzels to explain how land rights in this country are divided into separate sticks. These rights all start together, but you can separate them. For example, you can separate access rights and allow people to walk on your land. You can separate out mining rights, timber rights, or grazing rights. In the same way, you can own the land but not the development rights. That's where land trusts come in. These nonprofits can separate development rights, safeguard them, and preserve the land. I began to fall in love with land trusts.

It was clear to me that meaningful habitat protection needed a broad approach. Nature preserves were great, but you couldn't turn the whole world into a park. Also, try explaining park boundaries to a whooping crane. Whether you were talking about an orchid or a box turtle, wild species needed entire landscapes to survive. Land trusts, or land conservancies, seemed to have an answer. They could safeguard habitat on private or public land, they could buy land or separate development rights, and their work was permanent, voluntary, and local. I designed my graduate program around land trusts.

In class we scrawled matrices and population charts on the board, the axes labeled with songbirds, turtles, or butterflies. It was one thing to do the math. It was another thing to actually save their lives on the ground. Land trust work took more than calculus. It took everything I'd learned, everything I had.

But before my time with land trusts began, it was Glen's story.

Traverse City, Michigan
1991

The Grand Traverse region was already chock-full of Glens: Glen Haven, Glen Arbor, Little Glen Lake, Big Glen Lake, Glen's Landfill, Glen's Market, and artist Glenn Wolff. And now a newcomer: Glen Chown.

When Glen Chown took the helm of the newly hatched Grand Traverse Regional Land Conservancy, he was twenty-nine, sandy haired, cocksure, and in over his head. But Rob had promised to stand beside him, so here he was, sharing Rob's office on West Grand Traverse Bay. It was 1991, and GTRLC—or simply the Conservancy—had just been legally incorporated. It was Rob Collier, head of Rotary Charities in Traverse City, who had singled Glen out to be the Conservancy's first executive director. Dark haired, curly headed, and bespectacled, Rob was a strong environmental champion. He had noted Glen's passion and wanted to bring someone with conservation experience to Traverse City.

Over the past few years, this sleepy northern town had started to wake up. Suddenly new roads and developments inched over old hunting spots and favorite fishing holes in the Grand Traverse region. Business folks at the Traverse City Rotary Club got to thinking. How could we balance growth with a network of protected areas? Could we boost tourism by saving views of lakeshores and cherry orchards? Further north, in Petoskey, a land trust had been set up in the 1970s. What if we had one here? When Rob took charge of recruiting a leader for a fledgling Grand Traverse conservancy, he called north to Petoskey, where Glen worked as a land protection specialist at the Little Traverse Conservancy. "Glen, it's Rob Collier. Let's have ice cream."

They met at Baskin Robbins in Charlevoix. Glen ordered vanilla with nuts and chocolate swirl, known regionally as Mackinac Island Fudge. Rob stuck to chocolate. Over the hum of the ice cream freezers, Rob outlined plans for a new conservancy in Traverse City. But Glen was content in his job. No thanks, he said.

Rob persisted. He called again and they shared more ice cream. As the weeks went on, Rob changed tactics. "I have Interlochen tickets," he said.

Glen said yes to the tickets. It was Van Cliburn, the legendary concert pianist, playing at the Interlochen Center for the Arts. Glen played piano himself and dreamed of owning a grand piano someday. As he settled in his theater seat, Rob extolled the virtues of the Grand Traverse area, which included cultural gems such as Interlochen and great hiking at Sleeping Bear Dunes National Lakeshore. After the concert, Rob kept calling.

Glen, it's Rob Collier.

Again: Glen, have you given some thought to what we talked about?

And again: It's Rob. Look, Glen, I want you to think about this seriously. We could use you down here.

Glen sighed and scanned the land projects on his desk. After a stint at the Nature Conservancy in Virginia, then a move home to Michigan, he'd just landed what he considered the ideal job: contacting landowners in peaceful, remote Petoskey. "I don't know, Rob. I've got my job here. I'm just not sure I want to make the move."

"Chown, you're incorrigible!" said Rob. More than six months had passed, and still his recruit was reluctant. "I'll be with you, Glen," said Rob. "I'll help you make it work. I'll open doors for you. I'll introduce you to people at Rotary, to people in Benzie County. You'll have Rotary's financial support and my personal help."

Glen gave in and sent in his résumé. He toured the land. He learned that his main competition for the director post was a fundraiser for the Presbyterian church, someone who could raise big bucks but knew nothing about land work. When the interview committee offered the job to Glen, he was still uncertain. Should he take it?

Back at his rented lodgings, Glen snapped open a Labatt's and passed the corn chips and salsa to his roommate, Wil. The two of them had rented a cottage on Walloon Lake for the off-season. Tonight they sat up late as Glen grappled with the life choice before him. "Traverse City will be an urban jungle. I won't like it," said Glen. "Plus they need me here—I've got so many deals going, I can't just leave them."

Wil, an advocate for water quality, looked at him. The two had shared many talks about how best to protect Michigan's natural land. "This place will be fine, Glen, whether you're here or not," said Wil. "On the other hand, the Grand Traverse region could go either way. If they don't hire the right person, that could set things back twenty years or more. A lot of land could be lost."

Glen stared at the lapping waves on Walloon Lake. He thought of his conservation heroes, John Muir, Aldo Leopold, and Henry David Thoreau. He knew his answer. It would mean fewer hikes, fewer swims, and fewer camping trips in his future. He would have to say good-bye to his own freedom in the outdoors to save it for others. Wil's words echoed in his mind. *This place will be fine, whether you're here or not.* But if he didn't accept the challenge, what would happen to the land around Grand Traverse?

Glen packed his khakis and good shoes, his assortment of ties and polyester sweaters. He boxed up his books, including old favorites that had charted his course to date: Edward Abbey's *Desert Solitaire,* John McPhee's *Coming into the Country,* and Stewart Udall's *The Quiet Crisis.* He was single, but about to commit himself to a nonprofit. Taking this job meant pouring his life into the needy, newborn Grand Traverse conservancy, drop by precious drop.

The new conservancy covered four counties surrounding Traverse City: Antrim, Benzie, Grand Traverse, and Kalkaska. Rotary gave Glen orders to "hit the ground running." Natural land was disappearing fast, and landowners needed immediate options. Down at Watervale, for example, the innkeeper Dori Turner was eager to protect her property, and there were others. Her uncle Oscar had been so impatient he'd restricted development on his Lake Michigan shoreline property two years ago, in 1989, before the Grand Traverse land trust even existed. The land management branch of Rotary had agreed to hold the conservation easement temporarily, until Glen's group could take over. There was no time to wait.

True to his word, Rob took Glen under his wing at first. It was Rob who secured $100,000 as a three-year start-up grant from Rotary and lodged Glen in his own office, part of the Great Lakes Petroleum Building. Rob also helped Glen solicit matching grants from the Biederman, Borwell, Grainger, Oleson, and Seabury family foundations so the new conservancy would have a healthy start. But it was not Rob's way to foster dependency. Not many months had gone by before Rob nudged Glen to separate from Rotary. "You need to get out on your own," he said.

"I don't know what I'm doing, Rob," Glen protested. "I don't know how to run a nonprofit!"

"You'll be fine," said Rob. "I won't abandon you."

The Conservancy's new office was a grey-sided house on Third Street in Traverse City. Glen shared the first floor with another nonprofit director, Tom Kelly of the new Inland Seas Education Association. Tom and Glen shared an assistant and a copy machine. They also shared long hours and headaches as each coaxed a new nonprofit to life. Glen bought a house nearby on Webster Street, but he was rarely home. He merged his soul with the Conservancy, so it was impossible to tell where the person ended and the organization began. His days, evenings, and weekends were consumed as chief jack-of-all-trades, leading field trips, meeting potential donors, negotiating land deals, sending fundraising letters, and hauling trash to the dumpster.

He was so busy, in fact, that if Rebecca Martin hadn't walked into the Conservancy offices, he might have stayed single. Becky, who held a summer journalism internship at the *Lake County Gazette,* stopped by the West Bay Drive office to drop off some pamphlets. She had straight blond hair, sparkling blue eyes, and talked two miles a minute.

That day Glen knew he would marry her.

Traverse City, Michigan
1998

Glen and Becky Chown's first son, William, was one year old when I arrived at the Third Street office. It was February, and more than a foot of snow sagged over the eaves. Glen, thirty-six, had been married for four years now. He commanded the whole Third Street house as well as a staff of five. I drove in from Wisconsin to become the newest staff member, making it six.

Back in December in Madison, I had spotted the job listing while nervously passing the time before my thesis defense. I couldn't settle to anything, so I began scanning job lists down in my basement office. The environmental studies department occupied the brick-walled bowels of Science Hall. For two years I had typed on my computer in a windowless basement room as the radiator pipes clanked and cockroaches scuttled along the floor. "Used to be the medical school morgue," a department staff woman told me as she first handed me the key. "They stored the bodies in here. Have a good night!"

Now I was preparing to turn in my key. In two hours, a trio of professors would convene to grill me on conservation principles: What's the difference between alpha, beta, and gamma species diversity? When a forest is fragmented, how far do edge effects extend? How do changes in forest structure affect habitat for ground-nesting songbirds? What are the pros and cons of several small nature preserves versus a single large one? What legal land protection tools work best for landscape-level conservation? Assuming I fielded the questions well, I would graduate with a master's degree in land resources: debt-free, but also income-free.

That's when I spotted the ad: "Land Protection Specialist in Traverse City, Michigan." Traverse City? I had never heard of it. I reached for a map. Although I'd grown up in the Midwest, Michigan was alien territory to me. Once I had hiked the length of Isle Royale—a stray piece of Michigan located in Lake Superior that's closer to the coast of Canada—but otherwise I'd never stepped foot in Michigan. The job's posted deadline was a month ago, but I dialed the number anyway and asked for Glen Chown.

His voice rumbled with powerful warmth. Yes, the job was still open. As we talked, he painted a picture of lakes and forests, strange sand dunes, and clear fly-fishing rivers. Clearly Glen was a man on a mission who loved his corner of the world. "We've got some unique land up here. Not just natural land, I'm talking about farmland. The Grand Traverse region has some of the country's best cherry orchard land."

I scratched the words "Farmland—cherries" on my notepad. To me, that was a strike against the job, but I stayed mute. I yearned to save the natural world, not land converted to farms. Still, this job in cherry country might give me the chance I was looking for. Glen changed the subject. "Do you like snow?"

"The more the better."

He laughed. "Well, you'll love it up here. Last year we got 200 inches."

A month later I was standing in my snow boots next to Glen at the Pyatt Lake Nature Preserve. His wife was there, along with baby William trussed up in a snowsuit, and Ty, a land protection staffer. This was the outdoor portion of my interview. We hiked by the buckled roots of a cedar grove and emerged at the frozen edge of Pyatt Lake. Glen and Ty leaned against the overlook railing, gesturing with mittened hands as they spun tales of land protection. How schoolchildren had rallied to save Pyatt Lake. How the Conservancy had saved a river parcel called Seven Bridges after a series of close calls with developers, timber trespass, and a heartwarming appeal to grant makers in Lansing.

"So there we were in front of the Trust Fund board, and we've talked about water quality and how it's great trout habitat, and then I scrapped most of my speech and just told them what my little brother had said to me the night before." Ty was talking. His treble voice squeaked to an even higher pitch with excitement. "My little brother, Reb, he's thirteen. He said: 'If we lose Seven Bridges, where will we go to fish? Where will we go?'"

"The Trust Fund voted it in," Glen broke in. "The staff had recommended against funding it, but the board approved it on the spot."

I gazed out at Pyatt Lake. Fishing spots were what mattered. Favorite wild places. Simply remembering them could cause a state-appointed board to reallocate thousands of dollars.

What would it feel like to be Ty? To be Glen? How would it feel to stand there, on a piece of land that you personally helped to protect? To know that by your own actions, trees were standing that would have been felled? That a lake or a river meandered through its seasons because of you? That porcupines would still climb into tree cavities and the air would still tremble as barred owls and pileated woodpeckers gave their haunting calls? Would I get the chance to join their ranks and find out? To me, Glen and Ty were honorable warriors. Loraxes.

Glen started me as a land protection specialist at $23,000, full-time, with the understanding that most weeks I'd be working overtime. "You'll be leading field trips on the weekends, plus going to township meetings and giving talks many evenings," said Glen. "It's not a nine-to-five job. Summers are crazy. And things get busy at Christmas, too. That's when most donations roll in."

With the job, Glen had handed me a slice of the world to take care of. "You'll be working in Benzie County," he told me. "It's beautiful country; you'll love it. The Betsie River, the Platte, plus Crystal Lake, that's an eight-mile-long lake, you'll get to know it. And Lake Ann. We're doing a big project on Pearl Lake right now. And of course there's the sand dunes on Lake Michigan's coast."

I traced out the contours of the Benzie County lakes and forest on a map. Two rivers, six major lakes, multiple minor ones, forests, wetlands, dunes, and shoreline. All that land, mine to care for. The responsibility felt like the solemn weight of a graduate's robe and stole on my shoulders. A fierce swell of protective love engulfed me.

On Third Street, the Conservancy's office bristled with passion. The building itself was humble and homey. It had dull grey siding, a screen door that banged, and a mourning dove nest above the entrance. The front window was framed by two cedar bushes. In the backyard, a plywood door tilted lopsidedly over a corrugated metal tool shed. Crammed inside were a jumble of weed whackers, gas cans, shovels, and nature preserve signs leaning on their posts.

A great behemoth of a copy machine dominated the main floor of the house, and above the walls of the copy machine hung newspaper clippings and children's drawings saying, "Save Pyatt Lake." Upstairs, four of us squeezed offices into the bedrooms: Ty, Kieran, and I, all land protection specialists, plus Kieran's wife, Anne-Marie, who juggled the newsletter, field trips, and their new baby. We erected assemble-it-yourself chipboard desks under the dormers and took turns using the three phone lines. The home wiring system sagged under the pressure of too many computers. Ignoring the fire hazard, we stuffed precious land deeds into overflowing desk drawers.

Downstairs, Birgit handled the money and Arvida handled everything else, including the white-haired volunteers from the senior center. One of Arvida's jobs was to deliver endless platters of sugar cookies. While the cookies lasted, volunteers folded fundraising appeals and sealed the envelopes' edges with moist, yellow sponge pads. We lugged full mailbags to the bathroom, stacking the grey, bulgy sacks in the bathtub until someone was free to make a post office run.

It was a young nonprofit, only seven years old. Like any young thing, the Conservancy was full of unfocused dreams and bursting with energy.

Driving that energy was Executive Director Glen Chown. Glen was a fireball. He pounded energy down the rickety stairs. He bellowed it through the halls. He purred it into the phone when he had a VIP on the line. And so many people were VIPs in the land trust world–landowners, Conservancy members, board members, local politicians, new donors, and philanthropists with family foundations. Glen needed them all, and his personal charm captured person after person. He drew them toward the Conservancy's mission without their conscious consent, until folks who had given no thought to land protection before found their heads nodding and their mouths saying, Yes, yes, that's exactly what we need to do.

Glen lured people hungry for hope and passion. He was like a sugarer, tapping through the sinewy bark of a maple tree to find sweet sap and then transforming it into the melt-away pleasure of maple sugar candy. When he made home visits, he tapped into childhood memories of summer cottage life and walks on beaches and transformed that rush of sweet warmth into dollars for the Conservancy's latest project. When he talked, wallets opened, and when he began "chowning" it up, donations really poured in. As one couple watched Glen's rusty maroon Honda drive away, they rubbed their eyes and turned to each other. "What just happened?"

By the end of Glen's first year, the Conservancy had 492 members. Three years later it had swelled to nearly 1,300. When I arrived, more than

2,300 people sent in money every year, and the Conservancy's influence was growing. It grew despite his crowded desk that toppled with papers and his earnest exaggerations. Glen blazed a fiery commitment to land protection. He charged ahead with a "Ready—Fire—Aim!" approach, but he charged with such cheerful zeal that supporters gave more money than they had intended, and gave it gladly.

Glen's office jutted out next to the porch at the front of the house. It was an airy room with windows on three sides that all rattled in their casings as Glen pounded around the building. He was a man in motion. Tethered by his phone cord, he would pace the office, as the cord stretched out of its coil and grew more tangled with each call. Every now and then the door flew open and Glen's voice bombarded us: "Ty! What's Suzanne's husband's name? Kieran! Get me a map of the Boardman River! Quick! Birgit! Where're my sunglasses?"

A bulky word processor dominated his desk, plus towers of paper that slipped and spilled and competed for attention like kids in a busy family. Glen knew all about competition in a big family. He had grown up with four brothers and a sister in Bay City. With six kids, Glen learned to hone his assertiveness and pitch his voice loudly at the dinner table. These days he stuffed maps, papers, and good intentions into a weatherbeaten leather briefcase, always meaning to enter notes about his last donor visit into the computer database. The database languished while Glen's stacks of paper mounted. He marked important notes with an angular, left-fisted scrawl: *Call Rob Monday* or *GM vice president cottage on Torch Lake*. His secondhand table, already wobbly on its axis, tipped precariously during every staff meeting.

"That's it! Focus!" Glen would say, banging his fist down with every syllable. "Laser beam focus! Are we ready to save some land? Who's going for lunch? Will you pick up a sandwich for me? And an iced tea. What's that?" He would wave his hand in dismissal. "Oh, don't worry about it, I'll pay you back later."

Like Glen, I arrived at the Conservancy single and sacrificially devoted to my job. I was twenty-eight, wore round-framed glasses, and had dark brown hair reaching to my waist. I was a quarter inch shy of making it to five foot four. Back in Madison I'd packed my turtlenecks and hiking boots, my new skirts and jewel neck tops. I sold my secondhand furniture to my roommate, Ellen, and left behind a broken heart and a bushy Boston fern, too big to travel. Mostly, I shipped books to Michigan: *Principles of Conservation Biology, Doing Deals: A Guide to Buying Land for Conservation, The Fragmented Forest, A Sand County Almanac,* the *Ramayana,* and my newly printed thesis. I marked each box "Traverse City" (a name I had just learned to pronounce like a local) in black permanent marker.

Coming from Columbus and Madison, I found Traverse City a far cry from an urban jungle. With an official population of only 17,000, the town was smaller than half the size of either city's college campus. Besides being small, it felt parochial.

Traverse City in 1998 still had dirt streets close to downtown. The population was ninety-seven percent white. Area schools closed on the opening day of deer hunting season but didn't close on Martin Luther King Jr. Day. Hispanics lived here, but many worked seasonally as migrant farm laborers, living in cinder block pickers' barracks tucked away on remote farms. Native Ottawa and Chippewa were the largest minority. Downtown, if someone walked by with a fishing pole and bait bucket it didn't raise eyebrows, but when an African American family strolled by the sight caused heads to swivel. In 1999 the *Traverse City Record-Eagle's* lead story profiled local kids who had gone out of state for college. One blond freshman had never met an Asian person before. Petrified when she was assigned an Asian American roommate, she called her mom. "I was so scared," she said. "I was like, 'Mom, I can't do it.'" Traverse City boasted a new mall, a dammed river, and an all-night box store.

But the land was beautiful, and that's what grabbed me. Northern Michigan was filled with unearthly lakes: spring-fed lakes, glacial lakes, Great Lakes, bar lakes, tiny pothole lakes, chains of lakes, and the enormous Grand Traverse Bay, a giant lobe of Lake Michigan. In the days when French traders and Ottawa and Chippewa canoeists crossed the waters, the bay was the *grand traverse*—the big crossing. The voyageur canoes were gone. These days the shimmering blue bay distracted drivers along Grandview Parkway three seasons of the year; in winter ice chunks floated in a watery honeycomb and waves froze at the shore. "A view of the bay is half your pay," people joked as they hunkered down to face the lean winter months.

Lake Michigan itself glowed like a vast tropical sea, dazzling the eye with Caribbean teals and blues. But looks can fool. For those brave enough to swim in July, the water was still chilled to fifty or sixty degrees Fahrenheit. Rugged white pine trees clung to the shore instead of coconut palms, and the water was fresh, not salt.

The first time I set foot in Michigan I walked on the solid, lichen-covered granite that forms Isle Royale. But here on the "Gold Coast" of lower Michigan, sand covered the landscape. Even from outer space you can see the Great Lakes sand dunes. They rim Michigan's west coast in a distinct band. Sand attracted a million tourists a year to Sleeping Bear Dunes National Lakeshore. Local businesses like Cherry Republic elevated sand into their motto: Life, Liberty, Beaches & Pie. Locals buzzed around town with bumper stickers that read "Got Sand?"

Besides a landscape of lakes and dunes, I had entered orchard country. Northern Michigan was part of the "Fruit Belt," a swath of land well suited for growing stone fruit, thanks to the vast watery bed of Lake Michigan moderating the climate. Honeycrisp apple trees formed neat lines along with Jonagold, Northern Spies, Yellow Delicious, and Macintosh, and the Elberta peach was first developed here.

But the king of orchard crops here was the cherry. Sweet cherries for munching and spitting out the pits. Tart cherries for pies and cobblers. Each July Traverse City crowned a Cherry Queen who rode in the National Cherry Festival parade decked out in a cherry-red dress, satin sash, and sparkly tiara. The Queen's job was to wave to parade-goers, then tour the country for a year touting the antioxidant benefits of eating cherries. Neighborhood elementary schools anointed Cherry Princes and Princesses from the first grade—a time-tested method for getting cherry moms and dads to spend their summer evenings twisting chicken wire and tissue paper into parade floats. Meanwhile, on the farms, migrant workers from Mexico trekked their families north to pick apples and shake cherries, where they mixed with local teenagers on their first summer jobs.

The Conservancy was engaged in saving Pearl Lake when I arrived. At risk was unspoiled forest, 250 acres, with glacial wetlands, loons, and osprey plus a bald eagle nest with two young. Developers had plans to build ninety-seven houses. "We didn't get a call on this parcel until the developers already owned it," said Glen. "It's always more expensive to chase bulldozers."

I nodded. I loved Pearl Lake. It was perfect wild habitat and backed up to state forest land, forming an even larger natural area. Pearl Lake was worth saving, but the key was to find other big parcels before the developers did. That meant getting out in front of the developers by talking to landowners.

Before coming to Michigan, I'd studied landowners. I'd written papers labeling them "stakeholders," "property owners," and "taxpayers." I had even talked to one over the phone, but my voice had shaken. Truth was, I was terrified of them.

But there was no way to get around the fact that the business of saving land was all about people. If you wished to preserve habitat you had to talk to the people who owned the land. During my first months at the Conservancy, I wished I had studied more human psychology and less forest ecology in graduate school. The math and science set the direction, but if I wanted to act rather than be academic, I would have to find new courage. But first, I needed to find a Benzie County plat book.

"Here's what we have," Kieran told me. "It's five years old."

"We need an up-to-date plat map," I said. "Ownership changes all the time."

"Talk to Birgit."

The finance director looked overwhelmed. Fundraising appeals covered her desk and mounted high from postal trays on the floor. I stated my case.

"How much do they cost?" she asked.

"Thirty dollars."

"Can't you use the old one?"

I waited and didn't answer. *If I have to, I'll use my own money and buy a plat book myself,* I thought.

She sighed and wrote out a check.

My new plat book was a slim, spiral-bound volume with ads for foresters, sawmills, and excavators mixed in with landownership maps. "This book sponsored by the Benzie County 4-H club!" the cover said. I scoured the booklet looking for large parcels with 100 acres or more held by the same owner. Conservation biology principles drove me on: save big blocks of habitat. Look for natural links between protected areas. Habitat fragmentation is the enemy.

The canopy of a big forest shades the forest floor and creates the right conditions for spring wildflowers to flourish and songbirds to build their nests safely. When roads and houses punch holes in the forest canopy, the forest degrades. Bit by bit, foot by foot, the air dries out along the edge, changing the microclimate. Deer stroll down the new openings and munch their way through the vegetation, killing the next generation of young trees and clearing low brush as effectively as a vacuum cleaner. When too many deer move into the woods, they eat the forest into submission. Predators like cats and raccoons prowl the edge areas and gulp down bird eggs and young. Birds that used to conceal their nests on the ground inside bushes are now fatally exposed to predators. Their genes direct them to build low nests, but each clutch of eggs is wiped out as soon as it is laid. Roads bring in weeds and disease—seeds roll in on tires and create new patches of aggressive foreign plants like garlic mustard and spotted knapweed. The newcomers carpet the ground and spread so effectively that local plants can't compete. With invasive species hogging the sunlight and nutrients, native wildflowers die out and the ground layer becomes a solid mass of usurpers.

I was new to dune and cherry country, but I knew about fragmented forests. For most natural habitat preservation, it all comes down to this: big is better. Big blocks are better yet.

At the bottom of Benzie County lay the biggest block of land in the plat book. I couldn't keep my eyes off it. Why was there such a big parcel of land in Blaine Township? The land stretched six miles across. Two thousand, maybe three thousand acres, all with one name marking it: CMS Arcadia Land. "What do you know about this land?" I asked Glen, showing him the plat book.

Glen glanced at the map and smiled. "Ah, so you've found Consumers."

"Consumers?"

"Yeah, Consumers Power, the biggest public utility in Michigan. The parent company is called CMS Energy," he said.

"It's big," I said.

"Oh, it's big," Glen agreed. "It goes into Manistee County, too. The whole thing's 6,000 acres."

"You mean I'm only seeing half of it?"

That afternoon I sat in Glen's office as the April wind rattled the windows. The snow had melted into a slushy heap and flooded the grass, just as Consumers might have flooded the Arcadia land. I learned how Consumers had consolidated the land beginning the year I was born. How its plans had failed and the land lay idle, waiting for a new vision.

When I left Glen's office I had stars in my eyes.

The land was bigger than I had thought.

It was entirely clear of houses.

Most of it was natural, and the dune was bound to have rare species of global significance.

That day I determined to save Old Baldy and the back acreage on Dry Hill, land I had never seen. *This* was what I had come to Michigan for—the chance to tackle conservation on a scale that made a difference. In the Midwest, where land was mostly chunked up in forty-acre squares, a 6,000-acre tract was something grand. Here was a rare opportunity to reknit the patchwork landscape. A chance to make a global contribution to habitat protection in our own backyard. In Glen, I recognized the zeal of a fellow conservationist out to save the world. Glen shared my drive for big parcels, and this was the biggest of the lot. The leviathan. To tackle the quest, first we needed a Manistee County plat book.

5 Dune Dreams

Whatever you can do, or dream you can do, begin it.
Boldness has genius, power and magic in it.

—Attributed to Goethe

Northern Michigan
1998–2000

Of all the natural wonders in Michigan, the Great Lakes coastline and sand dunes are exceptional. Not only are they stop-in-your-tracks-and-stare beautiful, they're a boost for biodiversity—species live here that are unique on earth. Not many species can tough it out on the dry dunes. The ones that thrive here have adapted to the specialized habitat. The Great Lakes dunes offer a home to more than thirty rare plants and animals, including a few endemics: plants and animals that live nowhere else.

Our world is richer for these unique specialists. All the extreme and unusual places have their own cast of characters, whether it's polar bears and penguins in the polar regions or one-of-a-kind geckos and tortoises in the tropics. True, our silver-leaved Pitcher's thistle isn't as adorable as some of the world's other rarities, but it adds unique genes to the world's soup mix. It's a Great Lakes original.

Here I could embark on a task of global importance. Here was a slice of the world's ecology where I could make a difference.

Yet sometimes we neglect what we care about most. For two years I dreamed of the Arcadia land but took no action. This is often the case. Lovely dreams seem out of reach. We dream about what we might do in a wouldn't-it-be-nice way, but then we busy our days with other things. For me, staff meetings swamped my Tuesdays, field trips took over my Saturdays, and I was frequently out in the evenings running to township and county meetings. Land deals at the forty- to ninety-acre scale occupied my days. Glen, too, dreamed of the Arcadia land, but was distracted with constant fundraising, staff issues, budgets, and board meetings.

When it came right down to it, a mammoth project like the Arcadia dunes never seemed convenient.

Conservation on this scale would demand enormous energy and new methods. We were talking about the largest privately owned parcel on Lake Michigan. Saving Arcadia would not be routine. How could we even possibly begin? After my first two weeks on the job, I'd overcome my fear of meeting landowners. I felt confident picking up the phone and talking to any landowning family, but how would I knock on the door of a giant corporation and attract its attention? It was too big. Too out of reach. The dream of Arcadia languished.

By now I had hiked the dunes and understood firsthand the magnitude of the project. At stake was one of the world's most vibrant populations of Pitcher's thistle. An unbroken canopy of near-old-growth forest. A view of eternity from the top of the dunes. And possibly the whole local orchard economy, for those who cared about agriculture. Yet week after week, the Arcadia dunes only hovered at the back of my mind.

It was a local bank that finally brought sand dunes into my life. "I have a client in our trust department who owns some land on Lake Michigan," said the trust officer, who had called out of the blue. "I think your group might be a good fit."

It wasn't Arcadia, but the dunes at Pt. Betsie were also globally important. The Nature Conservancy had been chipping away at land protection for years on a small swath of dunes near the Pt. Betsie lighthouse. The lightkeeper's house had a picturesque red, cedar-shingled roof and whitewashed light tower, and around it lay habitat for threatened dune plants and insects. Over the years, the Nature Conservancy had amassed a network of parcels to create a nature preserve, but its plans called for adding priority parcels in the vicinity. The largest of these, sixty acres with a quarter mile of prize shoreline, was owned by the Laney family.

Soon I was walking the land with Jonathan Laney. We crunched through a carpet of beech and maple leaves, and I gazed in wonder at the sight of the sand dune burying a living forest. Some of the sixty-foot trees had sand smothering them up to their hips. The active sand dune would keep covering its prey until the leaves and top branches dropped off, and the tree trunks stood mummified in sand. Up the beach a stretch, the sand was simultaneously *un*covering a ghost forest that had suffered the same fate hundreds of years ago. As the sand blew off the old forest it exposed the skeletons of trees—stark bone-white trunks against the blue sky. This was land worth saving.

But something was wrong with the landowner relationship. I watched my guide warily.

Jonathan plied me with tubs of yogurt from his pickup truck. His flatbed had groceries crammed to the ceiling, and in the cab more groceries overflowed across the vinyl cushion, leaving scant seat space for the driver. Inside his house, junk piled high against the kitchen door. It was obvious he didn't read his mail: envelopes were strewn about the bushes. He favored bright orange vests, neon-green shirts and striped ties.

"You didn't walk there *alone* with him, did you?" asked the bank trust officer, horrified. I discovered that Jonathan was unpredictable: brilliant but not stable. The bank managed his finances in trust. He could suddenly turn irrationally angry and violent.

But having met Jonathan, I also knew that he loved the land deeply. He talked lucidly about the Lake Michigan land, and his trust officer understood. Together, with the help of the trust and Jonathan's siblings out west, we crafted a deal. The Conservancy would buy the land, the Nature Conservancy would help fundraise and likely add it to its existing preserve. The Laney family –and all the public—would have access to hike it. There promised to be no land management costs for us. We signed a contract to buy the Betsie Dunes land.

With more and more land deals completed, the Conservancy was thriving, but the little house on Third Street began to bulge past capacity. Since I'd arrived, the staff had grown to ten and we squeezed intern desks in next to the kitchen sink. It was clear the era of being a start-up nonprofit was over, and it was time to move into larger offices up the road.

Our new space was laid out with pale green padded cubicles and looked businesslike. Glen had longed for a quaint log-cabin office with paths leading out to nature trails, but he realized that could wait. There was land to save, and we needed a modern office to do it. It was a tremendous relief to move in to our new quarters. For the first time we had an electrical system that could handle our computers without overload. We had plenty of outlets, enough phone lines, and a fireproof safe for land deeds. We didn't have to take turns using the phone or store fundraising appeals in the bathtub anymore. With our new office we could concentrate on the business of "reverse real estate"—preserving the earth.

Glen and his family had moved, too. He and Becky bought a historic farm on Old Mission Peninsula, with plenty of room for their cats and dogs. Glen spent his off hours fixing up the barn, and they hoped to add horses one day. Their son, William, was two, and their second son, Martin, was born that Christmas Eve.

As for me, the time had come to see if I could make a major difference. While Glen was busy welcoming his new son, Martin, I took advantage of the quiet week between Christmas and New Year's to work on the CMS Arcadia land. Everyone else in the office was occupied with holiday plans, so the halls were nearly deserted. The last days of 1999 were mine to examine the giant property and devise a plan to save it.

First I needed a bird's-eye view from an aerial photograph. The property was so big it was hard to understand what it contained. I knew some land was farmland, some forest, and some pristine dune. But what was it really like?

These days, any schoolkid could tap a computer mouse and zoom in with Google Earth to see the landscape laid out like a gift. Up-to-date satellite imagery is available for every corner of the earth, twenty-four hours a day. But in the late 1990s, aerial photography coverage of northern Michigan was expensive and intermittent. The Arcadia land was also a victim of boundaries. One set of aerial photos showed the northern half, in Benzie County. The other set showed the southern half, in Manistee County. Edges did not match across the county boundary, the scales were different, and the photos were already ten years out of date. Yet acre by acre, I knit the trees and fields of the CMS Arcadia parcel together.

I stared in awe when I had finished. The new piecemeal map revealed the property's magnitude. There was the full extent of the Arcadia land stretched out before me—two miles long and six miles wide. A two-mile slice of shoreline with 700 acres of dunes perched on the high bluff, then a nearly 2,000-acre swath of unbroken forest, and finally 3,300 acres of farmland to the east. I traced blue, red, and yellow lines around each habitat, printed it out on an 11 x 17 piece of paper, and wrote a one-page vision statement for preservation. The case was simple. Now all we had to do was save it.

Glen's eyes locked on the Arcadia landscape the minute I rolled the map out on his desk in the New Year. Glen loved maps. He bestowed them on donors and grant makers with the enthusiasm of a schoolboy sharing his latest artwork. Glen waved the map with one hand and pushed my written case statement aside with the other. "This is great!" he cried. "Just what we need. Let me call Keith Charters."

Keith Charters was another Conservancy patron saint. Keith connected us to government, including natural resource policy in Lansing, the state capital, and the biggest source of land conservation funding: the Michigan Natural Resources Trust Fund. Every year the state gave out millions of dollars to selected projects. Keith was used to Glen calling him to talk about potential Trust Fund projects. Keith's heart resided in northern Michigan, and he had a soft spot for Glen's boundless enthusiasm. If we were to save Arcadia, we'd certainly need money from the Trust Fund in the future, but right now we needed Keith to get us an introduction to the CMS corporation. It took some time—big projects need patience—but Keith came through for us.

"Bill Parfet's on the CMS board," said Keith. "He'll be at Crystal Mountain in July for an all-day Natural Resources Committee meeting about tribal fishing rights. He's willing to meet you at 7:30 a.m. before the day's session starts. Get there early, and be ready. He won't have much time."

"We'll be ready," said Glen.

Our meeting was set for July 13, 2000. Our meeting place, Crystal Mountain, was a family-owned ski and golf resort in Benzie County. The Conservancy's good friend Jim MacInnes was one of the owners. I knew Jim from my job interview; he'd served on the Conservancy board. During my interview he'd asked me to draw a diagram showing how I thought the business world and the nonprofit's work were related. I grabbed a pen and quickly drew an intersecting relationship. Jim had nodded with satisfaction. Now I swallowed nervously as Jim led us down hallways decorated with Inuit art and meeting rooms labeled Cape Dorset and Baffin Bay. If we were about to meet with people like Jim, I wouldn't be so anxious, but the idea of business interests and nonprofit habitat goals intersecting was about to be tested.

Jim ushered us into an intimate conference room. Glen wore a suit. I clutched my stack of one-page case statements and maps. I'd tried to dress up our handouts for the occasion. The maps were in full color, printed on our new color printer, and I'd printed the case statement on special tan paper.

Four men wearing dark suits walked in, accompanied by Keith Charters. Bill Parfet took the head of the table. He was commanding and broad-shouldered. As he looked around the room sizing us up, it became obvious he'd endured too many tedious meetings in his life, and didn't intend this to be one of them. To his left sat George Burgoyne, a trim man with a hiker's build, who served as deputy director of the Michigan Department of Natural Resources.

Glen's eyes darted left, right, and down as he talked. He looked everywhere except in Bill's eyes. First he explained the Conservancy's founding, then described the CMS Arcadia land—how big it was, how we wanted to turn it into a nature preserve.

Keith checked his watch. "Wrap it up, Glen," he said. "We only have a couple more minutes."

"To make a long story short," said Glen, "we'd like to talk to CMS about buying this land."

"As far as I know," said Bill, "CMS doesn't intend to sell it. I think there is some interest in keeping the land and developing it ourselves."

"If you were to sell, would you consider us?" asked Glen.

"How do you propose paying for it?" countered Bill.

"That's just it, we don't know the land's value," said Glen. "Funding would come from a mixture of sources, some private dollars and some public funding from the Michigan Natural Resources Trust Fund"—here he looked at George and Keith, and they gazed back with no sign of encouragement—"We'd like to work together and order an appraisal."

"You need to talk to Bill McCormick," said Bill. "And also Rodger Kershner. Rodger is Bill's chief counsel." Bill Parfet stood up; our time was over.

Jim MacInnes lingered after the meeting. He was an engineer who used to design hydro and wind energy projects before he married into a ski resort family. Together he and his wife had built on her family's business legacy to become the biggest employer in Benzie County. Jim treated people right. His company badge said "Jim," and he greeted busboys by name as he moved through his domain. He hosted an outdoor art park, with sculptures dotted along wooded trails, and bicycled seventeen miles to work in the summers. Jim was always reading—books with titles like *The End of Oil* and *Guns, Germs and Steel*. At Crystal Mountain he promoted wind energy, land conservation, and the arts, and in politics he typically voted Republican.

Jim looked at my map and case statement. "It's a big property," he said. "How well do you know it?"

"Mostly from the aerial map," I said. "I've hiked the dune part and driven along the farmland."

"Get out and see it," he advised. "Do what the land tells you."

While Glen and I waited for Bill Parfet to pull strings and arrange a meeting with CEO Bill McCormick, I hiked the land. Sometimes alone, other days with biologists, ecologists, or other experts. We tripped over downed branches and traversed miles up and down hemlock ravines. We walked along the main ridgeline, discovered unexpected views of Lake Michigan, and marveled at a surviving stand of American chestnut trees. The shape of the land began to unfold.

In September, two local birders joined me. The scent of decaying leaf litter filled the air as we hiked. The canopy above was still green, and the day felt like summer, but the forest floor was tan with leaves from years past pressed together in a crumbling mat. The forest here had pillars of good-sized trunks along the slope down to Joyfield Road: deep-brown hemlock, elephant-skinned beeches, and scaly dark cherry. In places, young white pine, hemlock, and maple dotted the forest floor. A woodpecker drummed loudly. "Did you hear that?" asked Carl.

"The woodpecker?" I said.

"No," said Carl. "It's a black-and-white warbler. Listen."

Carl Freeman was the one who reminded me of John Muir: tall as a tree with a shaggy beard down to his chest. He was an artist who'd carved a hooded merganser to mark his mailbox, and he seemed more at home with dragonflies than people. "This forest needs to be in your nature preserve," Carl said. "It's just as important as the dune land west of here. Lots of songbirds use it. Look! Did you see that? A broad-winged hawk."

Carl lived a mile north and had tramped through the vast Consumers property for years. His companion was Keith Westphal, an avid fellow birder who was as bald as Carl was hairy. Before that day, I had never given much thought to the land east of the state highway, M-22. The coast lay west of the highway, with its dunes and majestic forest furrowed with ravines—land that was truly unbroken and wild. The land east of the road was more of a hodgepodge. Stretches of intact native forest stood next to abandoned fields, active cherry orchards, cornfields, and planted rows of pines. Much of it had been so greatly altered by humans that I had never stepped out of the car to look at it. Today that was about to change.

"We want to take you to see the land on Keillor Road," said Keith.

"Farmland?" I asked.

"Yes," said Keith. "There's a hayfield there that's great habitat for grasshopper sparrows."

The land at Keillor Road was wide open, nothing to break the prairie-like view except a cluster of sugar maples circling the ruins of a house foundation. I wondered who had lived there. There were dozens of these homestead remnants scattered on Dry Hill. Sometimes the only sign that a house had once stood there came from a circle of shade trees, a lilac bush along an old drive, or a persistent bunch of daffodils that pushed through the soil every April.

When we got to Keith's field, crispy bits of lichen crunched as we stepped on the dry ground. We were standing amid stubble, a mix of grass and weeds that barely reached my kneecap. It looked desolate. I found it hard to believe that hay could be harvested from this field. Yet life hid inside. Keith and Carl talked about the birds that nested here: grasshopper sparrows, vesper sparrows, savannah sparrows, and meadowlarks. These birds relied on this field to build nests in its short grass. Further up the road, bobolinks sought out the lusher, longer grass in another hayfield.

"Trouble is, the farmers are converting these fields to corn," said Carl. "They're in a hurry to get a cash crop, and the birds are losing ground."

I nodded. I knew about the one-year license arrangements. Now, looking at the Arcadia farmlands seriously for the first time, I could see how this short time frame had transformed the land. CMS pressured the farmers, and the farmers in turn pressured the birds.

But something else was troubling me. This was northern Michigan. Up here, the natural landscape was forests, lakes and rivers, not prairie.

"But shouldn't it all be forest?" I blurted out. "There never was grassland here. This habitat is all artificial."

"Yes, true," Keith agreed. "Grasshopper sparrows and bobolinks never used to live here, but now it's an active breeding spot. The birds need this land, especially grasshopper sparrows. This spot has the highest density of grasshopper sparrows in the state."

"So we should stop farming in this area?" I asked.

"Oh, no," said Keith. "We need the farming. They cut hay twice a year here. That's what's kept the trees out."

That night I went home with my mind whirling. I'd always thought I was saving native habitat in its native spot for native species. In some places that was still possible. But here the wild landscape had long ago disappeared. If we got the chance to save Arcadia, we'd have to play God. We'd have to decide whether to replant trees or nourish the grassland haven that had emerged to provide a northern breeding outpost for birds struggling for their very survival. Grasshopper sparrows were a species of special concern, and here was a field they needed. Somehow we would have to manage this part of the farmland for the grassland birds.

I wished I could be like Carl, out for long walks every day, attuned to birdcalls and deeply immersed in nature's patterns. Instead, I knew my job was to glean what I could from naturalists and fight for the species' rights back at the negotiating table. I longed to be a better naturalist, but my eyesight was poor. I'd worn thick glasses since age four and could barely tell a robin from a bluebird, let alone a chipping sparrow from a song sparrow in the field. I didn't have enough know-how, but I respected those who did. What I could do best was to draw in the right experts.

After Carl and Keith, next came Dave Ewert, a chief ecologist from the Nature Conservancy. He had five hours to spare to tour the Arcadia land. It was a chilly afternoon, and I scribbled notes as fast as I could as Dave drove. Five hours was not much time to cover 6,000 acres and glean all the information I hoped to for my Arcadia conservation plan, but I was lucky to have Dave's time. We drove down Joyfield Road, parked, and walked a few paces into the forest. Dave pointed out the mix of hemlock trees plus a plentiful batch of young trees growing in under the canopy. He bent down his lanky frame to examine an evergreen bush. "There's yew here," he said. "Lots of it, and it's healthy. Look—no deer have been chomping it. If you've got yew, you know you've got a healthy forest system."

I wrote down "yew" in my notepad. We sure had lots of yew. In some places it grew so tall it brushed my armpits.

Last, we turned to the farmland. I grew silent, embarrassed that our project area contained so much agricultural land. But Dave had worked three decades in Midwest conservation and was used to it. Dave agreed with the birders. He liked the idea of a grassland habitat area. Grassland bird populations were in severe decline throughout the Midwest, he said. Their nesting habitat was dry and flat, which made it easy for developers to build houses and shopping malls in the fields. Keep haying the field, he said, but cut the hay *after* the birds have finished nesting. As things stood now, the grassland birds were in danger of losing their young to the mowing machines.

We dodged potholes on Matzinger, drove east, then south on Taylor Road, and finally parked at the site of another bulldozed homesite on Butwell Road. Our route showed aging orchards, overgrown Christmas tree farms, alfalfa for hay, and open vistas of corn. Dave shook his head at the corn. "Farmland can be compatible with wildlife," he said. "But there's a hierarchy. Tree crops are best. Monocrops of a single species are worst. Of those, cornfields are probably worst of all. Nothing lives there. A cornfield is an ecological desert."

Back in the office, I typed up my notes from Dave's field visit:

> Encourage tree crops and pasture. Trees are long term,
> provide some habitat, allow animals sheltered
> movement between natural areas. Pasture is good
> for small mammals—ground doesn't get tilled often.
> Consider impacts on insects, birds, small mammals.
> Avoid corn.

Hierarchy of best crops for farmland:

- Christmas trees

- Pine plantations

- Orchard trees

- Pasture

- Hay and alfalfa fields

- Diverse crops

- Monospecies crops

- Cornfields

I flicked on the computer and typed a new section in the Consumers Power case statement. I was doing what Jim had recommended, I was getting to know the land well. Then I added a new color on the project map: lime green for grassland.

Meanwhile, Glen finally had a date with CMS Energy's CEO. He scrawled the appointment in his day planner with a ballpoint pen: "Friday, September 15—Meet Rodger and Bill."

"You got maps for me?" Glen asked.

I gave him the updated set of maps based on my series of hikes. "What's this?" asked Glen, waving at the lime-green line.

"It's a new area for grasslands," I said. "A lot of birds nest in that area and need that grassland."

"Like what?" asked Glen.

"Bobolinks, vesper sparrows, grasshopper sparrows, meadowlarks . . ." I recited the list Carl and Keith had told me.

"Bobolinks," said Glen, grinning. "All right. Add in the bobolinks."

6 Talking to Giants

Adopt the pace of nature: her secret is patience.

—Ralph Waldo Emerson

Dearborn and Arcadia, Michigan
2000-2001

Helen had agreed to join Glen for his first big meeting with CMS executives, held that same fall, September 2000. Helen Taylor was the director of the Nature Conservancy's Michigan chapter, and she brought with her the nonprofit's statewide, national, and international clout. Helen worked directly for the Lorax. Day after day, she quietly made connections, introductions, and endless phone calls to tap the talents of business leaders, Republican auto executives, Democratic political allies, Christian conservatives from Grand Rapids, and families living in the top one percent of wealth. Then she would pair up these contacts with conservation projects around the state—including Nature Conservancy endeavors or projects by smaller, partner land trusts like us.

Like Glen, Helen's love of nature was so strong she rarely spent time outdoors anymore. She lived her days behind walls in meetings and board rooms, or behind the steering wheel on state highways, catching up on phone calls as she worked late into the evening. At home in Okemos, Helen had two young sons who stacked Legos on the living-room floor. Her husband took the role of chief parent.

A philosophy major in college, Helen graduated from Northwestern University and acted as a corporate consultant before joining the Nature Conservancy. She grew up in Indiana and gasped when she first saw a Great Lake. "I took one look at that lake and knew I was never going back," she said.

She had long, dark hair that she invariably wore tied up in a bun squarely in the back of her head. Wisps of hair often escaped and blew about her face. Helen was warm, direct, and genuine, with an engaging smile. When she spoke, she looked right at you, and you forgot everything else and focused on her message. Her message was simple: Let's work together to save life on earth by protecting the land and waters living things need to survive.

Even though she moved around power—chatting to the governor or conferring with CEOs from Michigan's big industries—Helen remained Helen. She waved away thanks, instead heaping it on others. But she was bold. "Helen wouldn't blink at asking for $15 million," one grant maker said. "Even Glen would blink before he asked for that." We were delighted our team included Helen.

The day before Glen and Helen met with CMS, I couldn't sleep. I tossed and kicked my blankets, and my dreams were fitful and filled with corporate negotiations. At 4:30 a.m. I woke with a stomachache. I slipped outside for a predawn walk, pacing until I grew calmer. Glen was the one heading downstate, not me. There was nothing I could do. Nothing but wait.

Down in Dearborn, Helen and Glen met up in the lobby of the Hyatt, next door to CMS's corporate headquarters. Together they stepped through CMS's entrance. As the elevator whisked them higher and higher, Glen clutched his briefcase and grinned nervously at Helen. Showtime. They were ushered into a waiting room, a posh place showcasing corporate wealth, furnished with leather chairs and a fine wooden coffee table.

Glen and Helen glanced about, looking for clues to help press their case, or insights into Rodger's or Bill's interests to help break the ice. In front of them lay exactly what they were looking for. "Do you see that?" Glen pointed to a photography book displayed on the coffee table. The book featured architecturally distinguished homes along the Great Lakes coast.

Helen nodded. "That's just our thing," she said. "We'll have to ask about that."

CMS's Rodger Kershner appeared. He wore glasses and had a thick moustache and dark hair. He seemed like someone who would feel at home in a law library. "What's your interest in the shoreline, Rodger?" asked Helen, pointing to the book on the coffee table.

"One of those homes is mine," said Rodger. "I have a place up on the Keweenaw."

Glen and Helen exchanged looks. The Keweenaw Peninsula, the most remote part of Michigan's already remote Upper Peninsula, was familiar territory to Helen.

"You have a house on the Keweenaw?" said Helen. "We're just wrapping up a big shoreline project up there." Chatting like old acquaintances, they moved into the conference room to meet Bill McCormick.

I heard about it all blow-by-blow when they got back.

"Helen was great," said Glen. "They really hit if off about the Keweenaw. Can you believe Rodger has a cottage up there? Helen's going to be the one who talks to Rodger. They've got that connection."

"And?" I said.

"And Rodger wants $25 million. He's really stuck on that number."

Talks with CMS inched forward. A month later my phone rang with news about the Arcadia property. I strained to catch the voice of my caller through the crackly connection. Cell phones were new, and this call had all the markings of an overextended cell connection from somewhere in the woods in southern Benzie County. "Heather? It's Brad Hopwood."

Brad lived in Arcadia just south of the Consumers Power property. A local builder, he loved wildlife habitat and did his best to save it. We were lucky to have dozens of allies like Brad, people who understood the Conservancy's interests and acted as our local eyes and ears. Brad didn't call often, so he must have news to report. I pressed my index finger against my opposite ear and tried to catch his message.

"Hey! I was out by the Consumers property, and looks like they're doing some logging. There's a wood chipper parked there. Just thought you should know."

I stayed calm. Consumers had a forester stationed in the region, and under his direction, the company had been gently logging the Arcadia land for years. Nothing big. Nothing disruptive. In thirty years they'd hardly touched the best-quality forest habitat. The mammoth trees on the most prized acres had always been blessed with a secret mandate to grow.

"Just routine?" I asked. "Out in the eastern farm area?"

"Joyfield Road," said Brad. "Looks like they've started."

Joyfield. Carl's black-and-white warbler habitat. Instantly I could hear a replay of Carl's high-pitched voice, cracking with excitement: *"The warblers come here because they need an unbroken canopy, and a rich block of forest like this . . . it hasn't been logged in years."*

I sighed and stared out the window of our new office. The most affordable office we could find was located in a strip mall attached to a grocery store, so my view was an asphalt parking lot filled with morning grocery shoppers pushing carts. I shut my eyes and conjured up a picture of Arcadia instead: dark hemlock mixed with maple and beech—huge trunks—and the call of the warblers and woodpeckers. I turned away from the window and stared at the maps of Arcadia that lined my walls. On paper, the future looked rosy. My maps showed a giant nature preserve with hiking trails. But while I was up here dreaming about conservation for the Arcadia dunes, forty-four miles away logging scouts were lacing up their work boots, armed with cans of red spray paint to mark which trees would fall.

I set out to Joyfield to view the damage. The loggers had been there before me. Just a month after my idyllic walk with Carl and Keith, now I stumbled over huge bouquets of treetop branches littering the ground like debris from a giants' wedding. Fresh dirt roads cut into the landscape. Where last month an unbroken leafy canopy had covered the forest, now I gazed up into stark gaps of sky. The loggers had taken trees and also altered the chemistry and structure of the forest. It was drier, patchier, straighter, and more exposed to disease, weeds, and predators. The loggers had targeted maple and cherry trees, knocking down the hemlock to make room for more cash-friendly lumber. A "forest-improvement cut," it was called in forestry circles. It "improved" a forest as a moneymaking machine by favoring certain species and trees with the straightest trunks, but the forest itself did not improve. Now beech and maple would grow, but the overall variety of species would be diminished. I wondered about the warblers. Would they still come?

Checking on all the other forest stands, I came to our gem, an 800-acre unbroken block of coastal forest—the heart of our proposed nature preserve. I gasped. The loggers were here. Every large tree trunk was marked with a slash of red paint.

"You have guys logging the Arcadia dunes," Helen told Rodger.

Rodger said he didn't know about it. Logging matters were routinely left to Consumers Power staff in Cadillac.

"Can you get them to stop? They're logging some of the forest we really care about!" said Helen.

Glen relayed the information to me. "Rodger can't stop it," he said. "The timber contracts are already out. You'll have to talk to their forester and the loggers directly."

I called the Consumers forester in Cadillac. No, he hadn't heard anything about Consumers being in talks to sell the land. Yes, the timber contracts had gone out. What could we do? If the loggers were willing, we could buy out their timber bid. That would give the Conservancy the exclusive right to cut the trees for ninety days. If we didn't want to harvest trees, we could just hold the bid and nobody could cut there for three months. Sure, he'd be glad to meet with us on the land and take a look at the proposed cut. He'd meet us out there with the loggers tomorrow.

When it comes to logging, there are good cuts and bad cuts. I brought Steve, a trusted forester, along with me to offer advice. We pulled onto the highway shoulder, my Saturn sedan dwarfed by the loggers' four-wheel-drive pickup trucks. It was mid-November. The season's leaves were down, and the forest was a bleak mix of brown and grey trunks, with branches angling up to the slate sky. Underfoot, the leaves had lost their October luster. I shivered under my fleece-lined windbreaker and pulled the collar up. I felt small standing there in my hiking boots and ponytail. The loggers wore rugged canvas jackets, no gloves, and work boots scuffed at the toes.

Steve walked from pine to maple to cherry, examining the trunks, the heights, and the red paint marks. He studied the cutting plan and asked a few questions about how the loggers planned to drag the trees out, where the landing area would be, and what they would do about tops. Then he reported back to me. "This is a light timber cut," he said. "There'll be some big trees gone, but the Consumers forester has a light hand."

Next to Steve, the loggers stuck their hands in their pockets and formed a semicircle around me, waiting.

I gazed at a stately black cherry slated for cutting. By its girth, I judged it was a hundred years old. No one had harvested these trees since Michigan's logging boom in the nineteenth century. I could stop this. I could buy out the timber contract and stay the chainsaws for $30,000. Everyone was willing. All I had to do was say the word, and the loggers would drive their pickup trucks back to Manistee County. But three months from now the contract would run out, and the same trees might be at risk again. Three months. It might be just long enough to buy us time to cinch a deal with CMS.

"If this cut goes forward, will there be any lasting impacts on the forest?" I asked Steve.

"They're taking some big trees, but the structure will be good," said Steve. "There'll still be a strong mix of ages and species."

I scanned the array of trunks. We were in this for the long haul. A hundred years from now, there would be other stately black cherries and white pines interweaving their branches. I would not see it in my lifetime, but it would be there someday. Better save our precious cash for the immediate fight.

"Thanks for your time today," I said. "The cut looks fine. Go ahead with your plans."

I turned my back on the dune forest.

On the drive back to the office, I tried to shut out thoughts of the logging cut, but images of those mammoth black cherry trees rose in my mind. I tried not to picture them falling. What's more, tomorrow might produce a new timber contract. I needed to figure out what to do. The trouble was that our efforts to negotiate a purchase agreement with CMS were taking so long. Logging the very forest we were trying to preserve was like dumping paint on a dress just before you were going to buy it. You could still buy the dress, but it would take a while for the stains to fade, and some of them might be permanent. On the other hand, we weren't necessarily even buying the property. CMS was only talking to us. There was no contract, just wild hopes on our side. What good were wild hopes against the might of a billion-dollar corporation?

A cement mixer passed me, heading west. There was a new housing development going in nearby. Then a logging truck rumbled by. Change was coming rapidly to quiet Benzie County. I clicked off the radio so I could think better.

What we needed was for everything to slow down. Stand still. Just stop. Give the saws a rest, don't market the Arcadia land to new buyers, just put all plans for the property on hold and give us time to breathe, to dig into property records, appraisals, contamination issues, and most of all time to mobilize our supporters and scrape together financing. Three months was not enough. We needed Time.

"I let them cut the trees," I told Glen back in the office.

"On the dune side? West of M-22?" he asked.

I nodded.

Glen sighed and pulled his hand through his hair. He hated to see a tree go even more than I did. I was glad I could spare him the pain of personally seeing which trees were doomed.

"We need that money for the option," I said, voicing what we both knew was true.

We were angling to get an "option to purchase" from CMS. In exchange for some money, the landowner would agree to give us the exclusive right to buy their land for a set price, within a set time. If we decided to buy the land, it was ours. If we failed to move forward and buy the land within the designated time, the landowner would be free to sell it to someone else.

But neither the Conservancy nor CMS Energy was ready to agree to a purchase option. The property was so vast we had no idea what a reasonable price was. Millions, for sure. But how many?

"We need them to stop and give us time," I said. "Time to figure things out. We need them to agree to stand still."

This idea of buying time became our new strategy. I drew up a "Stand-Still Agreement" and Glen and Helen badgered Rodger on the phone. In between Consumers' normal business of energy contracts and rate structures, its chief counsel began hearing about northern hardwood forests and species diversity. I outlined a new property map showing sensitive forest areas and marked them: "High-quality habitat—no timber harvest." If CMS agreed and signed our document, the company would also be agreeing to a period of no logging in these designated areas. In January 2001, Glen braved the snowy roads to meet with Helen, Bill, and Rodger again.

Two days after the meeting, Glen and I huddled over the tan speakerphone. Rodger was calling, and he had Helen on the line in Lansing. "You want time to do a plan," said Rodger.

"That's right," said Glen. "We need some time to get some appraisals, figure out what the land's worth."

"The number's north of $25 million," said Rodger. "Maybe $30 million."

Glen laughed. "We think it's closer to $11 million."

"We'll see," said Rodger. "I'll sign your Stand-Still Agreement. You've got till the end of June."

I burst into an enormous grin. We'd done it! The world had stopped spinning. For six glorious months, we were free to get our act together without worrying about timber cuts and housing plans. Not only had we gained a breather, we looked like the number one candidate to buy the land. When the Stand-Still Agreement ran out, why wouldn't we be the obvious buyer?

But both the dunes and the giants had more surprises in store for us.

7 Dune Diligence

By failing to prepare, you are preparing to fail.

—Benjamin Franklin

Arcadia and Traverse City, Michigan 2001

Just when Rodger consented to our Stand-Still Agreement, another dune deal appeared to delight and distract us: Green Point Dunes.

I'd longed to preserve this gem for years. From the top of Green Point Dunes, you could sweep your eyes across the entire expanse of the CMS Arcadia land. It was Baldy's twin. A towering bluff and dune that faced Arcadia, with Watervale squeezed in between.

"It's the *Sound of Music* view!" Glen called out. He was standing at the top of Green Point, arms spread high in a V, mimicking Julie Andrews. This was Glen's first time at Green Point Dunes. After a hike through the forest we had emerged at the peak of a hilltop meadow. Before us lay a blanket of forest covering forty square miles, not a house in sight. An arc of golden dunes swept to the west, and then Lake Michigan's unending blue horizon. Glen feasted his eyes on the scene, a grin lighting up his face. "Doesn't it make you just want to burst into song?" he asked. He spun left and right, arms still upraised. "The hills are alive!"

My heart was already singing. Green Point included 250 acres of coastal habitat, a mile of pristine Lake Michigan shoreline, and a healthy population of Pitcher's thistle. Just a bit further south an active sand blowout, the Sugar Bowl, marched over coastal trees in a parabolic swath. Green Point was full of mature black cherry, sweet-scented cedar, and hemlock-draped dunes. I'd dreamed of Green Point Dunes' preservation in my sleep. Together, CMS Arcadia, Watervale and Green

Point shoreline added up to nearly a five-mile stretch of coastline. Dune habitat that size could begin to make a true ecological difference.

The Ranke family had bought the land as a rustic retreat for their four children, now grown. John Ranke, one of the sons, was then in his forties and settled downstate in Bloomfield Hills, an affluent Detroit suburb. An international tax attorney who traveled the world, he rarely had time to visit the property. For three years I had courted him, sending letters and once a photo of a cecropia moth with wings outstretched. "We found this beautiful moth on your family land," I wrote. He called the day he received it from a distant time zone.

But it wasn't until January 2001, in the same week Rodger Kershner okayed the Stand-Still Agreement, that the project surged to life. "Mrs. Ranke is ill," the family lawyer told me, referring to John's mother. "She doesn't have much time. The family would like to preserve the land and complete the deal while she is still alive."

Could we cope with the timing? This would mean three active dune projects: Betsie Dunes, Green Point Dunes, and CMS Arcadia (hopefully). Our commitments were starting to add up, and prime shoreline on Lake Michigan commanded a huge price tag. The Green Point property alone was valued at $10 million. Even though the family was willing to sell for less, the purchase price would still be far above our budget. Would preserving Green Point Dunes hurt our chances of saving Arcadia?

That was the risk. We said yes to Green Point. Then redoubled our efforts in determining the feasibility of saving Arcadia.

"We need to think big here," said Glen during yet another brainstorming session about Arcadia. Time was ticking on. We all knew we had to use our Stand Still time well to secure funding. "It could be a new state park!" Glen went on. "Or what about the Great Lakes Fisheries Trust? Maybe we can team up with a 'green' developer."

In the end, we tried all those ideas. Somehow we knew that to save Arcadia, we'd have to try every funding path available. First came the

New Urbanists. Helen introduced us to a new acquaintance of hers, Sam Cummings. Sam hailed from Grand Rapids and specialized in renovating old buildings. He believed in making cities vibrant centers and preserving wildlife habitat. Sam, Helen, Glen, and I met regularly at Sam's Grand Rapids office.

Perhaps an innovative, green-thinking developer like Sam could help us realize how we could afford to preserve the Arcadia land. Glen and I led a tour to the Arcadia coast on a snow-filled day, a day when the wind pounded the shore. Helen was bundled up in a scarf, her wispy black hair flying. Sam and his partner, wearing only baseball caps, froze their ears. This was Helen's first time on the land, too. Proudly, Glen and I led the way to a low point on the beach decked in white pine. "Gorgeous!" Sam said. "This is spectacular!"

My heart swelled. Old Baldy was as good as saved. It had been so easy—all it took was a map, some introductions, and now some green-hearted folks with money to invest.

Six months had seemed like a long time when we first signed the Stand-Still Agreement with CMS. But there was so much to figure out. It wasn't until spring that Sam had plans to show us. He'd been crunching dollars and sketching out views while up north I'd focused on habitat preservation areas. Now Glen, Helen, and I were gathered once again in Grand Rapids while Sam rolled out a wall-sized map of the property.

"We'll need some high-end homes here," he said, pointing to forest along the highway. The three of us steeled our hearts and nodded. We had to expect some compromise if we went this route.

"Then, to make the numbers work, we're going to need homes here" at the north end," Sam went on. We watched carefully. Sam had gone out of his way to help us during the past months, running multiple scenarios and listening to our dreams, always saying, "Okay, tell me what you need, tell me what I can do." Now here was his final proposal. He indicated the most sensitive beachfront area of the property.

"That's the dune shelf, Sam," objected Glen. "That's where we walked. It's prime dune habitat!"

"We need waterfront views," said Sam.

"But, Sam," said Helen. "That waterfront is ecologically unique. That's one of the things we're trying to *save*. We really can't have houses or roads there."

Sam looked grim. "I know it's not what you want, but that's the only thing that makes the numbers work. You'll still get the majority of the land preserved—you'll get all these back acres to keep open. Sometimes you have to cut off a toe to save the body."

The three of us stared in silence. The plan took all the good stuff. All the pristine forest and dunes were marked for houses and roads. Despite Sam's best efforts, it was clear the numbers wouldn't work for a joint project of preservation and sensitive development.

"That's not cutting off a toe, Sam," I said. "That's cutting off the head."

Sam's conclusions would be useful in future talks with CMS, but they wouldn't help with our present money troubles. We thanked him, and Glen drove seventy-five miles per hour all the way home. "Well, Heather, in a way I'm relieved that didn't work out," he said. "At least people can't say we didn't try the private options. Now we've got to try the public ones. We can't raise all that money ourselves. Maybe we can sell the dune portion to the State of Michigan as a new state park."

It took Glen two months to entice the chief of Michigan's state parks out to Arcadia. Rodney Stokes, a rare African American man in the largely white world of conservation, had risen to the top of the state parks department through twenty-four years of dedicated service. He wore khaki pants, brown dress shoes, and a moustache. His grown daughter was off studying in Thailand, and Rodney himself was inching close to retirement. Glen sensed an opportunity.

"It's been a while since Michigan's had any new state parks on the water," said Glen.

"That's true," agreed Rodney. "Most of them were set up in the 1940s and '50s."

"There's P. J. Hoffmaster, Van Buren, Saugatuck Dunes, Warren Dunes. What would you think about a brand-new state park?" Glen asked.

"I'd love to set up a new state park," said Rodney. "That's a legacy I'd be thrilled to leave."

"Do you see it here?"

"Oh, I see it," said Rodney. "The land is certainly big enough, and these dunes are great."

We walked along the beach some more, reaching the flat, level plateau where Sam had recently envisioned ranks of private houses. "Right here is where we'd put the campground," said Rodney. "Nice, flat land. We could put maybe 200 campsites here, with electric hookup."

"Right here where we're standing?" asked Glen.

"Yeah. People want to be near the water. We'd have a paved loop road here and 150–200 campsites leading off it."

"This is a rather sensitive spot," I mentioned. "Couldn't you have wilderness camping?"

"People need access," Rodney said. "And they need bathrooms." He went on to describe the other infrastructure a state park would need: concessions selling food and maybe a gift store, roads, parking lots, and maintenance buildings.

"What about the back forest and farmland?" asked Glen.

"We wouldn't be interested in that," said Rodney. "The state would only be interested in the dune portion, about 2,000 acres. You'd have to take care of the back land. Yes, this would make a great addition to the state park system."

Rodney drove back to Lansing in his car emblazoned with the State of Michigan seal. We waved and promised to be in touch. Soon after, media outlets blazed news about state budget shortfalls. Governor John Engler had one year to go on his term, and a looming crisis was at hand. No new programs. No new state parks.

I wasn't sorry. There must be a better way to create public access to this marvelous dune besides paving it.

During this time, talks with Bill McCormick and Rodger Kershner at CMS were still limping along. The last time Helen and Glen had gone down they had taken Sam Cummings with them to lend the practical business side to negotiations. CMS Energy met them in a different conference room, one with a long wooden table dominating the space. Bill and his chief counsel entered the room from a side door and took seats on one side. Glen, Helen, and Sam sat on the other. *It feels like North and South Korea,* thought Helen.

"Public access is not what's best for the land," said Bill McCormick. "The public will just destroy it. Look at state parks. It's better off with an elite private development."

I puzzled over this one. There was some truth to Bill McCormick's view. A public beach would soon be littered with used condoms, lost flip-flops, and shiny chips packages blown from pockets. Up at Sleeping Bear Dunes National Lakeshore more than a million visitors came each year and impacted the natural land. Hikers and their dogs startled nesting plovers. Pitcher's thistle and other rare plants got trampled as children scrambled over the dunes in delight, disturbing cascades of sand. Beaches with easy parking had even more trouble. In some cases limited private access could be best for the landscape.

But I also knew that people needed to experience the land. Not just the elite but all kinds of people. Public access was the only way ordinary people like me could ever see the world's wonders. If no one learned to love nature, no one would rally to save it. It was as simple as that. We needed to extend access to more people so more people could fall in love.

Meanwhile, the debate between private and public protection began to rage over at Green Point Dunes. It seemed the only way to save Green Point was to create a new county park using state funds through the Natural Resources Trust Fund. The Trust Fund might be willing to award us a sizeable grant for Green Point Dunes, but only if the locals wanted it. To prove we had hometown support, the local township had to weigh in.

Blaine Township Hall lay at the end of White Owl Drive. If you drove any farther, your tires would dip into Lower Herring Lake, and you might float over to Watervale. Mounted by the town hall door was a woodcarving of a snowy owl done by Carl Freeman. There were five township trustees, some of whom had held the post for thirty years.

"I pledge allegiance to the flag, of the United States . . ." After we recited the pledge, there was a scraping of metal folding chairs as the Blaine Township trustees eased back into their seats. The men replaced their baseball caps. Town hall meetings were alive and well in Benzie County, and today taxes were uppermost on the Blaine Township board members' minds.

I told the board what the county and Conservancy hoped to do. The county was officially applying for the grant to buy Green Point Dunes, but the township had to sign on. The state would never give the money with an unwilling township. Five impassive faces looked back at me. "Will this Green Point Dunes be on the tax rolls?" someone asked.

Well, no, the land would be county owned, so off the tax rolls. New access, a chance for people to hike down and see the water.

"We need a road," the supervisor said. "Blaine Township has five miles of shoreline and not one public access point to the beach. We've got older people who can't hike. We want to drive to the beach."

They made a motion to support the county's application, with one condition: a paved road to the shoreline. "Tell the county: No road, no nature preserve."

"No!" John Ranke sputtered on the phone from Bloomfield Hills. "No paved road. That's a deal breaker!" He worried that an easy drive would bring too many people down to the beach. People, dogs, and cars would destroy the fragile lakeshore. They'd trample the rare species and leave broken bottles behind. They'd drive dune buggies on the Sugar Bowl. "The land would be better off with a private developer," he said. "We're not selling to the county. The deal's off."

Glen and I stared at each other. The fate of the land hovered over the phone line. John was right in many ways—a paved road would impact the dunes—but private development would also break up the intact forest and mar the migratory corridor, and what started as a light development could intensify over time. The only other option was for the Conservancy to buy the land directly.

"John, John," implored Glen. "Stay with us here, let's think this through."

I thought back to how deeply John and his siblings loved the dunes. How a five-inch moth once brought them to call us. *Keep him on the phone, keep him on the phone*, I thought. *If he hangs up, we're lost.*

"What if we do it as a private nature preserve?" said Glen. "We can't afford the full price. How much can you come down if we do it 100 percent privately?"

We started negotiations all over again. The Ranke family agreed to lop off more than $4 million from the sale price and granted us a five-year land contract, the same method parents often use to bypass the bank and sell a house to their child. There would be no paved road. The Conservancy would own the land privately—but we would also have to find the money. And $5 million was the largest amount the Conservancy had ever attempted to raise privately before. Were we getting in over our head?

The day we signed the land contract to buy Green Point Dunes I drove out to the coast and tacked up small temporary signs telling people this was the future home of the proposed Green Point Dunes Nature Preserve. How I longed to remove the word *proposed*. Would this nature preserve ever be more than a beautiful idea?

These dune deals were getting expensive. We needed $1 million for Betsie Dunes and now $5 million or more for Green Point Dunes. What would happen when CMS Arcadia demanded funds, too?

We needed money. Big money. And to get it, we needed someone to raise it.

Glen cornered Lois DeBacker, head of the C. S. Mott Foundation's Environment Program, at the annual conference of the Council of Michigan Foundations. Lois was petite and serious on the outside, but her heart burned passionately for the earth and the people trying to save it. She cared deeply about nonprofits and understood just how tough a job it was to run a do-gooder organization.

Lois normally did not give out money for buying nature preserves, but Glen never took no for an answer. Just a few years ago, Glen and Lois had met on a snowy January day to discuss a new nature preserve at Antrim Creek.

"We don't make grants for land conservation projects," said Lois. "It's really a long shot." Not long afterward, Antrim Creek was preserved—with a half-a-million-dollar leadership grant from the Mott Foundation.

Now Glen pitched his latest land project. Lois listened. She saw the bags under his eyes. She knew how hard he worked: trying nonstop to raise money and managing a staff now grown to twelve.

"You don't need land project funding from us," Lois said. "You need to be thinking about a capacity-building grant."

"Capacity building?" said Glen. "But we already have two challenge grants."

"That's just it. How are you going to meet the challenges? You need someone who can help you make a plan. Think about building up your fundraising program."

Back at the office, Glen scratched off a grant proposal asking for funds to hire a development coordinator, plus some extra for operations to ease the budget blues.

Lois rejected the grant request.

"Look at this!" Glen fumed. "Mott turned us down! This is what Lois asked for and she turned us down!"

"I don't think you're listening, Glen," one of the board members told him. "This isn't a rejection. She's inviting you to resubmit for more money."

"She didn't give us money to hire a development coordinator!" cried Glen.

"You don't need a development coordinator. You've got grand plans. You need a director of fundraising."

"You mean she's telling me that I haven't been ambitious enough?" asked Glen.

"That's what she's telling you. Go back and ask for more money."

Chapter 7

Lois and the Mott Foundation fully funded the higher request. The Conservancy now had $225,000 spread over three years to professionalize its overall staff and prepare a campaign strategy.

Christine Arvidson saw the ad from Pittsburgh. She paused. The job involved field trips, newsletters, fundraising, and more. Field trips with kids weren't her cup of tea, but small nonprofits often asked for everything and then some. She wanted a job in Traverse City to be near her aging parents. Perhaps this was it.

Two weeks later, there she was, perched on one of the Conservancy's two waiting room chairs in the hall. She wore a grey tailored pantsuit. Glasses and strawberry blond hair partly shaded her eyes. She was tall—that was evident even though she was sitting down. But above all, she was watching us, observant as a hawk stationed on a fencepost. This stranger was eyeing every detail about the place. She had arrived early for the interview; just as on my interview day, a snowstorm was pelting the area.

"Several of the applicants cancelled today," said the receptionist. "Or they're running late because of the snow. The roads are really bad."

"But they're local," I pointed out. "The woman in the hall is from out of state."

"She rented a four-wheel drive," said the receptionist.

That summed up Christine. She liked to be prepared. She did her homework, and once she made up her mind, nothing would stop her. If the weather forecast was a winter storm, she simply rented a car capable of the drive and left a day early.

"I don't know," Glen said after the interview. "Should I hire her? How's she going to help us? She doesn't have any background in land conservation."

"You don't need that kind of person," his board advised him. "You've got a staff full of them. You need someone who knows campaigns."

Christine joined us in February 2001. Her job was to direct communications and advise campaign strategy. We called her Christine because there was another Chris in the office, but Christine was a Chris. Tough, no BS. Christine had helped steer political campaigns, directed capital campaigns for universities, and had worked with nonprofits like Habitat for Humanity. She lived by quotes such as: "Money talks; bullshit walks" and "Sacred cows make the best burgers." She knew how to organize and get things done, how to buoy up her coworkers and empower them to perform their best.

Christine spent her first weeks wading through the legacy of a busy start-up grassroots nonprofit. She stumbled over boxes of out-of-date newsletters and brochures in the storeroom, and discovered that no one entered donor visits or conversations into the computer system. "If you're doing a big campaign, you have to shine yourself up," she told Glen. Then she proceeded to organize the fundraising, computerize records, and add codes to fundraising appeals. The codes helped us track success and study what worked and what didn't.

Like Glen, though, I was worried that Christine didn't know much about land conservation. If she would be out there as a figurehead talking to supporters and reporters, she needed to be an authority on the natural world. Goodwill was not enough to be a land champion. My roommate had once given me a birthday card featuring purple loosestrife. She knew I loved nature, and the photo itself was stunning—an endless field of purple with tall flower stalks. But purple loosestrife is one of the greatest threats to native plants in North America. It invades wetlands with a voracious appetite, and millions of dollars go toward trying to *contain* the plant before it wipes out precious habitat for wetland plants, birds, ducks, insects, and frogs. As Aldo Leopold, Wisconsin's famous conservation son, said, "One of the penalties of an ecological education is that one lives alone in a world of wounds."

We signed Christine up to attend the national Land Trust Rally to learn more about the world of land trusts. "You should really go to this class on biodiversity," I said, showing her the brochure. It was a crash course, but hopefully it would be a start.

Christine laughed. "You want me take a nature class?" she said. "Sure, I'll go. But I know I'm not the expert. I'll still need to come to you guys when I have questions about the land."

I should not have worried. Christine was bright enough to pick up what she needed to know about land trusts. After the conference, Christine reported back to me. "You don't need me to become an expert in forests and birds," she said. "That's your job. You need me to be an expert on my area. If I don't know something, I'll have them talk to you directly. Give me some talking points and I'll be fine."

She was more than fine. With her help, the Conservancy team worked miracles for the dunes.

8 Beach Walks and Brick Walls

There is pleasure in the pathless woods,
There is rapture on the lonely shore,
There is society, where none intrudes,
By the deep sea, and music in its roar:
I love not man the less, but Nature more.

—Lord Byron

Traverse City and Watervale, Michigan
2001

When I'd first arrived in Traverse City, I'd met so many Conservancy board members, donors, and landowners it was hard to keep them straight. But one stood out: Reg Bird.

It had been Reg who'd told Dori about the new land trust in town and urged her to relieve development pressure on Watervale by giving away the development rights to the Conservancy. Watervale donated two conservation easements, first dune shoreline and then forest acreage. At the same time, Dori upped her protection of Watervale by getting the inn and cottages recognized as state-designated historic structures. Now there was much more than a liquor license standing between Watervale and CMS. Dori joined the Conservancy board, and her friend Reg became board chair.

Reg was gruff. He cracked jokes but hid his smile under his moustache. Reg had dark hair turning grey and a salt-and-pepper beard. A former advertising expert who had globe-trotted with Britain's Prince Philip on World Wildlife Foundation business, Reg now cultivated the casual look. He wore blue jeans and fleece vests and always had a little blue rucksack slung over his shoulder.

It was here at Watervale that Reg had fallen in love. As a youth, Reg had spent summers as a camp counselor at an all-boys' camp across the lake. Many a summer night, when his charges were in bed, Reg would swim across Lower Herring Lake to meet a young Watervale waitress named Ann, Dori's best friend. Reg married Ann in 1962. But his other love, the wild landscape of Old Baldy, remained vulnerable.

Reg liked to damn the torpedoes and charge full-speed ahead. He knew Glen shared his drive. As board chair, Reg was in on early negotiations with Bill McCormick and Rodger Kershner. He wanted nothing more than to protect the Arcadia land, but he also knew urgent matters of all shapes and sizes clamored for Glen's attention. "Glen, when you put your mind to something, it happens," goaded Reg. "You've got to put your mind to it."

While Glen focused on negotiations and funding possibilities, Reg put his mind to possibilities in his own neighborhood. Reg lived eighty miles from Watervale, on Torch Lake, a lake that stretched for nineteen miles and sparkled with the intensity of Caribbean teal and turquoise. Among the summer vacationers on Torch Lake were presidents of Ford and GM and executives from Proctor and Gamble. Torch Lake was also the summer vacation spot for Bill White, president of the C. S. Mott Foundation.

Charles Stewart Mott had made his fortune by transforming a bicycle wheel company into an auto parts manufacturing business. His company merged with Buick Motor Company, and Mott became a founding partner in General Motors. When he died in 1973, the C. S. Mott Foundation's assets totaled $300 million. By the time I joined the Conservancy, the foundation had become one of the largest charitable foundations in the United States, with more than $2 billion in assets. The Mott Foundation had strong roots in Michigan and a local connection on Torch Lake. Reg decided to talk to Bill.

Bill White's house was one mile up the beach from Reg's. Bill loved to swim. He came up to Torch Lake when the swimming was good and sometimes he attended neighbors' social gatherings. With Arcadia on his mind, Reg began to look for Bill at these lake gatherings. Some nights he would be rewarded. Bill would show up and flash him a smile, and Reg would gain a minute or two to extol a dune that lay eighty miles away, a dune Bill had never seen. The moment Reg spied Bill, Reg would sidle through the crowd.

"You again!" Bill would say. "How's your dune?"

"When are you coming down to see it?" Reg would ask.

There are routine grants, strategic grants, and extraordinary grants. Every once in a while, major funders depart from the ordinary and bestow an exceptional sum on a project—perhaps they establish a brand-new hospital in their hometown, or give most of the construction costs for a new library at their alma mater. Reg was seeking an extraordinary grant for Arcadia. If only he could pique Bill's interest.

Reg abandoned his stratagem of chance encounters one July day in 2001. He headed directly to Bill's house, pulled into his drive, and knocked boldly on the door., Bill's towering frame appeared. There was no use pretending this was a social visit. Both men knew why Reg had come.

"Look, I'm going down there today," said Reg. "If you want to go, let's go. At least take a look at it," said Reg. "Bring Claire."

Bill eyed the sunshine; it was a beautiful summer afternoon. "Let's go," he said.

Reg was stunned. He watched in his rearview mirror as the Whites pulled out of their driveway to follow him southwest to the coast. They were really coming to see Baldy! Not just Bill, but Claire, too—C. S. Mott's granddaughter who served on the foundation board along with her husband, daughter, and other family. After months of effort, he'd succeeded in coaxing Bill to visit Arcadia. Now the dune would have to speak for itself.

At Bill's request, they stopped in the village of Frankfort for ice cream waffle cones. Frankfort was a mere eight miles away from the Arcadia land. Reg launched into the history of the landscape: how Consumers Power had intended to flood the land; how Watervale used to be a logging camp.

Bill licked his ice cream cone as Reg spoke. "Do they have ice cream at Watervale?" he interrupted.

"You've had enough ice cream," said Claire.

"They probably do," said Reg, surprised.

Bill's cryptic comments made him inscrutable to us at first. But beneath his wry humor lay an extremely savvy, caring man. Bill grasped the complexities of doing good in the world. Philanthropy was hard work; it demanded vision, diligence, and insight. It meant understanding how to shore up nonprofits and invest in capacity building; it meant trusting local people to know what they needed themselves, and at the same time pushing them to make the most of their opportunity.

It also meant having a heart of passion that could be stirred when the right project came along. Could Baldy be that project?

Reg and his guests arrived at Watervale Road, which dead-ends into the sand dune. "Take your shoes off," invited Reg. "Put them on a log."

To Reg's delight, the dune's power took hold. First the little group shuffled through a narrow sand passageway, flanked by sand walls shoulder high. Clumps of dune grass waved and bowed beside them, the grass tips scraping semicircles in the sand. As the pathway dropped, the visitors focused on keeping their balance among the sloped holes of sand footprints until they emerged fully out on the beach. To the west the deep blue waves of Lake Michigan crashed, tumbling pebbles and drowning out small talk. To the north loomed Green Point Dunes. To the south stretched a wild and empty honey-toned beach. At the end of the beach towered a breathtaking view of Old Baldy.

Bill and Claire White fell under Baldy's spell. Unbidden, they began walking. They gazed at the dune, drawn to it, as they walked barefoot nearly a mile down the beach. At the base of the huge dune, Bill stopped and stared upward. Reg sucked in his breath and stayed silent, letting the dune speak for itself.

On the way back to Watervale, Bill told a story. "You know, I knew a place just like this when I was a kid," he said. "Out east on Cape Cod. Almost identical. Years later I went back, and it was all built up with hotels and bars and bowling alleys." He paused. "They didn't even save one dune," he said. "Not one." Bill stared back at Baldy. "Geez, I didn't even know places like this still existed."

Beside him, Reg took a deep breath. *Hot spit!* he thought. *Better to be lucky than good.*

Back in the office, we hovered on Reg's every word. Arcadia needed a champion, and it looked like Reg had just found one. The story of Bill's beach walk became an overnight legend.

But luck? I pondered this as I coasted my bicycle down Long Lake Road toward home. It was indeed lucky for Arcadia that Bill White had loved a sand dune as a boy. That the young boy who loved Cape Cod dunes had grown up to marry into the Mott family. But I knew if I reached into the corners of nearly any adult's heart, I would discover a piece of land that he or she loved from childhood. An open field here, a fishing hole there, a forest path that ended in a blueberry patch, or perhaps the wild crash of the coast. Nearly all of us cradled memories of a beloved place within us. When something strikes that chord, we respond. Will our children have a hallowed store of nature memories to draw on? We may indeed need luck in the future. The kids of the new millennium are increasingly divorced from the natural world. Once-a-year class field trips to a pond or park can only hopelessly skim the surface. Love of nature accumulates over lazy days and changing seasons. Love takes time. Unless a new generation gets time outside, land conservation may need *gallons* of luck in the future.

Meanwhile, the longed-for appraisals rolled in. The reports said the land was likely worth between $12 and $16 million. Now all we had to do was make a reasonable offer. But time was ticking by. In less than a month our temporary agreement with CMS would expire, and the property would no longer Stand Still.

"Come up to the office!" It was Glen calling my house on a Sunday night. "Reg is here. We've got to crank this thing out."

They were already at work on the computer when I arrived: Glen typing and Reg pacing back and forth. Both were yelling. I blocked out thoughts of an evening bicycle ride along the bay, forcing my head to focus on real estate numbers. There was no use telling Reg and Glen this was Sunday evening and the deal could wait until Monday. They were fired up now. The Stand-Still Agreement would evaporate in a matter of days. We simply had to have a new deal in place, and deals took time. The urgency was real.

"How are we going to close the gap?" demanded Glen. "We're 10 million apart. There's no way we can go much higher and maintain credibility with our funders!"

Glen deleted what he had just typed. Reg paced.

"Help me out here, Heather!" Glen cried. I paged through my file folders and recited appraisal facts and figures. Both Reg and Glen were in an agitated state, and the volume of the conversation crept higher.

More than two hours later, Glen swiveled his desk chair and pushed back from the computer. The June sky was darkening, but we had a one-page letter offering $14 million for the property.

Reg began to chuckle. "You know who you are?" he asked me. "You're Hermione. You keep us straight and know all the facts. I'm the old grey-beard, Dumbledore, full of worldly wisdom, and Glen has that boyish charm and fearless courage that no one can resist. Glen is Harry Potter."

But it seemed CMS had defenses against Glen's charm. "That's not even close," said Rodger. "The number's still north of $25 million. Probably $25-30 million with 100 exclusive homes."

"Have you ever walked the dunes, Rodger?" asked Glen.

"No, I haven't been out there."

"The views are blocked, the development potential is terrible," said Glen.

"We'll need to get our own appraisal," said Rodger.

The third appraisal, ordered directly by CMS, listed the value at $24.5 million. "That confirms our suspicions," said Rodger.

For the first time, the property felt out of reach. It was as if a slightly open door had been firmly shut, and the executives had retreated into their leather-upholstered offices. Had it been simply amusing for them to talk to the Conservancy folks for a while? Perhaps all our hopes were naïve. I went to bed early that night in despair and scrawled a few words in my diary: "Difficult day. Review appraisal high. Greedy. Looks dismal."

Our faithful advisors weighed in. That's an inflated price, they said. The bluff would be difficult to develop. The market up north was already oversaturated with golf courses. Words of business advice flowed in by email and phone:

"Don't cave in yet. Let him stew on it."

"Point out the alligators."

"Assume there's no competition."

"If they're still talking to you, that means they're interested."

Then Helen called with more bad news. Even though our Stand-Still Agreement had time to go, developers were sitting at the table again. "Hey, Glen. I just talked to Rodger. He met with the Granger development company today. They're proposing just 200 units total on the property, thirty of them on the dunes. He's talking about an exclusive-type development like the Huron Mountain Club with gates. Also, get this: Rodger says they have to sell by the end of the year."

"Did you tell him our money is as good as theirs?" asked Glen.

"Yeah. He says Granger carries less risk," said Helen. "Rodger said he's not very optimistic about your ability to deliver."

Gary Granger also carried God. A conservative Christian from Grand Rapids, he headed a development company called the Granger Group. His company listed Jesus as a major shareholder. Maybe God could be on our side, too. Following the premise that God helped those who helped themselves, we launched a quiet campaign to dissuade Gary Granger. Our business allies sprang into action: CEOs, company presidents, and energy businessfolks. We knew we needed corporate peers to approach Gary. One cornered him on a boat cruise. Another talked to him at a Young Professional Organization meeting at the House of Representatives. They reported back:

"Gary has four to five other projects going. He's not very serious about it."

"I pointed out the alligators to him. He's just looking, really, not sure it makes sense."

Glen, Reg, Helen, and I took a collective breath. Negotiations were only in the early stages with Gary, but there would be other developers. Meanwhile, our six-month Stand-Still Agreement with CMS rattled to a close. Foresters marked more trees to cut. We had no deal, and the world started spinning again at a pace nature couldn't take.

Still, we had Helen. If the conservation world were made up of leaders like Helen Taylor of the Nature Conservancy, conservation victories would double. Like Glen, she was expert at tapping into the childhood memories of donors and business executives. When people shook hands with Helen, their titles and assets melted away. "An issue like conservation levels the playing field," Helen liked to say. "Everyone wants that. Conservation involves people being outdoors, it's about their memories and experiences. All these people have places that matter to them, places where they grew up, places that are very, very close to the heart."

Helen's goal was to create a network of people who could open any door the Nature Conservancy needed. Helen opened doors we could not touch. She lived by the adage "My house is your house," and welcomed us to share her board's clout.

"They're not taking us seriously, Helen," said Glen. "Our money is as good as theirs! Who do you know who knows Bill McCormick?"

"Well, Jim Nicholson is on our board," said Helen. "He and Bill are friends."

"You've got someone who is friends with Bill McCormick?" said Glen. "Helen! That's it! Would you do that for us?"

"Sure, want me to ask him?"

"Get them in motion," said Glen.

Jim Nicholson, a businessman in chemicals and water treatment, was a longtime Nature Conservancy board member. He held positions on a variety of boards, including the Detroit Symphony Orchestra and the YMCA of Metro Detroit. He and Bill McCormick had both served on boards together, and both had houses in the exclusive Bay Harbor community up north near Petoskey. At Helen's request, Jim began regularly bumping into Bill during the fall of 2001 and asking him about the Arcadia property.

"This is what Jim says," said Helen, her voice breaking up as she talked on her speaker phone driving down the highway. "It's clear Bill wants lots of money. More than $30 million. If he can't get lots of money, he says he wants to develop it into something like Bay Harbor. But Jim doesn't believe him. He thinks they're just going to sit on it."

The news was puzzling. Why didn't Jim believe him? What was it about Bill McCormick that tied him to the Arcadia land? There was something going on we didn't yet understand.

Glen and I looked at each other, stymied. We wanted this dune, and we wanted the project to move forward at our pace. All this work, and things were going nowhere. In fact, the more we worked, the more things seemed to be slowing down. I couldn't understand it. Here was a company that owned a piece of land—seemingly for no good reason. Its business was energy, and this property was no longer connected to the energy business. We were offering good money. Why wouldn't they even talk to us? What could CMS possibly want with the Arcadia land? We needed more help. Somebody who understood corporate negotiations inside and out.

Helen came through for us yet again. "I can bring Max out," she said. "Max teaches negotiation at the Harvard Business School. He and his partner do negotiation workshops for us every once in a while. We'll set up a workshop and invite all the land trusts in Michigan. I'll see if he's free."

Our friend Jim MacInnes offered to host the event at the Crystal Mountain conference rooms. Soon there was Max Bazerman, with his black beard and round glasses, newly arrived in the Michigan northwoods in his dark blue suit, cracking East Coast jokes. With him was his partner, Len, who said he'd learned his best negotiation techniques from his ex-wife.

Max and Helen both had connections to Northwestern University, where Max once taught. He loved to help the Nature Conservancy, and offered free training if Helen would pay his travel costs. Max's tips on negotiation were like buckets of water for thirsty hikers. Every drop applied directly to the dune project. I lapped it up. Between sessions, we huddled together with Max and Len in a private room to enhance our dune-saving strategy.

Glen filled them in. "We still haven't heard about our offer," said Glen. "They want $30 million, so we're thinking of sending them a year-end letter and upping the offer."

"Don't bid against yourself," said Max. "You've got to stick to the appraised fair market value."

"But they said they have to close by year-end," said Glen.

"You want to close by the end of the year?" asked Max. "Don't bid against yourself. Be clear about $14 million. Silence is a tactic. Don't be overeager."

Glen sighed. He was good at charging forward. Holding back was trickier. The negotiation game got him stirred up, but after dashing toward the goal, it was infuriating to pause mid-race and "hold it right there." Besides, potential supporters couldn't be expected to stand by indefinitely. "It's hard to keep so much money warm," said Glen.

"Keep it warm," warned Max.

Keeping money warm for Arcadia meant constantly impressing funders with the project's high stakes and urgency. We needed to keep excitement up so donors would be ready at any moment when the time came. Keeping money warm for Arcadia also meant denying other land projects. While Glen was extolling Arcadia's virtues, other worthy land projects were also clamoring for funds. I accepted this. Development moved faster than our small nonprofit could step in and negotiate deals with private landowners. As land protection experts, we had to assume responsibility for making good choices. Triage was our daily fare. Elevating one landscape meant turning our backs on another: we had to choose which child to save. Because of its very size, the Arcadia project magnified this tension like never before. But what if our plan to buy the CMS land didn't work out? Were we wasting time and money on a dead-end dream? Were we forfeiting other vital habitat while we concentrated on a lost cause?

"Glen, it's Helen again. I just talked to Jim Nicholson. He says it's a bad idea to put any political pressure on McCormick. They aren't going to find a buyer. They're just stuck on getting $30 million. He says to save the Mott Foundation's interest for something else."

Ever since Bill and Claire White's beach walk, the Mott Foundation had become heavily invested in doing its part to save Arcadia. In fact, the board was considering a gift of $750,000 to the Conservancy as a first step. This critical gift would be the option money—risk money needed to lock in a purchase price. The foundation was also talking about a special multimillion-dollar grant.

The day before the Mott Foundation met to vote, planes crashed into the Twin Towers. Glen and Reg were shaken as they drove to Flint on September 12 for the meeting. The mood at the Mott meeting was somber. They voted to approve option money for the Arcadia dunes, but denied the larger multimillion-dollar request. Bill White explained the board's denial: "We need movement, Glen. We can't wait for this forever."

Glen nodded. He knew that attracting the Mott Foundation's interest had been a godsend, and that such an opportunity could not last indefinitely. Like the Conservancy, the Mott Foundation had other worthy projects waiting to be funded.

Why wouldn't the Arcadia project move? It all came down to Bill McCormick. Bill's appointed spokesman, Rodger, was happy to talk to us; he was affable and seemed to like Helen and Glen. But Bill McCormick was another story. Whenever Bill's name was mentioned, the price invariably climbed to $30 million.

As 2001 marched on, Glen grew despondent. Time and again, he rehashed what McCormick had told him in their first meeting. "He honestly thinks private development will protect the dunes better than a public nature preserve," said Glen. "He thinks the land will be better off under his scenario with houses."

Something was blocking the deal. Despite all our efforts, something had lodged in our path. We fumbled against the barricade, hoping sheer willpower would remove it. Then we launched a new wave of spies to approach Bill McCormick. Keith Charters asked Bill Parfet. Helen enlisted more board members.

That's when we learned what we were truly up against. Our CEO allies reported in with this dire news: Bill McCormick did not want to let the Arcadia land go. No matter what the price, he had a personal reason for his company to keep it.

Bill McCormick had also fallen in love with Arcadia.

The official CMS plan called for private development of upscale homes plus a golf course and equestrian center, but there was a personal interest. Bill had special plans for one plot of land. We were up against a man with incredible power who had selected his house site in the heart of our nature preserve. Bill planned to build his *own* house next to Baldy.

"It's Bill McCormick and he's not budging, Glen," Reg said. "You heard what they said—with Bill, once he gets something in his head, it's very hard to shake."

That fall, Glen and Reg had driven downstate one more time to negotiate with Rodger. Talks dragged on, but there was no progress. Even Reg acknowledged the blockade. "You've got a conservancy to run," he said to Glen. "It's time to turn our attention elsewhere. We've got to drop Consumers."

The reality stung. It was against Glen's nature to give up on something. Like McCormick, once he got something in his head, he'd drive forward until it was done. Reg was the same, and giving up on Arcadia meant failing to protect the land he loved. As for me, I felt as if I'd let down the thousands of unseen inhabitants of Arcadia. The hemlocks, the Pitcher's thistle, the black-and-white warblers, the bobolinks and grasshopper sparrows.

We couldn't force the corporation to sell. It was time to give up. *To everything there is a season,* I thought. Perhaps these ancient words applied here. A time to push forward, a time to hold back. A time to recognize defeat and quit spinning time and resources. A time to redirect attention elsewhere.

I took down the coastal maps from my wall and clicked shut the file drawer marked CMS. It was nearly 2002, four years since I'd arrived in Michigan, and our dream of buying the Arcadia dunes was done.

9 Waking the Giant

Alone we can do so little, together we can do so much.

—Helen Keller

Northern Michigan and Jackson, Michigan 2002-2003

The Enron scandal burst upon the scene. Next Dynegy, another energy-trading company, fell. The web of corporate corruption kept expanding and by early 2002 it had entangled CMS Energy. "CMS Energy Admits to Bogus Power Trades" blared the headlines on May 16, 2002. "CMS Energy Embroiled in Round-Trip Trading."

Glen and I gaped at the unfolding events in disbelief. CMS Energy executives had played a game of greed. They'd created imaginary corporate value by buying and selling energy within the company, artificially lifting its income by $5.3 billion. More than seventy percent of CMS Energy's wholesale electric trades turned out to be fake. The false trading had gone on for two years—starting at just the time when the Conservancy had first arranged a meeting with CMS. During that time CMS Energy's auditor had overlooked the sham—or rather, played along.

Glen and I tracked CMS Energy's stock daily on the computer, watching in wonder and horror as the corporate giant began to unravel. For the first time in my life, I devoured the newspaper's business section. One morning at breakfast I spread the newspaper out beside my cereal bowl, then set my spoon down, eyes glued to the page.

Chief of CMS Energy Says He Is Resigning
New York Times, May 24, 2002

CMS Energy, an energy trader, said today that its chief executive, William T. McCormick Jr., resigned after the company disclosed sham electricity trades.

Mr. McCormick announced his resignation at the start of today's annual meeting, bringing applause from some shareholders. At least six class-action lawsuits against the company have been filed since last Friday.

My cereal quietly congealed beside me as I read the article through three times. The world had just changed for Arcadia.

After Bill McCormick's dismissal, CMS board member Ken Whipple stepped in as interim chair to steer the company back to sanity. With McCormick gone, his dream house on the dune had also been toppled. Incredibly, our stumbling block was gone. Now, perhaps, we could ink the deal with Rodger. It was June, a short time after McCormick's resignation, when I called Rodger's office to schedule the next meeting.

"I'm sorry, Rodger Kershner is not available," said his secretary. She was juggling three phone lines. "He'll get back to you right away."

No one ever returned the call. The very next day after my attempted phone call, Rodger Kershner abruptly resigned.

I read the news at breakfast again, this time in a restaurant since I was on the road for the Conservancy. There was Rodger's name, stark and black, in the *Detroit News*. My fork clattered down beside my stack of buttermilk pancakes and I let out such a big gasp the other patrons stopped eating to stare. "Just reading the news," I explained meekly. Then I called the Conservancy.

Bill McCormick's departure had cleared the way, but Rodger's loss was devastating. Rodger had been our main man. Without Rodger, we were back to square one with no executive contact. No human face for the vast corporation, which was once again in motion.

CMS Energy announced a "back to basics" policy. The company moved its corporate headquarters from Dearborn to Jackson, dropped a $500 million project in Argentina, and sold its Falcon and Citation private airplanes. The new leadership talked about reining in spending and selling "nonperforming assets."

"That's us!" screamed Glen. "Arcadia is a nonperforming asset! We've got to move! This is it! Quick—who do we know who knows Ken Whipple?"

Within hours, our network jumped into high gear, searching until we established a who's who link. We found it: Glen's neighbor John, a musician and orchard farmer, knew Bill and Mary Swift, both retired Ford Motor Company executives who lived on Old Mission Peninsula. Ken Whipple now had a home on the neighboring Leelanau Peninsula. He had retired from Ford Motor Credit Corporation, and Bill Swift knew Ken well enough to call him.

We waited, anxious and unsettled, until the phone call had been placed.

"Ken needs a fast, simple cash deal, and the financing has to be credible," said Bill Swift after his chat with CMS Energy's new CEO. "And Glen, I think you're in luck. Ken Whipple is also a member of the Leelanau Conservancy."

A man who liked land trusts was the new CEO? We sent up a whoop of joy.

Our first contact with Ken Whipple had gone well, but we needed more allies among the new top executives . . . and we needed them *fast*. Ken had his hands full with the crisis. Any deal had to be fast. CMS Energy had assured angry shareholders that all major nonperforming assets would be sold by the end of the year, just seven months away.

"Word is the new rising star is David Joos," reported Bill Swift. "All the real estate has been assigned to Joos."

"Okay, we have a whole new crew," Reg told Helen. "We have to start over again."

"Helen!" said Glen. "We have to meet with Joos. Can you swing that? He's probably up to his ass in alligators right now."

"Sure," said Helen. "He lives in Okemos right around the corner from me. I'll see if I can get a meeting."

Helen reported back immediately. "Glen! You wouldn't believe how my meeting with Joos went."

"What? What did he say?"

"It was just too funny," said Helen. "He wanted to meet at the Coral Gables for coffee." She paused to laugh. "It's such a dive. No one would go there for coffee, but Joos suggested it. Can you believe that? He's so different from McCormick. He's just a regular guy. I think we can work with him."

Helen soon arranged a meeting at CMS Energy corporate offices to pitch the dune purchase to the new guard. "Can you do Tuesday, July 30?" she asked.

Glen paused, eying his overfull calendar, but Reg jumped up immediately and yelled into the phone. "We'll take the meeting! We'll take the meeting!"

Three weeks later Reg and Glen were seated in CMS Energy's headquarters—newly moved to Jackson to save costs and image. The waiting area was pleasant, but it no longer displayed corporate swank. They opened negotiation talks with the man Joos had assigned to the project: Joe Tomasik.

Tomasik looked at home in a suit. Whereas Glen and Reg squirmed in their seats, more at ease in the woods, Joe's favorite habitat seemed to be a room with cushioned swivel chairs and water glasses on coasters. He had a thick head of grey hair brushed to the right, a solemn grey moustache, and glasses. When we met him, he had sad eyes. Joe Tomasik had devoted more than twenty prime years of life to CMS Energy and Consumers Power, and was still reeling from the company's public humiliation. To us he was wonderful, for the simple fact that he did not care about the Arcadia property. He had no private house site selected. No personal stake at all. His job was simply to sell the dune to an appropriate buyer.

"We're trying to keep a lot of money warm," said Reg. "We'd like to move forward with a purchase agreement within ninety days."

"I'll take your offer to my management," said Tomasik. "But I also need to present them with a plan B."

"What sort of plan B?" asked Glen.

"A development plan," said Tomasik. "They need to be able to see all the options."

Back at the office, Reg tried to allay my fears about "plan B." "It's just a formality," he said. "Tomasik needs a second option so it makes him look good. Then he can choose to work with us."

But in our hearts we all worried. What if Joe Tomasik found a plan B he liked better?

While CMS examined a plan B, we focused on fundraising. One thing was clear: we had to be strategic. Already our operating budget was at $1 million and expensive dune deals were piling up. There was $1 million to raise for Betsie Dunes, $5.6 million for Green Point Dunes, and CMS Arcadia looming over it all.

"We have to bundle them together." It was Christine speaking. By now she'd settled into land trust life and we'd all begun to rely on her experience. She was the only one on staff who'd raised money through a capital campaign before. "There's no way we can fundraise for all these projects separately," said Christine. "If we let donors choose which project to give to, they'll all want their money to go to the big one. What we have to do is roll all three dune projects together. Turn it into one big coastal campaign."

"But people only give in their backyards," said Glen. "It's human nature. Crystal Lake people only give to Crystal Lake, Frankfort people only give to Frankfort. Land is very local. That's how it works."

"No, Glen," she said. Then she explained how Arcadia would eclipse small projects like Betsie Dunes. Donors would swoon over the high-profile big deal and leave the Conservancy without enough money to fulfill its other obligations. Creating a coastal campaign was the only thing to be done.

"That's brilliant!" shouted Glen, leaping from his chair, waving his arms. "That's brilliant!"

"That's survival," said Christine.

While we waited for a deal to sign, Christine helped lay the groundwork for the anticipated Coastal Campaign. No matter when the deal happened, we'd need influential friends. Watervale was a good start, but we needed more allies. It was time to introduce new people to the Arcadia dunes. What better way than a boat ride?

As the end of July approached, Glen fretted about the weather.

"We can't do anything about it, Glen," said Christine for the twelfth time.

The chance to use the *Inland Seas* schooner came up about once a year. Glen's old friend Tom Kelly captained the boat. His mission was to introduce Great Lakes ecology to schoolkids, but he liked to help out other good causes. Tom and Glen had once shared an office when they were both new executive directors, and now Tom called and offered Glen the use of his schooner. The *Inland Seas* carried life rafts for thirty passengers plus crew. That meant three Conservancy staff and twenty-seven donors.

I watched as the *Inland Seas'* bow approached the rickety pier. We were in the village of Frankfort, a coastal town just north of Watervale and Arcadia. During the Age of Sail, Great Lakes schooners would have been plentiful in Frankfort's harbor, but in 2002, prime docking space went to motorboats. Our boarding area was a crumbling parking lot.

Our guests gathered on the cracked pavement. Some were longtime friends of the Conservancy, but many were new faces, attracted by the chance to ride a schooner, mix with friends, and glimpse a secret shoreline. This was meant to be an evening of inspiration, not a fundraising trip. But inspiration and giving are always linked. Within a year, passengers from this schooner trip gave gifts to the Coastal Campaign totaling nearly $2 million.

Glen was all smiles. It was a perfect summer evening, the sky clear blue, the temperature in the seventies. The crew hoisted the sails and the schooner edged out into Lake Michigan, its bow pointing toward the dunes.

Among those onboard was David Reese. He'd received the invitation at his summer address on Platte Lake. The invitation showed *Inland Seas* with its deep reddish tanbark sails bright against Lake Michigan's blue horizon. "Please join Naomi Borwell as her guest on an evening sail on the *Inland Seas*. We'll enjoy light snacks and discuss the importance of the coastline to our way of life." David was a banker who carried enthusiasm wherever he went. He had a wide smile, a tall, runner's build, and a passion for the beauty of the natural world. A few months ago, David had sent the Conservancy a check via his family foundation to protect wetlands filled with cedar, maidenhair fern, and orchids. Now he was curious to see the Arcadia dunes.

Perhaps Remy, the French-speaking first mate, added to the spell of that evening's sail. Perhaps the historic boat itself reminded people of time horizons longer than the next week. Perhaps it was the story of Consumers Power's failed attempt to flood the land, which many heard for the first time. Or perhaps it was the event's host, Naomi, with her graciousness and her steady passion for land preservation. But the dune itself must have known it was on show, for it enchanted the evening. The dune glowed golden, basking in the sun's evening touch. Light blessed the dune. From the schooner's deck, the mighty dune looked mightier. Every time I'd hiked up the bluff and gazed down, I'd felt a powerful, on-top-of-the-world feeling. But now, gazing up at Baldy from the water below reminded me that there was nothing more amazing than life itself, the endless flow of water and sky, the cycle of generations. I looked around and saw the spell of the dune and sky settle on the other passengers.

At that moment the sun set.

Sunset. It's an event that happens every day, though we scarcely notice it. Up north, the midsummer sun dawdles on its way down, setting so late people forget to eat supper. When it does set, we shrug and flick on electric lights, then continue unhindered with our business. On that July evening, the sun touched down at 9:14 pm. For a moment, it hovered like a red pearl through the rigging. The golden glow on the dunes intensified to orange. David Reese snapped a picture. "Spectacular," he murmured. "That is the most spectacular piece of property I have ever seen in America."

The next morning he was on the phone with Glen. "We've got to save those dunes! We've got to do whatever we can do. I'll make a lead gift. I'll talk to my friends. I'll lead hikes. I'll do whatever it takes."

Glen had just got his first member of his Coastal Campaign cabinet.

About this time, Dori phoned. I'd become a regular visitor to Watervale's forest and dune land but rarely stepped into the buildings. "You're working so hard," Dori said. "Why don't you spend a night at Watervale? Bring a friend and you'll be our guest for dinner and breakfast."

I was delighted. There was no question who I would bring: Rick, a local timber framer who carried the fresh smell of wood chips wherever he moved. He'd built his own kayak and shared my love of adventure on bikes, hikes, and boats. I'd known him for four years now. Rick, with his shiny, shaven head and crinkle-eyed smile.

At Watervale we hiked the coastal dunes, picking up pebbles at Lower Herring Lake's outlet creek. The Arcadia land backed up to Watervale, but today the dune could take care of itself. Dori had left out rowboats for us to use. Rick and I rowed out to the middle of the lake. The lake was calm with the fresh summer scent of lake water. The oarlocks creaked and I shifted to the stern as Rick took a turn at the oars.

Then I proposed.

CMS negotiations lurched forward, then fell back. August ended and summer residents moved back to their winter homes in California or downstate Michigan. It was one thing to kindle new passion for the dunes and quite another to keep that passion burning. When Bill White left his summer home on Torch Lake, Reg visited him at the Mott Foundation office in Flint. "This is Reg Bird," he would say, as he introduced him to Mott staff. "He's trying to sell me a dune."

Glen conferred with David Reese and others endlessly, Dori chatted to guests at Watervale on their front porches, Reg tried everything to keep Bill White's memory of his beach walk alive. But months slipped by, then a year.

Meanwhile, Helen was busy with her own massive deal. A suite of 390,000 acres was up for sale in Michigan's wild Upper Peninsula. The landowner was Kamehameha Schools, an educational trust set up from the estate of a nineteenth-century Hawaiian princess. This area spread across more than 300 lakes and 200 miles of river shoreline and sprawled across eight counties. Helen was dedicated to helping Arcadia, but she also needed to cultivate the Mott Foundation on behalf of her own project.

What came next was a plane ride. Bill White proposed a barnstorming day. He must have figured: *With Helen coaxing me to see the Kamehameha land in the Upper Peninsula, and Reg and his dune project on the Lower Peninsula, what better way to view all these large conservation projects than by plane?* He could invite the Mott Foundation board and make a day of it.

We arranged to meet Bill White and his party at the tiny Thompsonville airport. The village airport building was about the size of a large living room, paved with 1960s linoleum. It served only small charter aircraft. Glen, Reg, and I watched the clock nervously as two hours crawled by.

Then the rumble of engines came from the north, and three King Air turboprop planes landed. Soon Bill White, his wife, daughter, and other Mott board members stood out on the tarmac, laughing and chatting, their hair blowing in the wind. The aerial tour of Kamehameha and Arcadia was done. In one morning, they had flown over Tahquamenon Falls, traced the length of the Two Hearted River, and flown west over the sandstone cliffs at Pictured Rocks National Lakeshore before heading south along Sleeping Bear Dunes and finally banking over Arcadia. Now it was our turn to showcase Arcadia from the beach and offer the visitors Watervale hospitality.

Bill White tucked his six-foot-three frame into the hired van along with Glen and a staffer from the Nature Conservancy. Flying had put Bill in a good mood. He turned around in his seat and cracked a grin at the two men sitting behind him. Each represented a different conservancy; each was eager and perched on the edge of his van seat. "Nice land," he said. "Can't do 'em both, you know. Which one is it going to be?"

Bill White led his fellow Mott trustees onto the dunes at the end of Watervale Road, just as Reg had done the summer before. Some slipped off their shoes and flexed their toes on the beach. We prayed the dune would work its magic.

Meanwhile, Dori hovered between the kitchen and lobby of the Watervale Inn, stirring up her own magic. The dining room was set with peach-colored linen tablecloths, handwritten menus, and sweet pea centerpieces. After the beach walk, the Mott board would dine at the inn. Our hope was that a Watervale lunch combined with a day full of images of dunes and forests would put our guests in the right frame of mind for approving our bold, $13 million grant request for Arcadia.

The trustees gathered in the inn lobby after lunch, the same spot where CMS real estate agents once bargained to buy Watervale over the ironing board and drapes. Glen, Reg, and I squeezed against the reception desk as Bill stood up and leaned against the dining-room doorframe to begin the meeting. First up was Kamehameha. An amazing property, lots of urgency, let's move forward on the request and approve an award of $10 million. Helen grinned with relief, and I smiled, too. The Kamehameha land was a fantastic landscape, and it seemed the board might be in a giving mood.

The next agenda item was Arcadia. Beside me, Glen and Reg were as still as churchgoers. I pressed my back against the wall. There was nothing to do now but watch and wait. We'd already outlined the rare chance we'd been granted by the change of guard at CMS and how we were taking advantage of it with our aggressive revised offer. It was our strongest chance yet.

"We have before us a request from the Grand Traverse Regional Land Conservancy for $13 million," said Bill. "However, there are some things to work out yet. I suggest we look at this again at the board meeting in September."

The board meeting broke up and Watervale's lobby was filled with chat and the scraping of chairs. Bill caught Glen's eye. "Go get a deal first," he said.

We did not have a deal. In fact, quite the opposite. Talks with the new CMS Energy leadership had dwindled. We were offering good money; CMS Energy wanted to sell. What was holding things up *now?*

Even though negotiations hung suspended, we charged ahead under the single-minded belief that the deal would happen. It *must* happen. If we couldn't move forward, we'd use this time to prepare by engaging potential supporters more deeply.

"Chris, you've done capital campaigns before," said Glen. "What do we need to do here?"

"I've done a traditional one," said Christine.

"What's so different here?" asked Glen. "We have a big project; we want to raise a lot of money fast."

"That's what's different," said Christine. "Our time frame is hugely collapsed." She looked at Glen and nodded. They both knew it took years of personal trust building to develop relationships that could support a campaign. "You look at a museum, a university," Christine continued. "Their campaigns go on for five to eight years. We're looking at a few months. Plus, we're not building a building. There're no bricks or plaques. People like sticking their name on a plaque or a building."

"But that's the nature of land deals!" cried Glen.

"I know," said Christine. "Land deals need a new type of capital campaign."

"Like what?"

"I don't know," said Christine. "We're in mostly uncharted territory, but there is a land trust in Maine that's in the middle of a huge capital campaign. I thought we should drop them a visit."

"Go!" said Glen. "Go to Maine!"

Soon after the Mott Foundation jet tour, Christine stepped off a commercial flight in Portland and drove to Topsham, a town of 6,000 on the craggy coast of Maine. The Maine Coast Heritage Trust office was housed in the Bowdoin Mill, an old restored mill right on the river. Unlike the Grand Traverse Conservancy, the Maine Coast Heritage Trust was an established land trust icon. It had been founded thirty-two years ago and had a Rockefeller as its vice chair. It had just publicly announced a $100 million five-year campaign to save islands and coastline. On that September day, the staff still had $50 million more to raise, but despite the demands of their workload, they welcomed Christine and treated her to a full day of campaign insight.

First the fundraising director handed her a campaign packet. Crisp, professional images of lichen-encrusted rocks, moss-coated forests, and red-veined pitcher plant flowers covered the pages. Maine's case statement was an oversized full-color packet with maps, stories of land deals in the works, and scenes of water and the rugged granite coast.

"Wow," said Christine. "You put a lot of money in this."

"Yeah, about $50,000," her host sighed. "To be honest, you're looking at one of our first mistakes."

"How so?"

"Everyone told us we had to create a posh case statement if we wanted to raise big money," she said. "So we did. Now we've got 5,000 copies of it in boxes, and it's already out of date. Land deals move too fast."

"Oh."

"Do you see this picture?" Maine's fundraising director continued. She pointed to a large framed photograph on the conference room wall that showed people on Maine's craggy coast and lichen-covered rocks. "We had to Photoshop the people in," she said. "We learned the hard way: you have to connect the land to people. Our photos were beautiful, but there were no people in them. They were failing to make the case."

Back in Michigan, we added pictures of people enjoying the Arcadia land. It wasn't empty land. It never had been. If we wanted to save the area, we had to recognize that people—farmers, innkeepers, and hikers—were part of the landscape.

Still CMS Energy would not budge. In fact, the flurry of calls and joviality between Reg and Joe Tomasik ceased. We had money in the bank for an option payment, but no one responded to our letters or answered our calls. Where was the deal?

CMS's nonresponsiveness made me think of the story of Kumbakarna, a giant in the Indonesian version of the Ramayana epic. A battle is waging, but the mighty Kumbakarna sleeps on and on, oblivious to the clamor around him. His brother desperately tries to wake him by pulling out the hairs on his enormous toes. Our situation was like that. We had a giant to rouse, but no matter how hard we tugged at the hairs on CMS Energy's toes, the giant slept on.

Glen buzzed Max Bazerman, aka "Our Man in Boston," for negotiating help. "Why aren't they moving?" Glen asked. "We have a good offer. We have the option money in hand."

Max agreed the silence was peculiar. "Their cash needs and slow response time are inconsistent," he said. "Make sure you bring the banks in. Bankers are in control of CMS's destiny right now."

We talked to bankers. In fact, we talked to everyone in our network of local spies who might help. Land is inescapably local. Being a local land trust meant we were rooted in the community. Any outsider contemplating purchase or alteration of a piece of land had to activate local channels, whether it was the county zoning office or a local gatekeeper. We smothered our local networks with pleas: if you hear anything about CMS Energy or the Arcadia property, please call us.

Bits of news trickled in, each like a separate puzzle piece. We watched with mounting apprehension as a picture of logging and development began to emerge. CMS wasn't giving the silent treatment to anyone except us.

The first local friend to call was the president of a northern Michigan Fifth Third bank. A logger had stopped by his office, and it seemed CMS Energy was accepting sealed bids for logging the entire property. Next a local businessman called: the downstate developer Gary Granger was back. He'd spent a week on the property, hiking and flying planes over it. The Benzie County zoning office phoned in next. "There's a realtor who's been calling about rezoning the property and concentrating all the development on the lakeside." A banker called with another tip: "Watch the county records—there's a deal pending that will show up in the public record in a couple of weeks."

That was enough. It wasn't the full picture, but a deal on the public record meant we'd fill in the missing pieces soon. We asked Linda, a Conservancy friend and local attorney, to watch the deeds.

The Benzie County Register of Deeds stamps page and liber numbers on all real estate documents and makes them available in the public record. Every house transfer, acreage sale, utility easement, gas pipeline easement, conservation easement, historic preservation restriction, deed restriction, survey, and mortgage or other land debt is recorded. Public records from the 1860s were handwritten, ones from the 1970s were stashed on microfilm, and modern ones are digitized. Land records make for dry reading, so title companies sprang up to search the public records before anyone sold a piece of land. Every week Linda would scan the land records at the courthouse to see if anything new had been filed on Arcadia.

Weeks went by. Linda kept searching. CMS Energy did not call.

Logging began again, targeting maple, black cherry and pine.

At my desk forty miles away, I tried not to imagine the Arcadia land as the trees began to fall.

"Hello, I'm Lynne Moon," said a new voice. "I'm a realtor. I have a client from Texas who's looking at a coastal property. You know about the CMS Arcadia land?"

"Yes," I answered, holding my voice steady. "We're aware of it."

That's the line we often used: "Yes, we're aware of it. We know about the property, we've been following it for years." No mention of the negotiation meetings, detailed ecological plans, or heartbreak. For really, what claim did we have? None at all, except that we loved the land.

Lynne went on. Her clients were Fritz Duda, a Texas developer, and his son, Fritz Duda Jr. They'd phoned her from Texas. "We're looking for virgin land," they said. "Large tracts of undeveloped land on the water, especially on Lake Michigan." She'd known just the parcel.

Lynne met Duda Sr. at the private hangar section of the Cherry Capital airport. Since she was there to give him a tour of the dune land, Lynne wore jeans and tennis shoes. Duda flew in on a private Lear jet. He was dressed in Italian loafers and a fine suit. As she drove him toward the Arcadia dunes, Duda stayed glued to his cell phone, ignoring her.

Lynne was a realtor, but she had concerns that transcended a sale. She loved hiking the dunes and her husband was the bay keeper, a local environmental steward. Lynne was contacting the Conservancy to see if she could "green up" Duda's plans and alert us to the competition.

My hand trembled as I set the phone down. I was thankful for the news but terrified, and details emerging from Benzie County's planning office confirmed my fears. Duda and Duda had hired the Traverse City engineering firm Gosling Czubak to evaluate the land—and CMS was funding half the study.

The rats! The new guard was turning out to be as slippery as the old guard. Glen and I put our local spies on high alert, and Brad Hopwood began calling in regularly from Arcadia. He knew the guy who guarded the key for CMS Energy, the key that opened the rusty road gates. "He's been asked to open the gates for this developer *again*," Brad told me.

For weeks we tracked every movement. Within minutes we knew when the Dudas or their representatives visited the land. We knew every step they took. But we didn't know why CMS wasn't talking to us. "This is just part of their plan B," said Reg, trying to reassure me. "CMS needs to show they've looked at all their options seriously."

"Then why are they footing half the bill with a Texas developer?" I asked. "Why aren't they doing that with us?"

"They just don't trust us," said Glen. "Our money isn't good enough. They don't understand a nonprofit's fundraising model."

"Be patient," counseled Max. "Wait until the plan is done. This new work could be helpful to you."

It was nearly Christmas when we reaped the real reward of being local. A staff member from Gosling Czubak Engineering Sciences called Glen to obtain an aerial photo of the Arcadia land. Glen held him on the line, teasing out nuggets of information. No, I can't tell you the name, the caller said. But it's a joint plan for CMS and a developer. Of course there's a preservation element in the plan. You can't do much with the back 4,000 acres anyway. Yeah, CMS has inflated ideas of what the property can hold; we're going to have to give them a reality check. What's the timeline? We have a big meeting coming up in two weeks to present our findings to CMS. Sure, no problem, I don't mind if you stop by.

The next morning Glen and I entered Gosling Czubak's offices. We huddled at the end of a table that stretched the length of a narrow window-less room. The walls were tacked with blueprint-sized designs of local trails, parks, and buildings. Like all the local firms in town, the Conservancy had done business with Gosling Czubak many times in the past. The firm sur-veyed land, developed open space plans, and plotted out buildings. One of the planners unrolled a sheet of paper. It covered the table. "You can't copy it, but you can take a look," he said, and left us with the prize.

Glen and I said nothing. Our eyes scanned the drawing and devoured the page, silently impressing every detail to memory. The Arcadia dunes coast was carved into rows of house lots. It didn't look like a dune, more like a strung-out parking lot. Behind the primo shoreline lots came layers of view lots ringing a dominant feature: a golf course centered on Baldy.

I scribbled notes in a small pad. Glen said nothing, took no notes. Perhaps he was already composing a new fundraising stump speech in his head.

"We saw it!" screamed Glen when we burst back into our office. Ev-eryone gathered around. "Almost 200 houses on the coast and Baldy is a sand trap! Duda and Duda, these guys are for real. What do we do now? CMS won't even *talk* to us."

"We call Max," I said.

"Call Max!" said Glen. "Get him on the line."

Out in Boston, Max listened carefully as Glen described the precarious position of the dune Max had never seen. Max was silent for a moment when Glen finished his explanation. Then Max—Max the Patient, Max of Play-Your-Hand-Close and Don't-Do-Anything-Now-Just-Wait—delivered his judgment: "Now's the time for a dramatic new offer."

"You mean we can go?!" asked Glen.

"It's time," said Max. "Here's what I suggest. The planners are going to try to lower CMS's expectations at this meeting coming up. You need to submit your best possible offer and deliver it *before* the planners' big meeting. They'll sit there in the meeting hearing bad news from the developer but knowing your offer is there. You want to make it as uncomfortable as possible for the developer."

"That's perfect," said Glen.

"The goal is to break the relationship between CMS and the developer," said Max. "Meanwhile, lobby the top executives all you can. The combination should get CMS back at the table with you."

"How do we know our best possible offer?" asked Glen.

"You'll figure it out," said Max. "It's the number you can live with."

We scratched through sheets of scrap paper, analyzed our cash needs, reread appraisals, and called our major supporters. "How far can you go with us?" we asked them all. Reg was assigned to call Bill White at the Mott Foundation.

"How's my dune?" asked Bill.

Reg grinned at the question. He filled him in on the engineering plan, and how the Conservancy needed to make a strong new offer. "Looks as if we'll have to raise the price tag a bit," added Reg. Bill told him to stay in touch.

Reg couldn't contain his delight. He paced the room afterward, repeating the sweet words he'd just heard. "He said *my* dune," emphasized Reg. "Not *your* dune anymore. *My* dune!"

No matter how we looked at it, one number rose to the surface: $18 million. Cash, clean and simple. I blocked out background noise from the office with a pair of industrial earmuffs and rewrote our old offer, striking paragraphs that complicated the deal with contingencies and donations. What was left was a straightforward cash deal. One week before CMS Energy's meeting with the Dudas and the planners, and ten days before Christmas, our bold new offer of $18 million landed on Joe Tomasik's desk.

Silence. Tomasik's secretary confirmed he had received it. The phones stayed mute as 2002 ended and the calendar strayed further and further into 2003. Then a brief item in the *Detroit Free Press* stated that CMS Energy intended to sell property in Argentina and *Arcadia, Michigan,* within the year. Sell Arcadia? To whom?

"I found it!" said Linda. It was January 2003, and Linda had been faithfully searching the register of deeds records for months. "CMS signed a deal with Calvin Foster," she said. "I'll send a copy over."

Calvin Foster. He was known for high-end resort developments on the coast. He was cozy with the current governor, a master at business partnerships, and excelled at convincing his partners to shoulder the risk in his development projects. Foster had previously partnered with CMS Energy and they knew and trusted him. His involvement was bad news for us.

"He's got a right of first refusal!" thundered Glen.

We read further, through fifty-seven pages of legalese. Settlement terms between Foster and CMS Energy unfolded concerning some unrelated business, but then there it was, on line A1(a): ". . . hereby grants . . . a right of first refusal to buy the Arcadia Property. . . . If CMS Energy sells the Arcadia Property . . . Calvin Foster shall have the right . . ."

"But look at this!" said Glen. "It's not so bad." He read on: "'The right of first refusal shall not apply to a proposed transaction in which the purchase price is in excess of twelve million ($12,000,000) dollars.' So that's what it is. That's us. They're covering their bases. Now we know their bottom number." He charged up and down the hallways, shouting out sayings from his high school track coach: "All out! Nothing left!" Then he settled down and pushed his energies into full-fledged lobbying, getting Helen on the line: "Helen, are you with me? Let's surround them!"

I updated Max on the lobbying plan and Max emailed encouragement: "Your plan sounds fine. Be patient! All the best, Max."

Then we launched the blitz lobby. Helen drew in Nature Conservancy board members and nonboard members from her Corporate Advisory Council and infused them with enthusiasm that they could help protect a dune area that was important to the whole state of Michigan. Helen tapped the chairman and CEO of General Motors, who agreed to have a chat with CMS Energy executives. She asked Jack Smith, General Motor's retired chief, to speak to Ken Whipple. She coaxed more peers, board members, business colleagues, and high-ranking government representatives. Her allies began badgering Ken Whipple at parties and at board meetings, all telling him: "You should do this. The Conservancy is a group you can trust."

In the political realm, Ken Whipple fielded phone calls from two former governors about the Arcadia land, John Engler and Bill Milliken. At the same time we threw our collective effort into contacting our new prize supporter: the brand-new governor, Jennifer Granholm.

Governor-elect Granholm took the oath of office on January 1, 2003. She was the Democrats' new rising star. She was blond, polished, poised, and not afraid to talk tough truths about Michigan's rusting economy. Young and fit, with three children in the care of the First Gentleman, she could sprint five miles across the Mackinac Bridge in the morning and debate policy in the afternoon. Glen arranged to meet Granholm's top staff before the election.

"Jennifer Granholm wants to help family farms and the Great Lakes," her advisor said.

"Well, this project has it all," said Glen. "Farms, shoreline, and a Great Lake."

"She'll be interested."

The Conservancy was not the only one trying to curry favor with the new governor. CMS Energy had also called the governor's office asking for help on an important matter. A meeting was set for March 12, 2003.

Glen and I were not present when Governor Granholm met with CMS Energy top executives Ken Whipple and David Joos. But afterward we heard so many reports of the event that I can picture every detail. Whipple himself delighted in telling the story.

Ken Whipple and David Joos were worried. CMS was still struggling with bad press and financial missteps from the McCormick era. They needed the governor's support for new electric rates to fund a $1.1 billion bond issue through the Public Service Commission. Bad press was still dogging their every move and the company badly needed a morale boost and cash. We need cash, they pleaded to the governor. We're the oldest utility in Michigan, we've got 11,500 employees, you need to help us. They talked rates, bonds, and jobs.

Governor Granholm talked dunes. "If you need money so badly," she said, "why don't you sell the Arcadia land to the Conservancy?"

Whipple and Joos stared at her.

"Don't you realize they have an offer on the table for $18 million with cash in ninety days?" the governor pressed on.

Ken Whipple stirred to life. "I didn't know the Conservancy could really come up with that kind of money so fast," he said.

"I've looked into it," said the governor. "They can deliver."

"Shoot, that's a good deal," said CMS Energy's CEO. "We should do it."

Memory has a way of slipping into lore. Was it forty-five minutes after that meeting with the governor that a CMS representative called the Conservancy office in Traverse City? Was it a day? What is certain is that the same week Governor Granholm challenged CMS executives in her office, the phone rang on my desk in Traverse City.

It was Joe Tomasik, whose voice we hadn't heard for six months. "I've been having an on-and-off dialogue with Reg Bird," he said.

On-and-off! That's an understatement, I thought.

"We've been under some limitations, certain commitments," he went on, "which prevented us from continuing that dialogue, but I'm calling today because we are interested in your offer from December."

I did my best to keep my voice steady for the rest of the call, then dashed out an email to our supporters: "The giant has awakened! Here we go!"

10 Dune Flowers

If you know wilderness in the way that you know love,
you would be unwilling to let it go.

—Terry Tempest Williams

Traverse City, Michigan
Spring 2003

After three years of false starts, CMS Energy was finally willing and eager to sit at the negotiating table with us. Speed was key to our offer. "A fast nickel beats a slow dime," Glen constantly chanted.

We boldly offered $18 million cash in ninety days. But our ability to deliver hinged on the goodwill of our lead funder, the Mott Foundation. As we edged closer to inking a deal, Bill White discovered accounting issues that might block his intended gift. According to Mott staff, the foundation could *not* give out a grant to Arcadia this year. The amount was too big. But by now Bill deeply cared about preserving this dune. There just might be a way to make it work. "Mott should just buy it," Bill said.

Buy it? thought Glen.

"We'll just buy the dune. Have it as an asset for Mott and give the Conservancy an interest-free loan for a few years to pay it back," said Bill. "Then if this doesn't work out, we'll sell it for development."

Glen looked at Bill's face to see if he was in one of his joking moods. He could detect no jovial twinkle in his eyes.

The deal took shape. The purchase price was $18 million. Mott would buy the dune portion for $13 million, then transfer the land immediately to the Conservancy for $6 million, effectively giving us a $7 million gift. Mott cared about the shoreline and dunes only. Its money could not touch the rest of the property, so of course, we'd need a lot more allies. The total Coastal Campaign would need public grant money plus millions from individuals.

We were pinning our hopes on the Kellogg Foundation to champion the back farmland. With a long-term interest in food, the Kellogg folks understood the importance of protecting farm acreage. They wanted to see prime orchard land stay in fruit production, see family farm businesses saved, and help us showcase the property as a model around the nation. Our plan was to restrict the farmland with conservation easements and resell it to local farmers—not that we'd met the Arcadia farmers yet. Our goal was to gain income and boost the local farm economy, but it was all just an idea at this point. I didn't know anything about the Putney home farm, or the Evans brothers' plans for new trees. The Putneys and other families were in the dark, too. We hadn't told them a word about our plans for Arcadia. I promised myself I would talk to local neighbors soon, but first we needed to make sure the deal went through. As Glen told me again and again, "It ain't over until the fat lady sings."

With Mott's strong commitment we gained new allies, two of the foundation's best attorneys: Mike Stack and Joe Kochanek. Mike, Mott's real estate counsel, spoke with a deep Russian bass. From our phone calls, I expected him to be seven feet tall with a black, curly beard extending to his chest. But Mike was a regular-sized, clean-shaven man with Polish roots who lived even further north, on the edge of the Mackinac Straits in Cheboygan. Mike was smarter than most people he talked to, and he knew it. He loved intellectual repartee and could revise a document incorporating new terms before the other party had even hung up the phone. Joe was the head of the Mott Foundation's legal team, and an ardent University of Michigan football fan who loved kidding Mike Stack about their shared Polish backgrounds.

On a Monday in March, Glen strode into the Jackson corporate offices once more, this time with the two well-seasoned C. S. Mott attorneys by his side. The game had turned. CMS Energy was conciliatory, ready to talk and listen. The negotiations went like this:

We like your offer of cash in ninety days, they said.

Well, as you know, there have been delays. We submitted that offer four months ago. We've missed key board meetings because of your delays. We can close by year-end, but not before.

Let's discuss price, they said.

Eighteen million is firm. We've looked at the numbers. Eighteen million is a fair price. We can't raise money unless the deal is fair.

Let's talk about that; can you explain your fundraising? We are concerned about your ability to deliver.

We can deliver, said Glen. But we absolutely need the summer. We need an option to purchase signed soon so we don't miss the summer fundraising season. That's critical. If we don't sign before summer, the deal shifts to 2004.

And, said Glen, stop logging that land.

I was assigned to work with the Mott attorneys to craft the all-important Option Agreement. The document grew to thirty pages including appendices and side agreements. I spent my days hunched over the phone with my finger pressed over my right ear to block out coworkers' chatter. I had never gone to law school, but I was becoming a lawyer through field trial.

Two months passed. April vanished, then May began. The deal CMS had verbally agreed to wasn't inked in writing. Mike Stack and I pressed on, and Glen began to pace. "You're making this more complicated than it needs to be," he told Tomasik.

"You're dealing with a very big company," responded Tomasik.

Glen grew more and more agitated. Not only was the precious summer season approaching, but our allies on the Mott and Kellogg Foundation boards met quarterly to approve grants. We couldn't miss another quarter. The CMS attorney was fretting over single words in the thirty-page set of documents, and Joe Tomasik was headed to Brazil on Sunday. "We simply cannot meet our funders' deadlines if this keeps getting pushed back while they dillydally over minutiae," said Glen.

Glen hauled in the weight of the Conservancy's board and shot CMS a formal letter: "We have . . . set a definitive deadline of signing the proposed purchase option for the Arcadia property by Friday, May 9, at noon EST. This deadline is necessary to meet the requirements of our lead supporters. . . . If we do not meet the Friday deadline then the closing date will have to be pushed back."

That Friday Glen sent an update to the board: "The hourglass shows less than three hours and counting." He paced restlessly, glancing at the clock. Much to our relief, emails from CMS Energy's legal team in Jackson began pouring in during the morning. One, two, three, four . . . seven emails plus faxes. But noon approached and there was no word from Tomasik, the man who could sign the deal. We stared at the clock. Noon passed. It was 1:30 p.m. now, then 2:30. Still no word from Brazil.

Fifteen minutes later, we heard the blessed words: "Glen, Joe Tomasik's on the phone."

We were so close we could smell the hemlocks and pines on the shoreline. All afternoon an avalanche of phone calls, faxes, and emails arrived from Brazil. We inched closer. Yet by the end of Friday the signature lines on the contract remained blank. CMS had missed the deadline.

That was the state we were in when I stood in Glen's office, armed with a final short list of negotiating points.

"Remember, I won't be in on Monday," I told Glen. "I'll be out all week."

"What?!" said Glen, swiveling around in his desk chair. "You're kidding!"

"You won't need me," I said, waving the sheet at him. "It's all here. Everything you need."

Glen continued to stare at me in disbelief, his arms leaning on the desk. "But surely you want us to *call* when we sign the deal?" he asked.

"No, Glen," I said. "No phone calls. No emails."

"But we're going to *sign* next week!" Glen cried.

"I'm getting married next week," I said.

A few weeks before, amid the flurry of the legal banter, I had slipped away for an hour. Around the corner, down the hill, to a little dead-end street called Hillcrest Court. The dressmaker was waiting for me, her hands full of folds of French silk. She placed the gown over my head and let it cascade down my body. The skirt rustled and swayed above my wool socks. "Here's the jacket to match," she said. "I think you'll be in luck. The weather looks clear this year—no snow in May." The lawyers were forgotten as I stood before the mirror draped in happiness.

Perhaps Glen had had a hand in the matchmaking as well as Dori. After all, he was there when Rick dropped by the Conservancy office at lunchtime one February with the weather report. Snowflakes were falling in huge crystal clumps. "Looks good for our camping trip," Rick said. This would be our second foray into winter camping. First we had cross-country skied to the Pictured Rocks' icy cliffs on Lake Superior with snowshoes strapped to our sled. Now we were aiming for the Pigeon River country. We could leave after work, in just another four hours.

Glen must have spotted the gleam in my eyes. Perhaps this was part of his strategy to ground me in Michigan. "Go! Go!" he'd said. "Go camping! Leave right now!" He'd waved his arms, shooing me out the door in the middle of the day.

The wedding was to take place at Watervale. On May 17 my family and friends would gather from eleven states and four countries to stay at the Watervale cottages, right at the base of the Arcadia dunes.

I slipped out of the office at the end of the day that Friday despite Glen's protests. On Wednesday, three days before the wedding, my brother and his family pulled into town. I ran toward their car to welcome them, and that's when I noticed a flash of color on my front porch. Someone had propped a bouquet of flowers by the door. When I bent to read the tag, I saw it was written in the rounded cursive of a florist shop staffer:

"Dear Heather, Now we know what Joe Tomasik's signature looks like. Love, Us."

Part III

Coastal Campaign

2003–2005

11 Watervale and Crystal Downs

Every creature is better alive than dead, men and moose
and pine trees, and he who understands it aright will
rather preserve its life than destroy it.

—Henry David Thoreau

Northern Michigan
June–July 2003

Fritz Duda was flabbergasted. How could a pipsqueak nonprofit group
like the Conservancy have snatched an option to buy the Arcadia land
out from under him? His realtor, Lynne, told me the story. She'd tried
to warn Duda. "There is another offer on the table," she'd said.

"That's a typical real estate ploy," retorted Duda sharply. "Don't give
me that."

"I don't play that game," Lynne told him. "I'm just telling you what
I know."

When Lynne told him that the Conservancy's deal was off if we did
not raise $5 million by summer's end, Duda relaxed. His chance to buy
the Arcadia dunes was merely postponed. "There's no way in hell they
can raise that," he said.

Could we deliver? That was the question in everyone's mind. Could a
small nonprofit achieve the impossible in one summer?

Up north, the winters are long. Snow sometimes starts in October,
smothering Halloween leaf piles, and doesn't fully vanish until April.
Children may hunt Easter eggs in the snowdrifts, and drivers leave ice
scrapers in their trunks year round.

But summers are short. The official summer season begins on Memorial Day, when the lakes are still chilled from frigid ice chunks that floated only a short month before. Summer tourist season ends on Labor Day, when the teenaged work crew heads back to high school and college. Ninety days. Ninety days to get all the swimming, beaches, and cherry pies in. Ninety days to find $5 million.

For this was our task. CMS Energy still doubted we could come up with the $18 million purchase money. The company had agreed to give us the summer for fundraising, but built a tall demand into the contract: give us written proof that you have seventy-five percent of the cash raised by September 15, or the deal is off. The Mott Foundation also wanted proof that our ambitious Coastal Campaign was viable. Yes, it was willing to consider a large gift in September, but only if local people could prove they truly loved the land. Show us that your donors care about the dunes, Mott said. Raise $5 million before our board meets in September.

"We've got to show them we can do it," said Glen. "It's just risk. We can manage risk."

We understood that every big donor would ask tough questions and seek reassurance. Donors needed to feel confident that we could pull it off, and that other major donors would support us, too.

The immediate person to convince was Lois DeBacker, head of the Environment Program at the Mott Foundation. If Bill White was determined to give millions to this small land trust, Lois was determined to see to it that the foundation's money would not be wasted. Known for her diligence and tenacity, Lois had to be pleased before the Mott board members would be comfortable enough to cast their vote.

Whereas Glen talked in hyperbole, Lois spoke in reality. Prior to signing the CMS Energy purchase contract, Glen and I had hunkered down in his office, locked in an epic conference call with Lois. The battle of wills dragged on for four hours.

"Lois! This deal is going to be a model for the nation!" said Glen. "It's the largest privately held coastal parcel in Michigan! It's the largest farm preservation project in the Midwest! This deal is going to be *transformative* for the Conservancy!"

"It's either going to transform you or it's going to kill you," said Lois matter-of-factly. "You'll have to prove to me that it's not going to kill you."

"Okay," said Glen. "What do we have to do?"

"Glen, you need to sit down and do a spreadsheet," said Lois. "Map out all your cash flow for the next ten years. Show me what impact the Coastal Campaign will have on your organization. Show me how you can pay the Mott Foundation back."

Spreadsheets and Glen did not mix. "Heather! Christine! Get in here! Lois wants a spreadsheet!" We huddled in Birgit's office and started in on the daunting job: calculating every known cost and documenting the reasoning behind our estimates. Birgit was the finance director. It was only five years since I'd petitioned her for $30 to buy a Benzie County plat book. Now we were sitting down to talk about $30 million.

Our task reminded me of Emma, the baker's daughter, who sold "pony cookies" down at the farmers' market. She wanted a pony with all her heart. Her parents rose before dawn and sweated through long days in front of their brick oven. They weren't the sort who could buy their nine-year-old daughter a pony. But they were enthusiastic entrepreneurs. "If you can raise the money for a pony, you can have a pony," they told Emma. "But you have to think through the full cost of the pony. It's the upkeep, not just the cost of buying it." Emma made a list of all the costs, from feed and vet bills to the expense of hoof trimming every six weeks. Then she bought seeds. She planted pansies and purple coneflowers and sold them at the farmers' market. She bought sunflower seeds, raisins, organic oats, and Belgian chocolate and baked hearty cookies. Next she drew a picture of a pony and propped a hand-lettered sign beside her parents' booth at the farmers' market: "Help me buy a horse, buy a pony cookie." She sold the cookies for $2 apiece. In just eighteen months, Emma was riding her new horse, Lacy.

We had to do the same.

What were the true costs? Five years from now we could expect some income from the land from sustainable forestry. In two years our bank loan would come due. Six years from now we had to live without Mott's interest-free money. Then there were the costs of surveys, attorneys, title insurance, additional staff, dump cleanup, trails, signs, and grassland restoration. The list seemed endless.

Stewarding the land was the biggest unknown cost. Our nature preserve stewardship staff was used to maintaining trails at our various preserves, but nothing on the scale of 6,000 acres. First we'd have to map the land and conduct a biological inventory. The dump cleanup was big—illegal dumping had proliferated during the decades the land had been left untended. We'd have to haul out rusted car bodies. If we wanted a native forest, we'd have to knock down overgrown Christmas tree plantations and create a sustainable forestry plan. The grassland would quickly turn to trees if we didn't manage it—we'd need fire training for controlled burns, plus seeding and mowing. Then there were the quick-spreading invasive species moving over Michigan. We might have to pitch battle against pernicious plants like garlic mustard that threatened the native forest. On the dunes, tufts of innocent-seeming baby's breath were already obscuring habitat for rare dune plants. We'd have to devise a way to rid the dunes of this florist shop escape artist and its hellishly deep taproots. Stewardship staff dreamed up the biggest budget they could think of: half a million dollars.

"We need more," said Birgit. "Should we double it to stay on the safe side?"

"Better triple it," I said.

The stewardship budget we eventually submitted was a staggering $1.8 million. Never before had we planned for so much land stewardship. Never before had the Conservancy built in *all* costs of the campaign into the budget. In the past, our goal had been the land's purchase price—we worried about raising funds for managing the property later.

"Better to build it all in," Christine advised. "Don't let people get the purchase price set in their minds. Simply tell them the truth: this is the cost to do the project."

This made sense, but I felt doubtful. The number was so big.

"Sophisticated donors are used to campaigns," she assured me. "They want to see the *real* cost. Don't worry if it's a big number. Sophisticated donors want to see that you've thought about it thoroughly and figured it out."

We eyed the full costs. Purchase prices for three dune properties, Betsie Dunes, Green Point Dunes, and Arcadia: $920,000, $4.8 million, and $18 million. Add in $1.8 million in expenses just to transfer the deeds: title insurance, surveys, recording fees, taxes, appraisals, and (the big one) attorneys. Land stewardship: another $1.8 million. Accomplishing all these tasks would take time, so we planned for new staff to help during the campaign. At the same time, the campaign would suck donations away from our annual giving pot. The campaign would have to transfer some money back to the Conservancy coffers to keep the ship afloat during the campaign years. We added in $1.4 million for regular operations. Then we had to consider fundraising expenses. Calculating fundraising costs at five percent to raise money from major donors and fifteen percent to raise the money from others, we needed another $1.6 million. It would take money to raise money.

As we worked, we overestimated our expenses (you never know what will come up in ten years) and underestimated our income (I know Glen says it's a sure thing, but what if that grant *doesn't* come through?). If our estimates were too far off, the Conservancy might collapse in fiscal ruin.

After four days locked away, we emerged with campaign answers. We could expect $7.5 million from individual donors. We could pay back the Mott Foundation on time. Ten years from now we would emerge strong, with extra money for other land projects. Grand total for the Coastal Campaign: $30.6 million.

Once we knew the campaign goal, Christine was firm on one point: our first fundraising efforts had to involve just a handful of major donors. "It's the quiet phase, Glen," she reminded him. "All campaigns start with a quiet phase."

Glen nodded.

"This has got to be top secret," warned Christine again. "We can't have people talking. No media. No mailings. Staff and board shouldn't even talk to their spouses. We're talking *quiet*."

"Right," said Glen. "Loose lips sink ships."

"And dunes," I added.

As summer began, the task looked insurmountable. For a campaign this size, our fundraising team was small and somewhat green. We had a couple of part-timers plus two new hires. Between Memorial Day and Labor Day we had to overcome the dual impossibility of raising $5 million in three months' time *and* not telling anybody about it.

Glen knew the monumental task ahead. Before summer broke, Glen had taken his wife and kids down for a weekend stay at Watervale. Dori hosted them in the Strawberry Box cabin, a cozy pink cottage perched above the lane. The weekend included a party with potential supporters of the Coastal Campaign and family time for hiking. Becky, eight months pregnant, gamely hiked the steep ascent to Baldy with Glen and the children. William, five and a half, and Martin, three and a half, scampered up the sand dunes in delight. Glen stopped them at the top as Becky caught her breath.

"This is Baldy," he told the boys. Then he warned his children that he was going to be busy this summer, really, really busy, and he wouldn't have much time left to see them or Mommy. He would be working to save this sand dune. "It's all about Baldy," he told them, hoping they would remember and understand.

The view Glen showed his children that day is what we had to offer. Memories. Colors. Shapes. Vistas of blue lakes. Hillsides bursting with trillium or cherry blossoms.

People did not come to northern Michigan for its ecological systems. The Great Lakes could be ecologically dead, yet the lifeless waters would still shimmer blue and people would still gasp and wonder at the endless horizon. It was the beauty that called. The flutter of a golden, tooth-edged birch leaf and the lap of the water against the dock posts as families stood by the cottage wishing summer could last longer. When September filled the air with the scent of freshly picked apples, cottagers would linger for a last look, trying to impress this moment—this one moment—in their minds so the image would sustain them through the weeks and months ahead when snow, jobs, car alarms, cell phones, and city traffic consumed life again. Here was an oasis, a spot on earth where nothing changed. The views today were as sublime as when Grandmother first dabbled her bare feet in the lake waters as a child.

But now change was threatening this oasis.

We had to tap that sense of beauty, family, and generations to get people to defend the dunes. We had to draw on the affection families felt for their own spot of land and extend that emotion down the coast to three unknown properties. Saving rare dune plants and protecting vanishing habitat was part of the story, but the message had to touch hearts. We had to sell beauty. We had to hawk heritage. We had to gamble on love.

In June the new Coastal Campaign launched at Watervale. Dori invited us to Wednesday Barbeque Night, a weekly evening when summer guests sit on folding wooden chairs by Lower Herring Lake's shore and feast on hamburgers, barbeque ribs, corn on the cob, sesame noodle salad, and ice cream sundaes.

The first Wednesday, Glen and I stood about the picnic tables wondering how best to break into the happy conversations around us. I felt conspicuous and awkward. We were the only ones with green plastic name badges pinned to our chests, and it felt like being on the wrong side of a sales phone call during dinner. Here we were, barging into a sacred vacation spot, asking people to stop licking barbeque sauce off their burger and listen to a pitch asking them to give away their money.

Dori settled Glen at a family picnic table and then reappeared at my side. "See that woman over there?" she whispered. "Sitting at the corner table? Go talk to her. Come on, I'll introduce you."

I described the dunes, the campaign. I mentioned that we needed pledges—$5 million by Labor Day. The woman smiled at me vaguely. "That's nice, dear," she said. Then she turned to chat with her granddaughter.

"This isn't working," sighed Dori afterward. "I thought people would fall all over themselves and say, 'Sign me up!'"

The next week we refined our approach. Dori posted signs on the inn door and invited everyone to attend a special presentation at the gazebo about saving Old Baldy on Wednesday evening. Free wine. She talked it up when guests arrived on Saturday, sat with them on porch swings, and ushered them toward the white-painted gazebo an hour before the barbeque was due to start. She enticed them with merlot and chardonnay, white cheddar, Brie, and tangy cheese from Switzerland.

"This is urgent, folks, we've got a real threat here," implored Glen. "A developer from Texas wants to turn Baldy into a golf course, and I've seen the plans."

After the talk people begged for pledge cards. The pre-barbeque talk at the gazebo had worked. Glen, however, didn't hand out any pledge cards. If people thought they could do their part by writing a $100 check on the spot, they'd do it. It was better to request a personal meeting and ask them to fill out the pledge cards privately. To have any hope of raising $5 million by Labor Day, the Conservancy needed multiple gifts of $20,000 or more.

Glen flung himself into the campaign whirlwind. The route to Watervale became automatic: south by the Interlochen Arts Academy, turn right at Frank Ettawageshik's pottery shop, then on through Thompsonville. Eighty-four miles round-trip between the Conservancy office and the coast.

Glen drove a Saturn Vue now, but his last car had been a junker. A Honda, partly rusted, but still mostly maroon after 300,000 miles. A Benzie County landowner had once kicked the tires in disgust. It had been Christine who stressed the importance of making his next car a domestic brand. "Glen, it's Michigan," she said, reminding him of the state's proud auto-manufacturing heritage. "You could be driving donors. It's just plain stupid not to be driving an American car." It was true, many of the people Glen was hoping to speak to were retired Ford or GM auto executives.

Glen's head was swirling. His third child, Leonard Lewis Chown, had been born on June 25, just five days before Glen's own forty-second birthday. He'd stayed home for a week and taken his two older children fishing and frogging on nearby Prescott Lake, but the Coastal Campaign was always waiting.

He played music from Greg Brown's *Going Driftless* album. His brother Bill had given it to him, and he loved the songs about the Midwest, about land and landscapes, and about John Muir. He let the lyrics wash over him as he turned down Watervale's gravel drive. Dori's hand-painted blue signs lined the roadside: Slow, please. Children. Walkers and Bikers. Glen parked by the inn and made his way to the cottage—Ursula, perhaps, or Johanna—where he had a date with a Watervale guest for a personal pledge meeting.

Hello there! Glen Chown! How are you? Yes, the porch is fine. What a *day* to be at Watervale! Were you in charge of the weather?

The Wednesday night gazebo talks at Watervale continued all summer. Every week a new group of summer guests arrived, and every Wednesday they learned that the dunes were in danger. Kate Pearson began to give the talks while Glen scooted up the coast to reach out to more donors.

Kate had joined the Conservancy less than a year ago. Her smile was electric, her every move energetic. She held her slim body straight as she strode down the Conservancy's hall, her long legs moving like a dancer's. Not ballet, modern dance. Kate had a knack for setting people at ease and listening to their stories. Kate had never raised money before, but listening, after all, is the chief hallmark of a good fundraiser.

The first time Kate took the gazebo floor, she was shaking. She took a breath and plunged into her spiel. "Now there's a developer from Texas, a Fritz Duda, yes, doo-dah, like the song," she said. "But he's real, you can Google him." *Why does he have to be named Duda?* Kate thought. *Doo-dah doesn't sound menacing at all.*

A Watervale guest raised his hand. "I'm a developer myself," he said. Kate gulped, thinking, *What did I say?*

"I've checked this guy out," he continued. "He's for real. This threat is real. So if any of you are thinking what I thought, that these Conservancy people are inflating the threat, take it from me. They're not."

Each week Kate presented at Watervale's gazebo before the barbeque. Each week Joan Wolfe, a local bird-watcher, attended and cried almost on cue as she gave her personal testimony about her love for the Arcadia dunes. Each week the same questions came up.

"Why isn't this in the paper?"

"Don't you care about small gifts?"

"What about Oprah?" someone would invariably ask. "Have you reached out to Oprah?"

"I didn't know she'd ever been to Baldy," said Kate. "Just because someone has money doesn't mean they're inclined to give. *We* are the ones we need to ask. We need to stretch ourselves."

Watervale guests stretched. Pledges started pouring in.

A college student who'd spent childhood summers at Watervale tallied her living expenses and made a monthly pledge. Artists banded together and sold original watercolors. The kitchen staff at Watervale was not to be outdone. The waitresses, prep cooks, breakfast cooks, and dishwashers collectively donated a chunk of their summer earnings. Together these gifts inspired others to increase their pledges, and some Watervale families pledged $25,000 or more, for that was the minimum to add their names to stones in a new Watervale garden.

Not everybody was motivated by rocks, however. Nancy, a summer guest, had already pledged a gift but was considering giving more. "Could I have some blankets?" she asked Dori.

The Watervale blankets were Pullman blankets from the days when Dori's uncle Walter used to work for the Pullman line. They were wool, dense and solid relics from the days of rail. Guests had hauled these mocha-brown blankets to the beach for years, and beach fire sparks had branded them here and there. Many blankets bore neat square patches where Vera had covered up holes caused by nibbling mice. Nancy's husband loved trains, and they both loved Watervale. In exchange for three Pullman blankets, Nancy raised her pledge fivefold.

Stories of impressive gifts from Watervale inched their way up the coast to the enclave of Crystal Downs. The entrance to the Crystal Downs Country Club is modestly marked by two pillars built of sandy-colored brick. A mile-long driveway leads to the clubhouse. First it passes through cedar hedges stretching like long, green caterpillars, then winds through birch, hemlock, white pine, and maple forest. From time to time the leaves part enough to catch a glimpse of the world-class Alister MacKenzie–designed golf course.

Business, finance, and banking families from Chicago, Columbus, Cleveland, and other Midwest points gather at Crystal Downs each summer. The waiting list to join is about eight to ten years. The dress code bans jeans, and good manners ban cell phones on the golf course. Cream-colored golf carts purr along the pathways. Jaguars and BMWs line up in the parking lot, and more than one car sports the green cedar leaf logo of a Conservancy bumper sticker.

Crystal Downs had nurtured the Conservancy since its founding. Glen needed to draw on the critical support of these families. Here he had gathered his volunteer Coastal Campaign cabinet, a trio of sophisticated businesspeople and seasoned fundraisers: David Reese and Nancy and Chuck Brickman, strategic thinkers with big hearts.

Nancy Brickman loved nature. Her mother had nurtured that early love and made cloth and wood models of birds mounted on pipe cleaners—cardinals, nuthatches, and ruby-crowned kinglets. Now a grandmother herself, Nancy liked nothing better than to gather neighbors to her home, greet them with a kiss on the cheek, offer fried chicken and drinks, and then afterward hike out into the darkness with Conservancy staff to call for barred owls.

Nancy had been one of Glen's earliest supporters, and for years her husband had stood to the side, smiling supportively, as Nancy hosted cocktail parties for the Conservancy. Now with the dunes at stake, he was ready to take an active role. Chuck was past president of Crystal Downs and together they knew families who had been summering here forty, fifty, or even ninety years.

David Reese added contagious enthusiasm and connections to the campaign. He knew Chuck from college, and ever since that sunset schooner ride, he and his family had blazed with a steady passion for saving the dunes.

Twelve years of owl-hooting field trips and dinner parties had set the stage. The Conservancy was twelve years old when the Coastal Campaign began in 2003. Fundraising experts say that typical donors will support a group for nine to eleven years before upping their gift to an extraordinary level. We had more than a decade of trust built up, but could we become extraordinary?

Glen charged out of his office with a yell. "Two and a half million from Kellogg!" he cried. "We got the Kellogg Foundation!"

This early gift from the W. K. Kellogg Foundation gave us a tremendous boost. It didn't count toward our summer $5 million goal—that had to be donated by private individuals—but now Mott was not alone. We could proudly announce two lead gifts in our fundraising pitch. Also, and this was essential, Kellogg had awarded money to the project because of the farmland. Most other donors fixated on the dunes, but as king of breakfast cereals, Kellogg cared deeply about sustainable farming and believed our dream of protecting the orchards and selling them back to farmers would work.

Glen and I had spent a Saturday touring Rick Foster, Kellogg's vice president, and his wife around the Arcadia farm fields. Rick had been impressed with the scale of the project, but as we walked through the shin-high corn plants, he kicked the stalks. "This is no place for corn," he said. "Look at this! Corn should be grown in places like Iowa, not here in this soil."

We agreed, and explained CMS Energy's one-year license arrangements with the farmers. The short time frame had forced growers to abandon their orchards and turn more fields into corn. Under the Conservancy's plan, the landscape could be different.

Rick was intrigued. Arcadia's sheer size was compelling. With so many acres, what happened on Arcadia would clearly impact farms beyond its borders. If this land stayed in agriculture, farms around it could also flourish. There'd be no neighbors or golf course members complaining about tractor noise or farm smells. No added pressure to sell for housing. The cherry-processing plant on Joyfield Road would benefit with a steady supply of tart cherries. The local farm-equipment supplier could keep selling hedgers, forklifts, and pruners to local fruit farmers. The whole system was linked, just like any ecosystem. This was what sustainable agriculture was all about.

Meanwhile, Conservancy staff scurried to produce campaign packets worthy of attracting more million-dollar gifts. We created a practical, not posh, storybook from a slim spiral binder. Inside we slipped dramatic photos of dunes, misty forests, and sugar sand beaches. Glen made sure maps were included. The three coastal properties—Arcadia, Green Point and Betsie Dunes—shone in bright highlighter yellow. We presented the full campaign goal and what we'd secured so far. After Kellogg's gift, there was only $28.1 million—or ninety-one percent—left to go.

Chuck Brickman saw the draft materials and immediately called the Conservancy to stop the presses. "We need to lay out the numbers differently," he said. "People are going to think it's a pipe dream and will just say no. Emphasize the lead gifts and public money. Give private donors a *realistic* portion. Show them it's doable—and do it on one page. These people don't have a lot of time."

The revised fundraising storybook featured Chuck's one-page sheet of numbers and broke the campaign down into bite-sized responsibilities. No longer did it focus on "ninety-one percent left to go." The figures were the same but laid out differently. Public dollars would cover so much, reselling farmland would add income, Mott, Kellogg, and other foundations would contribute sizeable amounts, leaving a manageable portion for private donors. This mini goal was highlighted with a bright yellow text bubble: "$7.5 million of individual gifts provide leverage for the entire campaign."

Leverage. We had to let folks know they were in good company. The Coastal Campaign was doable and something they would want to be part of.

Across the wooden footbridge at Crystal Downs that links the clubhouse with the golf shop stands Fred Muller. There, amid the pyramids of stacked golf balls, display of striped golf shirts, and issues of *Golf World*, *Golf Week*, and *Golf Digest*, Fred flashes his broad smile and greets every member by name. Fred Muller is Crystal Downs' golf pro. He gives lessons, manages the golf shop, and is an expert in golf course architecture. But ask anyone, and they'll tell you Fred is something more. He took the job in 1977, and during the past decades has earned his place as Crystal Downs' heart and soul. During the Coastal Campaign, Fred became an unofficial member of the campaign team. As members set out for the golf course, Fred dropped hints in their ears: Have you heard? Do you know about the dunes? He suggested names of potential donors to Chuck: Go and see Art. I talked to Mike today. Why don't you call Norm?

Chuck was skilled at drawing in donors. First, following the primary rule of fundraising, the Brickmans and Reeses gave large pledges themselves. Second, they concentrated on a core group of about five major donors. Once these leaders came onboard, others would surely follow. One man they hoped to attract was David Grainger, who governed a family foundation with $45 million in assets. The family had historically been generous with gifts.

"Well, I wouldn't be interested in that," David Grainger said when they approached him. "I've done a lot around here, and it's time for other people to step up and do their part."

"That's fine," David Reese responded. "It's a wonderful project. If you ever do want to get involved, we'd be glad to have you."

Meanwhile, Chuck was dropping off Conservancy packets and setting up appointments. He met a potential supporter for breakfast at Joann's Restaurant in Frankfort, and walked away with a leadership gift pledged. Chuck drove his blue BMW to homes along Crystal Lake's western shoreline, Glen beside him in the tan leather passenger seat. Chuck lined up four or five visits in a row, tracking the growing list of donor visits in a little appointment book. Each visit lasted twenty minutes. He knew families came north for the beaches and golf games, and he didn't want to waste any donor's time. Summer was beckoning.

The dunes were beckoning, too. David Reese made sure of that. The Reese family had arrived in northern Michigan in the late 1990s and reveled in area hiking. David made it his personal charge to get people out on the dunes, leading field trip after field trip.

"You heard about what we're doing?" he said. "We're trying to preserve 6,000 acres down near Arcadia. Have you ever *seen* two miles of beach with nothing on it? My wife, Weezie, and I feel so passionate about this ourselves that we've decided to give half a million dollars. Your family's been coming here for years. It's time to make sure your children and grandchildren can continue to enjoy it. Here are the people involved." Then he angled for a field trip: "At least come down and look at it. What day is good for you? I'll take you for a hike."

Glen and David both hiked the dunes. They preached on the dunes. They coaxed people to stray from the comfort of their summer cottages for a precious summer afternoon. "Just come and see. Bring the kids."

Perhaps the Coastal Campaign took a page from Lewis Carroll's *Through the Looking Glass,* the sequel to *Alice in Wonderland.* At a great feast, the Red Queen politely introduces Alice to each entrée. After the plum pudding and lamb chop have made how-do-you-do bows to Alice, the little girl can eat nothing at all. They are acquainted; their relationship has irrevocably altered. As Lewis Carroll knew, it is much harder to destroy something once you have been introduced. If our dunes stayed anonymous, no one would rush to rescue them. Our job was to introduce people to the dunes.

12 Arcadia

i thank You God for most this amazing
day: for the leaping greenly spirits of trees
and a blue true dream of sky;and for everything
which is natural which is infinite which is yes

—e. e. cummings

Benzie and Manistee Counties, Michigan
Summer 2003

Across from Watervale Road stood the Blaine Township Cemetery.
Township clerk Charlotte Putney sold a set of eight gravesites for $200.
It used to be only $2 when she started the job thirty-three years ago, but
costs were rising, and Blaine Township was obliged to adjust its fees.
Perpetual care was extra.

Despite the project's secrecy, I instinctively knew we had to reach
out to locals like Charlotte as early as possible. She was a township trustee and I knew she held a lease to some of the farmland on Dry Hill, land
she and her husband had once sold to Consumers Power. There were a
total of three township boards to consider, plus two counties and scores
of local farmers. What became of the CMS property directly impacted
these neighbors' lives and businesses. *These people ought to know what's
going on,* I thought. It was only fair. *And they ought to know sooner rather
than later,* I concluded. It was only wise.

Glen and Christine agreed when I brought it up; we couldn't talk
to the media but we could talk to farmers. But how should I go about
it? How could we reach locals in a way that did not spoil the campaign's quiet phase? How could I walk into a new neighborhood and
announce that soon the Conservancy might be the biggest private
landowner in the region? Speculation and rumor had hovered over

the Arcadia land for thirty years. My announcement was sure to be a bombshell.

I decided to start with a community-wide meeting, inviting all the Arcadia leaseholders, plus local farm families and neighbors. After that, I would make the rounds of local township governments. I had no idea what I would say, but trusted that my instinct to go to the people was the right one. Local landowners still bore grudges against the National Park Service for its heavy-handedness when the federal government created Sleeping Bear National Lakeshore a few miles north in 1970. The farmers and neighbors were the *last* people I wanted to blindside with our news, but the deal making had all been so secretive. At this early stage I still had few answers, but at least I could be frank, respectful, and open to ideas.

At first I agonized about location. A local town hall would fit a crowd, but it might link the project with government. Someone's living room? Not big enough, plus it might look like an endorsement. We needed a community meeting ground where locals felt comfortable. That's when a Conservancy friend suggested the church at Putney Corners. "That's the farmers' church," he said. "That's their gathering place."

Perfect, I thought. We meet on their turf, not mine.

The Blaine Christian Church stood on the southwest side of Putney Corners. A white painted board with the church's name sat between two bushes along Joyfield Road. The church was white with a grey shingled roof and a spire that poked above the orchard trees, like New England spires in a Currier and Ives painting. I brought coffee and cookies along with a trusted board member who added a level head and a connection to Manistee County orchard farmers.

The first curious farmers showed up half an hour early. Some were clutching the yellow postcard invitation I had mailed out to about forty-five households. "Dear Neighbor," it read. "Please come to an evening of information about the Consumers Power land. June 30, 7:30 p.m. I look forward to seeing you. Heather Shumaker, Grand Traverse Regional Land Conservancy."

I had signed with my married name, my new signature somewhat wobbly.

"Oh, it's you," one of the farmers whom I knew slightly said. "I wondered how many Heathers the Conservancy had."

A steady stream of neighbors filed in, and soon they filled all six rows of the church's folding metal chairs. Tonight I'd have to remember to talk about Dry Hill, since that's what the farmers called the Consumers Power land.

Still more people came, lining the back of the room, standing and leaning against windows. I counted about seventy. Some were white haired and old enough to have farmed Dry Hill in the 1950s and '60s. Others towed young children behind them. The crowd was a mix of baseball caps, blue jeans, and canvas jackets among the men, and curler-rolled hair, jeans, and T-shirts among the women. Everyone was quiet, voices hushed; there was hardly a sound in the room except for the creak of metal chairs as people shifted their weight. The room held thirty years of nervous anticipation. These people had loved, farmed, hiked, and hunted Dry Hill since before I was born. Some had been born there; some remembered the one-room schoolhouse perched on top of the ridge before Consumers knocked it down. It was as if the community were holding its breath, waiting to hear the sentencing after a trial.

I took a deep breath. There was nothing for it but to spill the beans. "I wanted you to be the first to know," I said. "The Conservancy has signed an option to buy the Consumers Power land. If we can raise enough money, we will be buying it in December."

There was not a sound in the room as I outlined our plan to make a new nature preserve out of the dune and forestland, and sell the farmland portion back to farmers, subject to conservation restrictions. "We welcome ideas you have," I concluded. "I wanted you to know about our plans upfront. We'd like to work together."

That night I didn't know what the farmers were thinking, but they told me later. From his seat next to his wife, Brian Putney was inwardly fuming. It wasn't the Conservancy he was mad at. It was Consumers.

Hadn't he asked the company time and again if he could buy some land back? Now here he'd been sideswiped.

Near the back, cherry farmer Mike Evans viewed the proceedings with a skeptical eye. Sure, he and his brother had been hoping to buy Dry Hill land for years. But would this work out? The Conservancy rep seemed so young and naïve standing up in the church meeting hall with her ponytail and glasses. *Is she up for this? Can the Conservancy pull it off?*

That attitude captured the mood of the room: prove yourself.

But just as the meeting ended, a Manistee farmer spoke up from the back row. "I just wanted to say that Consumers never would have come and talked to us like this. They never told us anything, or asked our input like the Conservancy's doing now. This is a big change, and I think we ought to help them out."

The meeting broke up on that note, but few attendees headed for the door. Instead they gathered around me in a thick bunch, mobbing me with questions. "*When* are you going to sell the land? I need to plant young trees," said one orchard farmer. "I'm forty-five now, and by the time those trees start producing I'll be pushing sixty. We can't wait around."

More farmers jostled for position, all trying to bend my ear. I tried to sort out names and absorb the avalanche of opinion. "*How* are you going to sell the land?" asked another farmer. "Locals should get preference, you know. We can't compete with outsiders. If you let just anyone buy that land it will end up as hobby farms."

"You shouldn't sell the land at all," said one corn farmer. "We can't afford to buy, we can only lease it. If we lose that land we're leasing, we'll be out of business."

An older farmer squeezed my arm and led me out of earshot of the others, speaking in a conspiratorial whisper. "That land should go back to the original landowners," he said. "All the families who owned land in 1970 and got threatened by Consumers. They're the rightful owners, not the leaseholders."

As he launched into a story about former owners, another farmer barged in to counteract that idea. "Whatever you do, *don't* let the original owners have first dibs," he said. "They sold their land fair and square to Consumers and got a good price for it. Really good money. Don't let them fool you."

My head was reeling, dizzy from so much direct lobbying. I promised we would try to come up with a fair process. The farm families all wanted access to me since I held access to the Dry Hill land.

At the end, a young woman my age with short, dark hair approached. "I'm Dodie Putney," she said. "Brian's wife, with Putney Beef or Fruit. I just wanted to tell you to take Dave off your invitation list. That's Brian's dad. He died last year."

I nodded, grateful for the information. I had no idea how things would work out, but I was certain they would. People wanted to help.

The next week I made the rounds in Manistee County. Manistee was new territory for the Conservancy. So new that our board had only recently voted to accept Manistee County into its service area. "We're working there anyway," I pointed out. "Half the CMS Arcadia land lies in Manistee."

Unlike Benzie County to the north, Manistee had no long history of owl-calling field trips and dinner parties with the Conservancy. We had nothing to build on. We needed brand-new friends in Manistee County—or rather, we needed instantaneous best friends. This was not the traditional way to fundraise.

My first stop was Pleasanton Township Hall, a white clapboard building with a bell steeple that had been a schoolhouse in the 1880s. Besides the five township planning commissioners sitting around a folding table, I was the only one in the room. We were a mere eight miles away from the church at Putney Corners, but across the border here in Manistee County, no one in Pleasanton Township had heard a whiff about what was going on.

"We've got a chance right now, but if we don't raise the money by Labor Day, CMS won't sell to us," I told them.

We talked taxes, we talked farmland. I pointed out that CMS hadn't been paying school taxes in their district for thirty years, so taking land off the tax rolls wouldn't cause any impact to the Bear Lake schools.

Pleasanton planning commissioner Gerard Grabowski caught the spark and urgency. He was also a baker, the father of Emma, the pony cookie entrepreneur. He loved the land. He and his wife picked blackberries there. He camped there on the sly and took his kids hiking. The sand dunes on the Consumers land in jeopardy! A chance to save it? That night he rushed back to his home next to the Pleasanton Brick Oven Bakery and told his wife, "We've got to do something!"

Gerard was as tall and thin as a lamppost, six foot three, with a shock of curly brown hair that seemed as healthy as the food he ate. Enthusiasm ran in his veins instead of blood. Maybe it was the bread he ate, carefully baked in his handcrafted brick ovens without yeast. "Yeast is high in gluten and phytic acid, which needs to be broken down before humans can digest it," he would explain in a rapid, mile-a-minute rush of information. "Humans can't digest yeast easily. People always used to eat grains that had been fermented first, which is a natural leavening process that takes ten hours or so . . ."

When Gerard took a cause to heart, he was unstoppable. The next day he began to make phone calls. He stopped by the kitchen at Camp Arcadia and talked to his friend who was a chef there. "You've got to listen to this. This is important." He spoke to a Manistee optometrist who was an avid birder in his spare time. He researched the Conservancy and dug into backgrounds of all the staff to make sure we were legitimate. He called the township treasurer to ferret out tax information.

In all his efforts, Pleasanton Township's longtime supervisor, Fred Alkire, supported him. Fred had served Pleasanton for forty years and cared deeply about his community. "If you need to get paid for travel, don't be shy," Fred told Gerard. "Go ahead and go to any meetings." Gerard took the message to heart. *It's my civic duty and charge,* he thought.

Just two nights later, Gerard squeezed along the back windows of Arcadia Township Hall, the third of three townships, for my presentation. He had to squeeze because unlike Pleasanton's empty meeting, this hall was packed. Gerard's phone calls and word of mouth had ignited the area. Township and village families filled every row of metal folding chairs. More lined the walls and pressed in from the front door, making about 180 altogether. I gazed at the swelling crowd.

I could tell we were swimming in foreign waters, unlike in Benzie County. No one in Manistee County knew us. Only a mile or two away, people south of the county line moved in different circles. Anxiety hung heavily in the room. After waiting for three decades, something was finally happening with the behemoth property in their backyard. The new potential landowners from Traverse City might as well have been from Texas. We were strangers.

A red-faced cattle farmer stood up in the back after I'd outlined our plans. "They're going to buy it up and do what they want!" he shouted. "You won't see that land going to farmers. They're gonna sell it above market value and soon there'll be condos on it!"

A woman from Arcadia spoke up. "What about houses? If you lock up all this land, we can't put houses on it. People need a place to live. We don't need more trees around here. We need jobs and houses."

Gerard the baker came to the Conservancy's defense. "We all rely on tourists here, like it or not. We need places like this to be preserved. It's good for our economy. Besides, I've looked into the Conservancy. A lot of groups are only an inch deep, but not these guys. You can trust them."

When I ended my talk the roomful clapped loud and hard.

Out on the sidewalk on Lake Street afterward, people jostled for position to say hello, extend a hand, give advice, or offer help. One man stood out. He was square-shouldered with rich dark hair and rectangular eyeglasses. He handed me his business card with a warm handshake. "I'm Chip May," he said, "director of Camp Arcadia. We'd like to help out. We'll do whatever we can."

I clutched his card, not daring even to tuck it in my pocket. This was a golden ticket. I didn't know much about Manistee County, but I knew we needed all the friends we could get from Camp Arcadia.

Camp Arcadia, lovingly called RKD, was a Lutheran family camp right on Lake Michigan. The courtyard had metal swing sets and seesaws on the beach. On most days, teenagers piled on the seesaws, Frisbees lay stacked on the front desk, and the gentle tap-tap-tap of ping-pong sounded from the rec room, where there were also stacks of board games like Candy Land, backgammon, and Scrabble, along with Bible Trivia and thousand-piece jigsaw puzzles of the Last Supper. Singing poured out from open windows and mixed with the constant sound of waves lapping or crashing from Lake Michigan. Campers lodged in the inn and began the day with reveille at 8 a.m., then Bible study after breakfast. Throughout the day the camp bell would clang to draw campers together for ice cream or three-on-three soccer matches. They ended their day with vespers at 10:15 p.m. and taps.

Every morning campers met for a Bible study program in the assembly room. The room was filled with white pillars and rows of wooden school chairs. Stacks of hymnals titled *All God's People Sing!* lined the shelves, and a broom closet was marked as the "Inner Sanctum." What dominated the room, however, were brightly colored felt banners hanging from the back wall, all stitched by the same woman. "This is the day the Lord has made. Let us rejoice and be glad in it," said one. Others proclaimed Lutheran values—Joy, Peace, Self-Control, Humility—or camp values: Praying, Playing, Fellowship, Service, Resting, Dining.

They might have added "Hiking." For generations, a weekly hike to the North Bluff called the Blowout Hike had been part of Camp Arcadia's official program. After all, Martin Luther said: "God writes the gospel not in the Bible alone, but on trees and flowers and clouds and stars." Women in the early days hiked the dune climb in long knickers. Camp directors staged late-summer sunset vespers services on the sand dune and led staff training amid its tranquility. In Arcadia, the gospel was sculpted on dunes.

Camp Arcadia. I didn't know much about the camp, but I knew it was key to our success here in Arcadia. Like Watervale, families had flocked to Camp Arcadia for a week or two of summer vacation for generations. What Watervale called Baldy, the Lutherans called the North Bluff. They loved the coastline fiercely. Besides the camp itself, which had more than 800 member families, there was a neighborhood of cottagers who had settled as close to the camp as possible. Chip May was opening the door to Camp Arcadia for us.

At the Conservancy, we were overjoyed with the news. But in Arcadia, fear of losing the North Bluff was spreading.

Kathleen Parsons stood with her bare toes chilling on the bathroom's white-tiled floor, the phone pressed to her ear. The rest of her was bare, too. She'd just finished a workout, and the phone call had caught her as she was about to slip into a bubble bath. As always, she'd propped the portable phone on a wooden stool near the tub before sinking into the bubbles. On the other end of the line, her neighbor dropped horrific news: "I've just learned about this developer from Texas."

The water jets churned and the bubbles frothed and burst at knee height, forgotten. The North Bluff in danger! *No, no, it can't be true,* thought Kathleen. *This can't be real. I'm dreaming this. This isn't really happening.* The North Bluff! It would be an end of an era.

"There's nothing we can do," her neighbor went on. "There's no way we can stop this. We're outgunned. This is so much bigger than we are."

Kathleen's stomach lurched with nausea. The threat to the North Bluff was a direct attack on her family. She set the phone down and began pacing.

Bill and Kathleen Parsons had met as teenagers at Camp Arcadia. Kathleen was only fifteen when she peeped out of the inn's window and spied Billy Parsons strolling across the patio in his black-and-white plaid shorts and white boater shoes. Now, forty-four years and three sons later, they were inseparable. Not just joined to each other, but rooted in Lake Michigan. Great Lakes water flowed through their cells and dune sand mixed with their marrow. "This runs in our veins," said Bill with a sweep of his hand. "The Lord's all around us right here." It was natural that they had a house in Camp Arcadia's Cottage Colony.

The day Kathleen fielded the call, Bill Parsons returned home close to midnight. He had spent the last few days giving a business presentation in Monterey, California, and struggled home through a string of late planes and cancelled flights. Kathleen waited up for him. He was ready to collapse in bed when he saw Kathleen's stricken face.

"It's the North Bluff!" she cried.

That night Bill and Kathleen stayed awake until dawn. Their emotions plunged from despair to anger to resolve. We'll never be able to do it! It would be the end of the world if we lost the North Bluff. What would it mean to the campers? To the community? The idea of bulldozers ruining it. The trillium! For the first time in their lives, they would be walled off from the place they loved so deeply. Was there a possibility of saving it? Could they do it? Would enough people come through? By dawn, the Parsons knew: "There are times when you just have to give your all. We have to do whatever we can do."

The next morning Bill called north to the Conservancy and grilled Glen for details. When he hung up, he was satisfied that Glen was seriously committed. On the spot, the Parsons turned their summer plans upside down. Typically they filled their summer days with golf games at Bear Lake or Pine Croft, tennis matches at Camp Arcadia, hikes, and games of bridge. Now the only thing that mattered was saving the North Bluff. In less than twenty-four hours, Kathleen and Bill cleared their agenda and became coastal crusaders. "This is our summer. This is number one," said Kathleen. "This is the fight we have to do."

News surged through the village of Arcadia and Camp Arcadia like wildfire. Developer from Texas. Three hundred homes, maybe a thousand. Five million to raise in just two months. Oh, we'll never be able to do it.

Besides the actual camp, the Cottage Colony neighborhood next door to the camp held 300 families, including the Parsons, many of whom had been coming to this part of Michigan's coast for five generations. A footpath linked the camp and cottages. There was a hush as you entered the cottage lanes. Bicycles leaned up against trees and cars were rare. Even the lake's surf became muffled in the leafy shade. The pace of life was dreamy in the Cottage Colony, like a never-ending week at camp. But financially, the neighborhood was tapped out. Camp Arcadia had just concluded its own $4 million campaign to add rooms, insulation, wiring, windows, heating, and new clapboard. People were still paying off their pledges for that sacrifice when the dunes called for help.

"How can we do it *again?*" people cried, and then continued, "How can we *not* do it?"

Bill Parsons, who had first arrived in Arcadia as a ten-year-old, now acted as president of the Cottage Colony. Together, Bill and Kathleen talked to everyone about the Coastal Campaign. They sought out parties, joined extra bridge games, and stopped people before services at the white-steepled Trinity Lutheran village church. They talked with the self-described "mayor" of Arcadia, and offered the village a challenge to match their own $25,000 gift. The village wasn't rich like the camp, and many people dismissed the idea of saving the land. Oh, it can't be done, people said. Forget it. Still, village families began to talk.

Next the Parsons turned to house parties. "We're having some folks over to talk about where we are on this project," Kathleen would say. "We're going to have a cocktail hour; will you come?"

The first party at Bill and Kathleen's home, "The Parsonage," was held on the deck under the shade of maple trees, birch, and hemlock. Twenty-five people gathered, filled with doubts and curiosity. Kathleen offered wine and cheese. Conservancy staff propped up posters on an easel as the guests settled in on bench cushions. Bill did the intro, then turned it over to the Conservancy. Kathleen was the closer. As a mother of three, Kathleen had perfected the art of Lutheran guilt. "If you don't do *everything* you can do, you are going to have to drive up over that bluff every week of every summer knowing that you didn't give it your all," she said. "If you had done a little more, if you had tried a little harder, if you had dug a little deeper, then *maybe* it wouldn't be what it is."

She looked at the faces of her friends and neighbors, many of whom had roots in the area reaching back five generations, too. "We must believe that David can slay Goliath," Kathleen continued. "It's not impossible. We can do this! But only if you reach down really deep and give it your all. Don't let it *disappear*," she pleaded. "*Don't* let it disappear!

"Let's join hands and pray," Kathleen concluded. She and Bill took their guests' hands and formed a prayer circle. Kathleen began to pray: "God, we know that this wonderful place should be preserved. We believe that. We're asking you to touch the hearts of those who can and will, those who can grab the vision and be a part of this project, to bless our children for generations to come."

"And save it for all eternity," Bill added.

"Amen."

North Bluff perched at the top of the prayer list for the campers and cottagers. Bill urged "prayerful consideration" and arranged for Conservancy staff to come speak at the camp's weekly dean's program when parents listened in the assembly room with their kids beside them. Involve the kids! That was Kathleen's mantra. It was the power of childhood love that caused adults to rally their friends and dig deeper and deeper into their pockets. To truly save the dunes, the next generation had to be included in the effort.

"Kids are part of this," Kathleen advised. "Their hands need to be on this rope for this tug-of-war. Ask them to do what they can, for whatever strength they can."

Her own children pledged $50 per month. Their pledges extended for years, but she hoped their pride in being part of the project would go on forever.

Bill and Kathleen hosted another house party and watched in amazement as even reluctant skeptics joined the fold. One neighbor declared: "I don't want to come. I'm not going to do anything," when first invited to the Parsonage. During the house party, she announced a sizeable pledge on the spot. "I had absolutely no intention to give, but I felt the Lord moving," she said.

Kathleen and Bill hugged their guests good-bye.

"Blessings go with you," said Kathleen.

"Blessings," said Bill.

Day after day, Conservancy staff trekked out to Camp Arcadia for follow-up visits after one of the Parsonage parties. The white Lutheran flag was always flying in the courtyard next to the American flag, its red cross and blue square flapping. We'd pass campers holding hands in the courtyard, spontaneously praying together, and heard campers thumping away at a piano, singing duets. Arcadia embraced us. The work became spiritual. Each time we left the camp, we passed under a wooden archway painted with these words: "Go forth, child of God, renewed in body, mind, and spirit."

Meanwhile, legends surrounding Fritz Duda and his development plans sprang to life. Arcadians told how Duda first discovered the property. He enjoyed the Great Lakes as a welcome break from the Texas heat, they said. He liked to cruise up Lake Michigan's coast in his yacht. A year ago, as he passed the Arcadia land, the lonely and magnificent North Bluff caught his eye. "Find out who owns that!" he called out.

At least that was the talk in Arcadia. The story buzzed through Arcadia, pulling comfortable second-home owners out of their sunrooms and summoning them to battle.

When helicopters flew overhead, pledges poured in. It must be Duda surveying the land! Then a yacht that could have been Duda's appeared, anchored in plain view. "Duda's there!" Bill Parsons cried. "Just go take a look! Just go out on the beach, and there he is waiting to get his fangs into it!"

To Bill, the yacht seemed as big as an aircraft carrier. Big enough, certainly, to launch a helicopter. For the Duda development plan called for a heliport, a golf course, and equestrian center. There would be hundreds of million-dollar homes on the land, maybe thousands. The image of this massive resort branded itself into people's minds. It was truly a story of David and Goliath: the dunes versus the destroyers.

Back in the office, my coworkers churned out campaign materials nonstop. Each major donor prospect received a white folder with a photo of the dunes printed on it. Kate and others customized the packets on the inside: parcel maps with the land in blazing yellow, Chuck's one-page leverage sheet, dune photos, and appeal letter. The dollar figures changed constantly as pledges came in, and the packet was customized for different areas. "What does a hike up the blowout on the North Bluff mean to you and your family?" one version read. Watervale families got the same packet, with "Baldy" substituted for "North Bluff."

After the house parties, Glen and others followed up with private appointments: We really need to meet in person. Yes, we'd love to have you both there. Once settled on a cottage porch, hearing the lap of Lake Michigan's waves, it was time to listen to stories. What brought you to this region? How do you and your husband make your giving decisions? What are the causes closest to your heart? These were standard questions to get to know supporters, but the Coastal Campaign had such urgency we had to go a step further. We had to be audacious.

Years later, Kate could still recite the bold request in her sleep: "Because of the immediate threat, we're asking that you put this project in your top three charities. Of course, your church is number one, and we know you have other favorite charities close to your heart, but we're asking you to place the Coastal Campaign in your top three list for only five years."

More and more house parties sprang up in the area to save Arcadia, including on Starke Point. The point was a narrow band of land between Lake Arcadia and Lake Michigan. When the Conservancy gang arrived at the Marshalls' house on Starke Point, the house smelled like fruit pies and coffee. Nancy Marshall was wearing white capris with a periwinkle sweater. Her chestnut-brown hair was cut in a round bob, and she bustled with enthusiasm as she set cherry pies out on the Formica counter. Nearby stood her husband, Bob, with his friendly, ruddy face, trim grey hair, and khakis. A pot of coffee gurgled. As it brewed, their brown and white cocker spaniel circled the floor in excitement over visitors.

Like Dori, Nancy knew food would help the cause. She served local cherry pie topped with vanilla ice cream, then stood by the fireplace and made an impassioned plea for the dune. "Bob and I hike there two, three times a week. It's just *gorgeous*. When I discovered it, I said to Bob, 'I have *got* to take you back,'" she said. "Now to think that it might be sold to a developer! I want you to know this land is important enough to us that we have made a financial commitment to the project."

Nancy had fallen in love with the North Bluff five years ago. But there was someone in the room that night who had loved it far, far longer: Ruth Starke Burkhead. Ruth's grandfather had founded the village of Arcadia and she was undoubtedly the town matriarch. Ruth had been born in the kitchen, eight houses north in the grey-sided Starke farmhouse on Starke Point. In her youth she had been crowned Ag Queen at Michigan State University. These days she spent her summers down at the Arcadia Historical Museum, a turreted Victorian building where she sat and sold 10¢ used books to benefit the museum.

Ruth sat on the edge of the Marshalls' pink plaid sofa, her tiny frame dwarfed by the sofa cushions. Despite her ninety years, her hair had a good dose of brown remaining. She brushed it back with a clip and it swept to her shoulders like an early twentieth-century schoolgirl's. Her face was a mass of crinkles and wrinkles, and she stood as high as Glen's belly button. Ruth radiated enthusiasm. She bobbed her head like a bird, clapped and smiled and hung on every word as Kate rolled out the story. All this talk about the North Bluff stirred up a flood of memory. Why, it was up on that very sand dune that she had first became intimate with a young man, she said. A ripple of laughter swept through the room.

Ruth gave her full support to the Conservancy and the Coastal Campaign, a huge endorsement. As she got up to leave, Ruth grasped Nancy's hands in her own. "Thank you, thank you for hosting this event," she said. "This has been so wonderful!"

With people like the Queen of Arcadia on our side, the Coastal Campaign might just be possible.

Not everyone became a coastal convert. In Arcadia, a vocal population preferred development on the dunes. When the Marshalls called some friends to invite them to a Conservancy house party, they declined. "No, we're not supportive. We don't want to come," they said. "We've talked to a lot of people here who say the town is just going to wither and die if we don't get some development in here. We all could benefit from development."

Others lost faith or doubted the Conservancy could pull it off. In the village of Arcadia, Tom Jass, usually an optimist, shook his head. His wife and daughter had both served as Camp Arcadia's directors in the past, and he knew the community intimately. "It's not going to happen," he said sadly. "They'll never raise the money."

A few miles north at Watervale, guests also shook their heads as they sat on the green wicker porch swings. "$30.6 million! How could the Conservancy ever do it?" they said. "Things like this don't happen in the Midwest."

It didn't help morale when a Watervale guest who had pledged $50,000 sent a registered letter to the Conservancy's office in Traverse City. After ripping through the green postal stamp, we found a short note inside: "I know you can not possibly meet the deadlines, therefore I am withdrawing my pledge."

Meanwhile, Gerard the baker was frustrated. All the attention was going to big donors. He felt shut out and helpless.

Fundraising wisdom divides people into givers and nongivers. It doesn't matter how much money you have, it depends on what type of person you are. Gerard was a giver. He gave money. He gave time. He gave his endless, infectious enthusiasm. He gave his bread. Loaves and loaves of it: manna grain, spelt kamut, golden wheat, and cranberry pecan. He stopped by the Conservancy office, his two homeschooled kids in tow, bowing and offering loaves of goodness, handing them freely out to the staff. "To sustain you!" he cried. "To nourish the soul! You look stressed. I'll bring more next week."

But he wanted to give even more. The Conservancy had said it could focus only on gifts of $20,000 or more for now. Logically, Gerard understood that only larger gifts would help reach the goal. But Gerard couldn't wait.

He trekked to the bluff in an agitated state. Gerard had hiked the CMS land for twenty-five years and frequently dodged past the faded "No trespassing" signs to go camping. *How much longer can I come here? What if the Conservancy can't find the money? What if the Conservancy can't buy it?* His eyes rested on a delicate spiderweb draped on an enormous beech tree. Like the spider, something small could still be powerful. "We ought to *do* something!" he cried. "We don't have $20,000, but let's raise it!"

That night on the bluff overlooking Lake Michigan, an idea took shape. The people of Arcadia and Pleasanton would host a harvest dinner. His friend Kurt would cook. Camp Arcadia would host. The camp dining room could fit 200 people. Usually, local fundraising events in northern Michigan depended on $25 for a plate of spaghetti, but with 200 people and $100 tickets, they would have $20,000 to present to the Conservancy. It was possible to become a big donor. Gerard phoned Traverse City the next day in great excitement.

"Don't talk to anyone," Christine said when she heard the plan. "Don't say anything. We'll come down."

Kate and Christine met with Gerard and his friends in the Trading Post building at Camp Arcadia. Kurt appeared wearing his double-buttoned white chef's jacket and a broad smile. Their wives were there, too. Christine saw the joy and eagerness on all four faces. She wanted the dinner to happen, but public events like this were supposed to take place *after* the quiet phase. She'd have to bring them into the inner circle.

"You've got to understand what we're doing," she began. Then she dropped her voice to a whisper. "We're in the *quiet* phase of the campaign." She showed them the gift lists, the estimates and assumptions. She explained how campaigns needed people to pledge major gifts in the early stages. How it worked best to gather leadership gifts without media exposure. Gerard agreed to make the dinner a general benefit to welcome the Conservancy to Manistee County. It would be a community harvest dinner with all local foods. No mention of Baldy or the North Bluff at all in the advertisements. They would do the dinner entirely themselves since Conservancy staff were already stretched beyond the limit.

When the talk turned to guest lists, Gerard grew more and more amazed. The Conservancy didn't know *anybody* in Manistee County. This was highly unorthodox for a major campaign. They were trying to raise money in an area where they were complete strangers. The true magnitude of what Gerard and his friends could offer with the harvest dinner became clear. "We can give you a sense of being welcome! We can open doors and introduce you! We can give you love!"

The Conservancy would need all the love it could muster. It was already August, and the $5 million was due by Labor Day.

13 August

Those who contemplate the beauty of the earth
find reserves of strength that will endure as
long as life lasts.

—Rachel Carson

Northern Michigan
August 2003

Across the bedroom, the clock radio blinked 3 a.m. Glen stared at the red glowing numbers and tossed in bed. His mind raced with worry. He had been out at Watervale with donors past 10 p.m., then retraced the dark route home for an hour and a half, entering the silent house at midnight. The intensity of the campaign never left him—it plagued him even in his sleep. Becky was asleep beside him, but the campaign climbed into bed with Glen, wedging itself between the pillows and pounding his mind. He slept fitfully, grinding his teeth, and jolted awake an hour or two later.

It was August. By the end of July the Conservancy had eked in $2.2 million. Not even halfway there. Nearly $3 million had to materialize in thirty days or the Arcadia land would be lost.

What are we not doing? What should we be doing? Glen pushed back the covers and, leaving Becky's sleeping form, made his way to the computer room where he started typing. *Might as well get something done,* he thought, and pounded out campaign emails. At 4 a.m., he caught an hour and a half of sleep on the sofa, then sprang awake for the day as usual at 5:30.

Down the familiar path to Whispering Trail, Glen jogged his daily circuit: out the farmhouse driveway, right on Old Mission Road, then tracing the Grand Traverse Bay shoreline along Whispering Trail. He passed Leo Ocanas's apple orchards, Rob Manigold's tart cherries and grapes. *What are we not doing? What should we be doing?* As he jogged, the fog lifted from his mind. He gained clarity with each step. More determined purpose. He thought of his high school track coach urging the team on with his Irish lilt. He thought of Heartbreak Hill in the Boston Marathon, the point at which so many distance runners lose heart and give up. *No! Not here. We're going to gut it out.*

But despite his determination, the campaign was taking its toll. Glen squeezed extra hours in the day, trying to cheat time. Most nights that summer he got by with four or five hours of sleep. Food was something he snatched when he could, wolfing down open bags of chips or grabbing a random sandwich in the staff refrigerator. He tried to eat at donor gatherings but spent most of his time greeting people and answering questions, so that food became a hindrance. Often he arrived home, tie askew and collar undone, and paced the kitchen floor, shoveling pretzels in his mouth, suddenly hungry. A mild headache blazed constantly. Bags hung under his eyes. But as summer went on, those eyes burned with an even fiercer passion.

I was involved in the fundraising campaign, along with many others, but Glen lived in its vortex. He carried the full responsibility and strain. Glen's inner drive did not accept failure. Work harder. Push on. Always meet the goal. Never falter.

To the Chown family, that sunny hike Glen took with his children to Baldy felt long ago. The campaign devoured family life. Becky and the boys ate dinner alone night after night. Glen often rolled his Saturn home at midnight and slipped through the sleeping house. After his morning jog he would see the children briefly before dashing to the office. Even when he was home for an hour or two, Glen's mind was absent. He remained a thrall to the campaign. He nodded vaguely at the boys and murmured "mmhhm" to Becky. Becky sighed and trundled the children off to bed on her own again.

Glen was worried about the family's annual vacation, too. Summers were always busy at the Conservancy, but usually Glen managed to snatch one week away with his family on the shores of Lake Superior. The Chown clan gathered up at Little Lake every August. They swam, picked blueberries, and shrieked in the frigid waves. But this August, Glen knew he would have to stay behind. The timing was too critical for the Coastal Campaign. He couldn't afford to miss a minute.

He broke the news to Becky. "You'll have to go without me." She sobbed, and Glen cried, too.

It wasn't just missing the week at Blue Cabin. In early June, Glen's mother had been diagnosed with cancer. The thought of not being with his mother at Blue Cabin, plus missing six-week-old little Leonard's first time there, was unbearable. It was family time, especially precious now with the specter of cancer hovering. The doctors had said the treatment was working. There was no cause for worry. But still . . .

"I can't let myself think about what I'm missing," he said to Becky as she packed the boys' swimming trunks and clothes for the trip.

The next morning Glen left for work early. A few hours later, Becky pointed the family Pontiac minivan north without him. It turned out to be his mother's last visit to the cabin.

It was early August when Glen rode down to yet another coastal donor meeting. Glen was agitated. He had not slept well the night before, awake for hours with worry, his mind racing with campaign pressure and fatigue. With each mile, he talked more loudly, barked orders to staff in the car, and waved his free arm. "What should we be doing?" he asked for the thousandth time. "What are we *not* doing?"

Outside, the hilly forests of Benzie County rolled by. Everywhere they looked new paved roads and housing developments encroached on the landscape.

"You know, we may fail," said Glen.

Silence hung in the car.

"We may actually fail," he said again, and swallowed hard. The idea was foreign and it jabbed nastily in the throat.

"We may fail," said Glen, his voice now regaining its normal passion. "But it won't be for lack for trying! We will do everything we can possibly do. We will talk to every possible person we can talk to. We're going to put our hearts and souls out on this. We're gonna pray. Cry. Do whatever we have to do. And we might still fail. But if we do, we won't be able to look back and say, if only I had talked to one more person. It's okay to fail, as long as we did everything possible we could do to make it successful. If we failed because we didn't try hard enough, then it won't be okay."

When Glen stepped out of the car, his face shone with a new intensity. The energy he brought with him had changed from desperation to pure inspiration.

"The campaign took on a spiritual tone then," Glen told me later. "People responded to that energy. We literally put our hearts and souls on our sleeve. We prayed. We cried. We shared our burden, and it was no longer staff driven. It became a spiritual cause for the whole community."

It was certainly spiritual for the Lutheran families at Camp Arcadia. They continued their stalwart support, and every week the whole camp gathered in the assembly room after morning Bible study to put their ethics into action and save the North Bluff. They gathered in cottages in the evenings, talk of the dunes on their lips. *Let's pray for the dunes,* someone would say. They reached out, linking hands, including Conservancy staff in their circle of prayers.

The intensity increased at Watervale, too. Guests talked to guests. Dori had people flocking to the gazebo meetings. One week a guest stood up during Kate's presentation. "I'm a computer programmer," she said. "I make $43,000 a year. I've examined my budget and looked at all my expenses for the next five years. I'm going to make a five-year pledge. I'm taking the difference between my income and my necessary expenses and I'm giving it all to Baldy."

Up at the clubhouse at Crystal Downs, stories like these circulated. Did you hear that the waitresses down at Watervale are donating their wages? I heard about a woman who examined her earnings, kept just enough, and gave the rest to Baldy. Nancy Brickman cried with joy when she heard about the generous gifts from Watervale and Arcadia. *Oh, goody!* she thought. *Someone else who cares as deeply as I do.* Heroism became contagious.

In the frenzied days of August, the Conservancy sent out a desperate plea for boats. Would you lend us your boat and sail donors by the dunes? Soon various craft set out from Frankfort and Arcadia harbors, including a red Maine lobster boat. One of these boat trips included Rick White, a Conservancy friend, who captained his own boat with a few passengers and David Reese as a guide. The dunes amazed him. Rick gave a passionate speech for the Coastal Campaign and pledged a six-figure gift from his family before the boat docked.

Yet despite the generous gifts, Glen grew more desperate. Time was ticking on, and still the pledges were a far cry from $5 million. The sheer beauty of the dunes obviously touched people's hearts, but what would motivate more people to give additional huge gifts?

The answer lay an hour's drive north, near Petoskey. Just outside town was Bay Harbor, an assemblage of top-dollar mansions and shopping outlets collectively called a "village." It was built on old cement plant grounds on Petoskey's southern border. CMS Energy owned the land and had teamed up with a developer to dredge out a marina and build gleaming tan condos, a white hotel, and a golf course on Little Traverse Bay. Cobblestone streets aimed to create a historic feel, but for those used to the timeless and elegant privacy of Crystal Downs, Bay Harbor appeared to be nouveau riche.

Ernie Behnke was curious about Bay Harbor. An influential man with roots at Camp Arcadia, Ernie was also part of the Crystal Downs world. Spurred on by campaign talk, Ernie rented a van and organized a group field trip for Crystal Downers to take a peek at Bay Harbor. What they saw stunned them.

"We can't have *that* down here between Frankfort and Arcadia!" Ernie exclaimed later to David Reese.

Fired up by his visit, Ernie spread the word around both Crystal Downs and Arcadia. "You don't want Bay Harbor down here, do you?"

Suddenly people envisioned the true stakes. The Arcadia dunes wouldn't just be changed, they would be obliterated. A Bay Harbor–type development would eclipse peaceful Arcadia. The specter of Bay Harbor jolted sideline supporters into action.

Bay Harbor gave Glen the miracle he needed. When David Reese got home from a round of golf in August, his son greeted him. "Dad, Mr. Grainger called you."

Oh! thought David, and dialed the number. All summer long, David Grainger had inquired about the dunes. "We're working on it," David Reese would answer him, and list all the Crystal Downs members involved.

"David!" Grainger's gruff voice was on the phone now. "That project you're working on. I've been doing a lot of thinking about that, and I want to get involved. I want to help you out." The Grainger family gave a large gift.

Then another miracle happened. The Dow family began to catch the excitement. This family was part of the Dow Chemical company fortunes and had initially favored development in Arcadia rather than preservation. Their change of heart may have come from David Reese's irrepressible passion. Or perhaps Barbara Dow caught a spark from Glen's eye as he waved his arms and expounded on visions of a new economic model, one based on nature tourism and agriculture. In August the Dow family transformed into enthusiastic supporters, donating from two family foundations for a total of $1.75 million.

It was then that David Reese knew they would succeed. With big names from Crystal Downs making lead gifts, other members rallied to be part of the excitement. The project caught fire. It was something people *wanted* to be part of. Members chatted about the Arcadia dunes over dinner in the Sunset Room amid the clink of glasses. They spoke of Baldy on the golf greens. "This shoreline is as beautiful as any view in the world," they told each other. "Have *you* seen it yet?"

Gifts came in. Heroic gifts. The miracle of August continued as donors enlisted donors, and initial skeptics embraced the cause. Villagers in Arcadia, whose median income was $23,000 a year, met their challenge match. At the end of August, John Woollam, a physicist and land conservation philanthropist, offered $600,000. Keep a bottle of champagne handy, Glen told people. When we meet the goal on Labor Day we'll all pop our corks.

In late August, semitrucks rumbled through town streets and back roads bearing white metal tanks of picked and washed cherries. Each crate weighed one ton. They were bound for fruit-processing plants to become the nation's cherry pie filling and to adorn its breakfast cereal. Orchard farmers parked their cherry shakers back in the barn and prepared for fall apple picking. Already maples lining the road to Watervale bore leaves tinged with red and orange. The air turned crisp. The monarchs left Michigan and began their long migration along Lake Michigan's sand dune coast. It was the week before Labor Day weekend.

On Old Mission Peninsula, Glen could not sleep. At the Parsonage in Arcadia, Bill and Kathleen Parsons lay awake, too. They had already hosted two house parties and donated a five-figure gift. Now they stared at the ceiling and spoke their fears aloud in the dark: "We've turned our world inside out for the North Bluff. How can we prevent it from becoming a golf course? What more can we do?"

The Parsons checked in with the Conservancy every day and made countless calls to neighbors. "We're so close," Bill urged. "We just need a little more. We just need you to dig a little deeper. I know you've already committed, but couldn't you just commit another thousand?"

With five days to go, a two-inch bell rang in the Conservancy hall. Christine had mounted the bell to give a cheery ring each time a new gift arrived. Someone from Beulah had just offered a major gift, and this time the bell rang as I had never heard it rung before. Designed to dink out a feeble *ding ding*, under brute force the little brass bell burst into a new sound: *Clang dang dang! Clang! Dang!*

"We did it! We reached 5 million!" Glen was shouting and beating the bell with all his might. Hooting, hollering, and waving his arms. "And it's only August 27! And it's before *noon!*"

I don't know what happened next. Everyone was jumping up and down, a mass of exhausted, ecstatic bodies, hugging, leaping, and screaming. The bell kept ringing with joy.

On Labor Day weekend supporters clogged the Conservancy answering machine to check in. Donors called Glen at home, panic in their voices: How are we doing? Is it looking good? Are we going to make it? Additional pledges came pouring in over phone lines. Glen scurried into the office to gather pledges left on the answering machine. On Wednesday, the Conservancy made the $5 million mark. By Labor Day itself, the figure was $5.4 million.

The next day we jammed the phone lines calling our supporters to report the news. Kate, clutching her notes, could barely choke out her calls. "Hi, this is Kate from the Regional Conservancy," she began. "I'm calling to share the good news that . . . oh!" she cried, gulping back tears. "I'm sorry! I can't talk. I'm just so excited!"

Then she realized that the woman on the other end of the phone was crying, too. They hung on the phone line, crying and laughing through their tears, until the woman called to her husband. "Roy! Roy! Come to the phone. Get the champagne! It's the Conservancy!"

From around the corner, Glen's voice boomed down the hall: "Pop your corks!" Across the Midwest, corks popped, and the phones kept ringing all afternoon.

We'd met the first goal, but would it be enough? The week after Labor Day, the C. S. Mott Foundation board assembled in its headquarters in Flint. Reg and Glen sat in the audience, suited and tied, listening. The board was embroiled in debate over funding programs in Flint versus awarding such a large grant to the dunes.

The Mott Foundation traditionally supported four areas: civil society, the environment, "Pathways out of Poverty," and a special effort to improve life in its hometown of Flint. The loss of auto parts jobs in the

1980s had left Flint in distress. The Mott Foundation loyally did what it could to improve local family lives year after year. In contrast, it had never contemplated such an enormous land grant, ever. The environment was certainly one of its four priority areas, but this was not a regular request. The Conservancy was asking for $13.65 million, $6.15 million as an interest-free loan, and $7.5 million as an outright gift. It was an audacious request.

Glen shifted in his chair, still exhausted from the weeks of campaigning. The Conservancy had met the mark. He had in hand more than $5 million in pledges, pledges that proved local people cared about the dunes. More than that—pledges that proved local people *adored* the dunes and were willing to sacrifice. But would it be enough?

Then Mott trustee Claire White spoke up. "If we don't do this now, the dunes will be lost." Claire made the motion to approve the Arcadia Dunes project. The room quickly filled with "aye's."

The next week CMS Energy extended the option agreement. We had proved ourselves. With the help of the Mott Foundation, the Kellogg Foundation, and local dune donors, in just three months we had raised what CMS required: seventy-five percent of the purchase price. It looked as if we were on our way to buy the Arcadia land in December.

14 Sand Bag

In order that I respect a man, it is
necessary that he has participated
in the passions of his time.

—Oliver Wendell Holmes Jr.

October 2003

Despite our summer's success, we still couldn't talk about the deal. The burden of the secret was unbearable. It was like winning the lottery and not being able to spill the happy news.

"It ain't over until it's over," Glen said again and again. During the heat of CMS Energy negotiations, board members and key players got weekly updates accompanied by security warnings marked "CONFIDENTIAL." "Don't tell anyone," he instructed board members. "Not even your spouse. Our job is hard enough."

That was particularly hard in my case. I had poured my soul into Arcadia Dunes nonstop for four years. The very week CMS signed the deal, I had stood with my brand-new husband and ninety wedding guests right at Watervale, at the base of Baldy. But I never said a word. I hung my wedding dress in the upstairs closet of the Mary Ellen cottage, changed into shorts and a T-shirt, and led my wedding guests on an afternoon hike to Baldy. My hair was still bedecked with delphiniums as I ran down the dunes, leaping toward the teal water below in sheer and silent joy.

For Baldy's sake, everything had depended on raising the bulk of the money in time and in silence. A news leak would have hurtled the Conservancy prematurely into the public phase of the campaign, taking up staff time and decreasing gift size. Part of the buzz at Crystal Downs, Watervale, and Arcadia came from being trusted insiders.

We also had a pledge to keep with CMS Energy. If the Conservancy failed, as CMS partly expected, the corporation did not want to look like the bad guy for selling its land asset to a new buyer. The company wrote a code of silence into our purchase option.

Now, after years of silence, it was time to talk. Christine quietly arranged a splashy public announcement, a press conference starring the governor on the Baldy beach. It was time to go public. Governor Jennifer Granholm immediately said yes. She'd helped with the deal once during negotiations, and she'd like to get some sand underfoot. But the splash had to be timed right. Too soon and we would lose big dollars. Too late and we would lose our splash. While staff juggled the governor's schedule, the date for going public hovered into October.

"We can't wait that long!" moaned Christine. "It's not viable. Someone's going to spill the beans!"

Indeed, the coastal secret was bubbling so loudly it was a miracle the news media could not hear. The Conservancy had a near miss when a *Detroit Free Press* reporter came north to do a generic story on protecting family land. Glen and Christine toured their guest around a Benzie County nature preserve and asked a local board member to join them. Before they knew what was happening, he began to tell the reporter the CMS Arcadia story. "Shhh!" whispered Glen fiercely when the news guy was looking the other way. "Shhh!!"

Reporters from Detroit to Manistee were beginning to catch wind of the project and grow restless. Amy from *Crain's Detroit Business* lived up north, and Peter from Booth Newspapers had a cottage in Arcadia. An AP writer living locally called in. Christine banked on their goodwill. "Here's what's going on," she said. "We've been talking to the owners, but this is a very sensitive deal. If we make our interest public it could kill it. So please help us, and weigh that against your need to scoop a land conservation campaign."

Meanwhile, CMS Energy staff scouted out the beach site with Christine. They noted every detail: remove the campfire rings, check handicapped access, enlist the sheriff's help for parking, run a generator for microphones, and rig satellite feed for TV media.

Just when we thought we could not keep the dunes secret any longer, Gerard and his friends in Arcadia staged their harvest dinner. Since the governor had not made her announcement yet, the event had to be a hushed affair. The poster depicted the dunes in blue and purple oil pastels but made no mention of the North Bluff. The words simply said: "Harvest Dinner to benefit the Grand Traverse Regional Land Conservancy." Gerard talked it up and sold tickets from his bakery stall at the farmers' market, but the real purpose had to be kept secret.

Yes, we'd reached the Labor Day goal, but fundraising could not stop. There was still a huge need for private donations like the harvest dinner. The dinner was a work of true community. Pleasanton Brick Oven Bakery donated the bread, the Ware family farm donated organic salad greens. Shetler's family dairy gave milk and cream. Crystal Mountain resort donated the linens. Camp Arcadia's Bryan Ulbrich donated cases of wine from his winery Peninsula Cellars, and the camp itself provided everything else. Chip May even wrote to the Lutheran synod in Missouri to get permission for the camp to have a liquor license especially for the event. On the menu were local turkey and chicken with peach sauce, with chocolate mousse for dessert.

One hundred and forty people bought the $100 tickets ahead of time, including business leaders, county leaders, farmers, mountain bikers, and former state representatives. Manistee Republicans arrived, Democratic Party leaders came. They all came for the North Bluff, although the name was only whispered.

Out in the lobby, Gerard counted the ticket money. The night of the event, forty more people had walked in, swelling the ranks but keeping the numbers just shy of the goal. Kitchen volunteers dug deeper and bought tickets themselves to boost sales, even though they never sat down to eat or enjoy the mood music. Glen was out in the camp dining hall speaking to the dinner guests, and in a minute Gerard would take the stage to announce the total contribution.

Just then Charlie, a local dentist in Benzie County, approached. "I hear you had ten tickets that didn't sell," Charlie said, and laid a check on the table.

Gerard bowed his astonished thanks.

"I was going to say we had raised $19,000," he announced to the crowd a moment later. "But thanks to a generous donor at the last minute, I can say we met our goal and raised $20,000 for the Conservancy tonight!"

Washing dishes among the stainless steel counters in the camp kitchen as the guests went home, Gerard marveled at their success: $20,000 raised by bakers, cooks, and farmers in five and a half weeks. *Now we've done all we can possibly do,* he thought. *This was a huge effort. We did what we could do. We did our best. Now it's up to other people to come through.*

The Baldy beach was being braced for the press day when news came that the governor could not leave the capital. Her staff hurriedly picked a new location: the Michigan Historical Museum in Lansing. It was indoors, no sand, but the room had some fake fir trees and a massive map of Michigan from floor to ceiling. It would do. The date was set: next Monday. It was finally time to go public.

Christine phoned people and checked off names with a fat green highlighter. Can you be there? There was no time for formal invitations.

It was still dark when a bus rolled out of Traverse City down US-127 for the three-hour trip to Lansing. We'd hired the bus to make sure this was a community event. On one of the bus seats sat Don Tanner, the ponytailed Benzie County chair, and on another Janice, the red-haired "mayor" of Arcadia. Farmers were invited, along with Conservancy staff, donors, and board members.

The event room was a swirl of people. The official Mott Foundation photographer milled through the crowd, snapping pictures. I spotted Helen Taylor from the Nature Conservancy. Glen's mother and father were there, along with Becky holding three-month-old Leonard. Brian and Dodie Putney stood near the back looking uncharacteristically stiff in their navy collared shirts embroidered with "Putney Beef or Fruit." The Putneys had dropped their kids at Elaine's early that morning and taken the day away from their cattle and orchards. My new husband, Rick, stood in the back near the farmers, while I joined the crowd. Like the Putneys, I was also feeling a bit stiff in my dress clothes. This was only the second time I'd worn a suit jacket.

Like clockwork, the governor appeared just in time for the event to start. "This is a great day for Michigan!" she sang out. "Today we are here to announce a major campaign that is a historic effort to preserve 6,320 acres of Michigan's finest land."

Beside her, Ken Whipple, new CEO for the CMS Energy Corporation, stood beaming. "I could not be more tickled that we're able to turn this stewardship over to this wonderful conservancy," he said.

Everything was going as planned. Then it was the Mott Foundation's turn. Bill White was dressed in a grey suit spiced up with a rainbow-colored tie striped in pink, lime green, orange, and magenta. He had a mischievous twinkle in his eye and was clutching a white canvas bag, the kind you get free for joining a new nonprofit.

"I hope you don't mind," Bill said, looking at the governor. "I committed a little felony and stole some of your sand." He held up a Ziploc baggie stuffed with dune sand. "I thought I should remind us what it's all about," he said. "First point: I've seen some world-class beaches in my time. This beach reminds me of one on Cape Cod. I grew up loving that beach. I went back several years later and I couldn't even find the beach, let alone the salt marshes which led up to the beach. It had been fully developed. That won't happen here.

"Second point: This has been a great partnership. We have the private sector, government sector, philanthropy sector, and the nonprofit sector. Together we can leverage our talents.

"Third point: Effective organizations. We've all read books on effective organizations. Well, the Regional Conservancy is a very effective organization.

"They're smart, they're creative, they're diligent and persevering, and they turn in results. We've worked with the Conservancy on several projects and they always deliver. I wish every organization we work with was as effective as you guys are."

When the cheers had died down, the media crowded round the Conservancy members. Radio reporters affixed lapel microphones on Glen. Newspaper journalists scribbled in flip pads. It all unfolded just as Christine had planned.

In the buzz that followed, CEO Ken Whipple made his way to Helen. "Helen, so nice to meet you," he said, shaking hands. "I expected you to be ten feet tall!"

Helen laughed.

"This has got to be one of the finest lobbying jobs ever," said Ken. "More important people from across the state of Michigan have called me about this deal than anything I've ever worked on."

Helen grinned at Ken Whipple. She could see how much Ken had enjoyed his involvement with this dune conservation project. Perhaps he would be game for more. She drew him in. Perhaps he would be willing to donate his time as a corporate advisor to the Nature Conservancy?

The next morning we savored the glory. The Arcadia Dunes story flooded more than thirty news sources across the state: "Deal Saves Arcadia Dunes," "CMS Sells Lake Michigan Land," "Deal Would Preserve Dune Area Forever." Arcadia made front-page news in the *Grand Rapids Press,* the *Ann Arbor News,* the *Jackson Citizen Patriot,* the *Flint Journal,* and the *Detroit News* business pages. The story reached as far as the *Sault Ste. Marie Evening News* and the *Daily Mining Gazette* in Houghton, 500 miles away. Back on our home turf, the *Traverse City Record-Eagle* gave us the front-page headline and devoted its editorial to us, "Arcadia Land Purchase Is Conservancy's Gem."

After our day in the spotlight, the rest of the week was back to business. For Governor Granholm, that meant meeting with the Queen of Jordan and other dignitaries in Dearborn. Up north, Christine staged a local announcement and press day at the Watervale dining hall for those who couldn't travel to Lansing. Two days later, Glen and I headed back downstate, this time to Jackson. It was time to focus on CMS Energy again.

Although the basic purchase deal was signed, we had outstanding business with CMS Energy. The deeds showed large swaths of utility easements crisscrossing the land. The energy company could clear out trees wherever the legal lines appeared and fragment the forest. The worst was the dune area. Baldy and the surrounding forest looked like a tic-tac-toe board with the X team winning.

All my passion from graduate school days in Madison blazed out. Fragmenting the forest like this would kill it. Even if we owned the 6,000 acres, the area could become nothing but a chopped-up landscape. We had to clear up the title.

"You'll never get CMS to give up a utility easement," Mike Stack, the Mott attorney, warned me. "They're a utility company! They never give up an *inch* in utility easements."

Glen and I arrived early at the CMS Energy office tower in Jackson. We were ushered up the elevator and into an empty meeting room. In the center stood a table as long as five pool tables glued together. We sat together at one corner, expecting Bruce Rasher, our point man from CMS, to show up. But it wasn't just Bruce.

On the stroke of 3 o'clock, the door opened and a smart line of CMS Energy staff marched into the room. One, two, three . . . twelve people dressed in suits entered the room. As if following an invisible conductor, they all pulled out chairs and sat down in unison. Glen and I gaped.

Bruce Rasher was director of real estate and facilities for CMS Energy. Most of his dealings had to do with power plants, utility lines, and sites for electrical transformers. He had a ready smile, and was tough but seemed fair. I had a feeling he liked the change of pace working with a nonprofit. We were different. We knew next to nothing about utility infrastructure; but he knew next to nothing about land trusts. It would be an interesting chess match.

Perhaps Max's negotiating lessons prompted me. I left my chair and walked into the middle of the CMS bunch, all seated together. It was time to change the balance of power. I placed a map of Arcadia Dunes in the middle of the endless table, and immediately the staff unbent to take a peek. I stayed standing, expounding the natural wonders and painting a picture of Arcadia intended to wow men and women who had never been there. These were engineers and real estate experts. Glen and I spoke about the forests and grasslands. How CMS Energy had stewarded the land so well for the past thirty years. How our entire interest in buying the land hinged on guaranteeing that it could stay intact into the future. We delved into biology and forest fragmentation, explaining how ill-placed power poles near the Grassland Preserve could create a "killing field" by giving hawks a place to perch and attack grasshopper sparrows. How many of the company's existing utility easements ran to nowhere. We wanted to change that. By the end of the meeting we were no longer adversaries—we were a team solving a puzzle.

In November we met again, the number of CMS Energy staff now whittled down to seven. It took five hours, but Glen and I emerged from the Jackson tower with a new map of Arcadia Dunes. One hundred percent of the bad utility easements had been removed, and a few existing routes had been improved or revised.

After our negotiations, Bruce Rasher from CMS Energy made an offer of his own. "Would you consider working for us?" he asked me. "We have a job for you here."

"Sorry, Bruce," I said. "I'm happy where I am."

"Well, keep it in mind," he said. "We'd like to have you on our side."

The next one to call was Mike Stack from his law office in Cheboygan. "You've got a job here," he said. "Go to law school, and I'll hire you."

"But I don't want to be a lawyer," I answered.

"I'll start you at $90,000," he said, not listening. "Come on, it's a good starting salary," he insisted. "We'll start you there and you can move up."

"It's not about the money," I said.

"What do you mean?"

"There are other things I want to do with my life." *Like write books,* I thought.

Glen told the story of our success in Jackson when we got home, adding a few embellishments. Soon staff stories like these blossomed into campaign legend.

"Have any of you ever met our coastal director, Heather Shumaker?" Kate asked a group of donors. "She's about *this* tall, soft spoken, and has a ponytail. Well, she faced down all these attorneys. CMS sent in fifteen people around the negotiating table, there's Heather up against all these men in suits . . . and then they offered her a job!"

Supporters loved these stories and cheered, pouring in new donations. If my ponytail could help, all the better. These new gifts were vital. We may have met the initial deadlines, but the larger $30.6 million Coastal Campaign goal loomed ahead. We still had half the money to find.

15 Lansing

Act—act in the living Present!
. . . .
Lives of great men all remind us
We can make our lives sublime,
And, departing, leave behind us
Footprints on the sands of time.

—Henry Wadsworth Longfellow

Traverse City, Arcadia, and Lansing, Michigan
September–December 2003

The Conservancy needed more money than private donors could give. The support from Watervale, Arcadia, and Crystal Downs, not to mention the Kellogg and Mott foundations, was massive, but we needed something bigger. The Conservancy had to woo public dollars, too. Even during the mad dash of fundraising from Memorial Day to Labor Day, Glen had taken time to court the State of Michigan and its Natural Resources Trust Fund.

The Trust Fund was Michigan's golden goose. It now gave away $25–35 million each year to buy precious parks, wetlands, and forests, and to build playgrounds, bike trails, and swimming beaches. No matter how badly the state's general budget fell, the Trust Fund sat sacrosanct, protected by the state constitution. Trust Fund money was oil money. It came from oil and gas wells located on state land. Some years the wells gushed with natural gas among the Antrim County shale deposits, and the Trust Fund swelled with riches. Other years oil prices fell and the Trust Fund had less to dole out. Yet even on a bad year some of Michigan's best parks and natural areas were saved.

The Conservancy had presented multiple projects to the Trust Fund over the years, and so far had been awarded every one. But the Arcadia request took things to the next level.

Not only was our request huge, we were asking the state government to experiment. Don't buy the land outright, we said, just buy rights to the land. We asked for a cool $11.1 million. And we asked for something the State of Michigan had never done before: buy a public conservation easement on a private nature preserve. The Conservancy would own it; the State of Michigan would buy public access and restrict development. Moreover, we had to bundle Green Point Dunes land into the Trust Fund grant package so it would not be left behind. Our job was to show that both dunes were part of the same system, even though Green Point Dunes was two miles up the beach.

First we needed a high-ranking sponsor. Trust Fund grants usually go to small townships or counties that own and manage the new park. Our project straddled three townships and two counties. We knew we needed one unified owner, the Conservancy. We also needed political champions. Glen and I drove to Lansing.

Our first champion was none other than George Burgoyne, deputy director of the Department of Natural Resources. George had entered the DNR for all the right reasons—he loved the outdoors and believed in conservation. But George would be retiring within weeks. Already his successor had been named. If we could secure his active support, Arcadia's bid for $11.1 million might have a chance.

George did better than that. He personally sponsored our grant application. "Submit it under my name," he said.

The grant application itself took me weeks to write, but with so much money hanging in the balance, we knew a stellar application would not be enough. We set our sights on wooing each individual member of the Trust Fund board.

Our goal was to get as many Trust Fund board members as possible out to Arcadia. We had to find at least one or two champions who would go to bat for Arcadia, and also ferret out all the potential pitfalls ahead of time so there would be no surprises on the day of the vote. Luckily, the Arcadia landscape was so vast it had something to offer for everyone. The project was like the elephant in the fable of the blind men and the elephant. In the story, each man encounters just one part of the elephant—trunk, tail, ears, feet—and comes away with an entirely different impression of what the animal is. A tour of Arcadia could do the same. We could showcase cherry trees, beaches, or forest, depending on a person's interests. We could put on a strenuous hike or an easy stroll.

The first Trust Fund board member to come north was Bob Garner. Bob's passion was land for urban recreation. He was not keen on Michigan doling out more dollars for protected areas in the sparsely populated north country. Bob was no newcomer to conservation. For years he'd hosted a TV nature program, *Michigan Outdoors*. He also knew the Trust Fund intimately. He'd even helped draft the original law that set up the Trust Fund back in 1976. Friends told Bob: You should see this property. It's important. We were advised to show him passion and beautiful landscapes, so we staged a dune tour for Bob.

Glen, Christine, and I met Bob at the scenic turnout above the village of Arcadia. It was a great rendezvous—plenty of parking, restrooms, and a drop-off-the-earth view of Lake Michigan. Tourists milled around at the overlook and stared as Glen and I pulled out aerial maps for Bob's benefit. We showed him how this scenic turnout adjoined the CMS Arcadia property, and gave just a taste of the fantastic views at Baldy. Christine made mental notes about everything that made Bob tick. He liked to farm, he hated to fly. He had known the governor long before she became governor. He liked conservation projects near Detroit. We gazed at the dazzling blue lake, willing the view to do its magic.

Bob said: "Shoreline is interesting, but after a while it's all the same."

Next we piled into one car to show him the Watervale beach view. Glen was eager to get him past the road end so Bob could fall under the spell of the dunes with Baldy and Green Point looming north and south. But instead Bob stopped away from the beach and stared at a wooden painted sign sticking one foot above the sand. In blue letters on teal it read: "Private beach—no trespassing."

"This is Watervale's beach," I explained. "Dori lets us use it, but there's no public access to the shoreline in this whole township."

"No public access?" said Bob. "That's a very big deal."

Next to come was Steve Arwood. Steve loved to hunt. He was on his way north to go bird hunting but granted us an hour or two. "Show him good hunting land," said Glen.

I chose a field surrounded by forest, a spot any deer hunter would love. Steve bounced his pickup truck along the ruts of a cart track and waved as he met us. He squinted in the sun, and called to his two hunting dogs. In another moment, a German shorthaired pointer and Labrador retriever raced out, exuding energy and boundless joy. The dogs put Steve in a good mood. He glanced around the field, seeing the forest bordering the open area on three sides. "This is great," he said. "Great habitat for white-tailed deer."

We toured, looking for buck rubs. The forest here at the edge of the field was stacked with young maple trunks. In truth, this field was one of my least favorite parts of the Arcadia land. It broke up the continuous stretch of native forest and bore the scars of an abandoned farm. It was scruffy land, baked hard as rock, now filled with spotted knapweed instead of the lush maple-beech forest surrounding it. Gaps in the forest like this field were bad news for nesting songbirds and other forest dwellers. But it was good hunting ground, and today I loved the field. At the end of the tour, Steve whistled happily to his dogs and waved as he drove off.

That year the governor appointed a new board member to the Trust Fund: an author and environmental advocate named Dave Dempsey. Glen soon spoke on the phone to Dave, and to his delight, Dave already knew Watervale and had visited Baldy. He pledged his full support immediately.

We now had done our best with three of the five judges, but we weren't able to woo the other two north for a tour. Did we have enough support?

Sam Washington, the fourth board member, especially worried us. Sam was a dedicated conservationist and lifelong supporter of the Michigan United Conservation Clubs, a coalition of sportsmen that worked hard for public access and hunters' rights. Sam fully understood the value of protecting natural habitat, but he was leery of anything less than full access. Would a state-held conservation easement prove strong enough in his mind? Should the state spend precious funds on such mammoth projects? Sam was bound to ask tough questions and his opinion could sway the show.

Two days after the governor's press day, the Trust Fund convened its quarterly meeting at the Clarion Hotel in Lansing. This was our one chance to showcase the project before the board met in December to award the money. Glen squirmed in his burgundy padded chair. I sat beside him, trying to muster confidence. The dunes were depending on us today. We were billing this as a "once-in-a-lifetime" opportunity, but there were other worthy once-in-a-lifetime projects competing for the Trust Fund's money. One was Helen's colossal Kamehameha project for the Nature Conservancy. The project had been scaled back some, but it was still massive: 271,000 acres of wild forest and river land in the Upper Peninsula. Then down south near Saugatuck there was another dune, a fellow land trust's project. Too many multimillion projects could break the system. We had to be both bold and considerate. We had to walk a fine balancing act so that all the best land in Michigan would be saved. We offered to stage our enormous request over three years.

Sam Washington spoke up. Will a conservation easement on private land work? What if there's a violation? Will hunters get full access, or will the Conservancy create wilderness areas and cut off access? What about all these big projects—is it fair to tie up state funds for multiple years?

We gave our best answers for Arcadia, but the Trust Fund board did not vote. Things were left hanging until December.

Meanwhile, the project pressure had shifted from the crunch of summer fundraising to the real estate side of things, my side.

CMS Energy was far from done with us. During the fall, we wrangled through drafting a covenant deed plus forty-nine accompanying documents to be signed at closing. Surveyors traversed the land, soil testers drilled pits. We examined every deed from all the assembled farm parcels back to its earliest ownership. Each day my diary entry began: Busy day. In early at 6 a.m. (or 5 or even 4). I dragged home long after dark at 8 or 9 each evening. Rick greeted me with candles over waiting dinners. The next day I trundled back to face it all again.

One big worry was inheriting farmland with obsolete pesticides still clinging to the soil. With so much orchard land around, we knew what to expect. Every acre of orchard land in northern Michigan harbored arsenic and lead, sometimes in alarming levels. These chemicals weren't used anymore, but their presence lingered. The heavy metals would stay buried in the soil with minimal danger to other life, but unless the Conservancy could gain a grace letter from the State of Michigan, we could bankrupt the organization paying off sky-high cleanup and legal fees. No matter how much we all loved the Arcadia landscape, the Conservancy could not accept that much risk. It would mean selling all our existing nature preserves to pay the bills.

To help out the arsenic hunters, I boarded a four-seater prop plane at the Cherry Capital airport. We cruised low, twisting in tight circles for an hour to find abandoned well shafts, farmstead ruins, and likely dump sites.

As the plane banked for the twentieth time, I put my maps down and groaned.

"Stare at the horizon," the pilot said, and scrabbled to hand me an airsick bag just in time.

Above this due diligence still hung the question—did Consumers Power ever threaten to exert eminent domain and take the land from farmers? We needed to find out for sure before we forked over millions of hard-earned dollars. If we could prove any parcels had been purchased by eminent domain, or even under that threat, then the public already "owned" the land. CMS Energy agreed to open its records.

Mike Stack and I sat in a square, grey cubbyhole of a room inside the CMS Energy Jackson headquarters. A staff member had just wheeled in a dolly stacked with seventeen cardboard boxes and heaved them on the floor. "Well, might as well dig in," said Mike, cracking open the first lid.

Inside the dust-coated boxes lay stacks of files documenting each parcel's land transfer. Notes from Gerald Derks, Consumers Power's front man, legal descriptions and details about timber and mineral rights. The price each piece of land sold for. Sometimes a question from a landowner. Every response CMS Energy gave was courteous and correct. Not a scrap of evidence suggested eminent domain. The money had been generous. If Consumers Power had ever threatened farmers with eminent domain, it had been done verbally and left no trail behind. Mike and I shut the last box and drove back north.

December approached. This was the month when the Trust Fund voted on how to distribute millions of conservation dollars. The year 2003 was a lean one. The Trust Fund had only $18 million to award statewide, much less than in recent years, and Arcadia was asking for a large chunk of it. Glen and I filed into the burgundy chairs again at the Clarion conference room, this time with knots in our stomachs.

On Decision Day, Sam Washington opened the debate. Sam was one board member who'd never had a tour of the Arcadia property. Glen and I sat breathless in our seats watching the board members seated on their raised dais as our fate played out.

"There are too many 'once-in-a-lifetime projects' asking for phased commitments," Sam said. "Perhaps the board should set a limit and cap requests. Phased projects tie up our money with just two or three projects."

The Trust Fund was familiar with buying single land parcels to create new parks and preserves. Now the Trust Fund was facing a new era of conservation. Not just single parcels but entire landscapes were up for sale. Arcadia and Green Point Dunes, Helen's massive forest project up north in the Upper Peninsula, and more. The projects floating before the board this year were major, multiyear projects.

One by one, land came before the Trust Fund board. Lakes, marshes, forest, and shoreline on Lake Michigan, Lake Huron, and Lake Superior. Helen's Kamehameha project moved in quickly and received $3 million toward its total goal. Suddenly our joint request for Green Point and Arcadia sat on the auction block. More than $11 million was at stake, and we were asking for a first year's installment award of $4.5 million.

The Trust Fund board was in a mood to whittle down grant requests. The game was this: slice off as much money as possible from other people's projects in order to boost funding for your own. Much of the game had already played out backstage—who will support whose project, who will make a motion—but the final act was always performed publicly, sometimes with dramatic twists at the last moment. Where would we fall?

The debate raged. What if we knock down the request to $3 million? What if we shift the grant, and give the Conservancy a small amount this year and more money in years two and three?

Someone called for a five-minute break. This was no idle, get-a-glass-of-water and stretch-your-legs break. Like the final minutes of a football game, each timeout was deadly strategic.

Dave Dempsey hurried over to Glen and me. "How much do you really need this year?" he asked in a whisper.

It was clear the Trust Fund board needed to free up money for other projects. After months of lobbying and grant preparation, it came down to this one whispered conversation.

"Can you get by with $3 million?" Dave asked.

Glen started to say yes, but I broke in. The ten-year cash-flow sheet was branded in my head; I knew the numbers. "Anything less than $4 million this year, and we lose an extra $300,000 in interest," I told Dave. "We need $4 million to close Green Point Dunes."

The break ended and board members hurried to resume their seats. Before we knew it, there was a motion on the floor—to fund the CMS Arcadia / Green Point Dunes project at $3 million.

Dave Dempsey interrupted. "I understand this project needs at least $4 million in this cycle to make this work," he said. "I make a motion to change the award amount to $4 million."

"I support," said Bob Garner.

"Aye."

"Aye."

"Aye."

In a second, it was done. We had $4 million for the dunes, with a promise of more over the next two years.

Glen dashed out of the Trust Fund meeting as soon as the board voted, crumpling his papers into his leather briefcase. He was headed to Ann Arbor. The dunes would be fine; now he had to be with his mother.

Since surgery in June, she'd made a tremendous recovery. She'd been able to join the family—minus Glen—at the Little Lake cabin and met the governor at press day. But then the call had come before Thanksgiving. Grave news. The chemo had failed. The cancer was back with a vengeance and had spread.

Glen drove distractedly, grief in his throat. In Ann Arbor, Glen grilled the oncologists. He questioned everything. They weren't doing enough. Couldn't they try another treatment? There had to be something more they could do. *She's going to make it,* he told himself. *She's got to.*

Up north the Conservancy office was in shambles. Even though closing day for Arcadia Dunes was looming only two weeks away, the Conservancy workspace was in upheaval. The board had decided to expand our office.

The chaos of shifting offices slammed into the Arcadia Dunes closing like a tidal wave. Phone lines were disconnected. Computers slid in and out of service. Files got packed away into white cardboard boxes. I frantically gathered the fifty closing dune documents about me, worrying and clucking like a mother hen. We had moved into our new office space only three years ago, but we'd already outgrown it. The plan was to break down the wall between our office unit and the empty one beside us, immediately doubling our space. Staff members went around cheerfully wielding paint rollers as they decorated new offices in maroon, gold, and seafoam green.

I panicked. Nothing could get lost at this point. Each night I shuttled papers vital to the Arcadia land transfer home with me. I slept with CMS Energy documents by my bedside, guarding them through the night.

I was not the only one restless at night. At the Parsonage, Bill and Kathleen teetered on the edge of terror. Sure, the Coastal Campaign had gone well so far, but Bill's years doing international business deals had taught him to be wary. Sometimes the last second brought doom. The phone could still ring. Last-minute glitches could spring up. "You think it's over, and then . . ." His voice trailed off.

Just as Bill feared, eight days before the planned closing, glitches *did* strike. It was not the office move that jammed a monkey wrench in the closing. Another developer did.

The nightmare began on Thursday, the day after the Trust Fund vote. Glen had barely had time to see his mother in Ann Arbor and race back north. The worst had happened. Suddenly, on December 12, 2003, we had no deal—no legal claim to the property. CMS Energy dropped its contract with the Conservancy. The dunes hovered, their fate again unknown.

The day before, Glen and I had reconvened to file formal paperwork. Soon it would be Christmas and we could withdraw to be with our families and forget all this for a while. But there was still one small matter to take care of. December 11 was the deadline to exercise our option and turn our agreement with CMS into a binding sale. Just a routine letter, maybe a paragraph long.

Then Mike Stack called. The second Mott attorney, Joe Kochanek, was already on the line with him. I had never heard Mike so irate.

It couldn't be, I thought. *This isn't happening.*

" . . . the title's not clean . . . Calvin Foster still has a claim on the property . . . right of first refusal . . . can't remove it . . ."

I listened in disbelief. Glen began to yell.

That long-ago document that Linda had tracked down in the Benzie County register of deeds was suddenly rearing its head. An obscure settlement document between CMS Energy and Calvin Foster concerning other deals had buried within it a line or two about Arcadia Dunes. CMS had a legal obligation to sell the land to Calvin Foster instead of us under a right of first refusal.

"But his right only kicks in if the purchase price is less than $12 million!" wailed Glen. "We're safe! Our purchase price is $18 million! This has nothing to do with Foster!"

"His name is still on the title," said Mike.

"It doesn't apply!" said Glen.

"The title company says it does apply," said Mike. "They're refusing to remove it."

We stared at the facts. Before the Conservancy had signed its purchase option with CMS Energy, CMS had granted Calvin Foster the right to buy the land first if the purchase price was $12 million or less. We knew that. Then trouble crept in without anyone noticing. When the Mott Foundation decided to *buy* its portion of the land rather than give the Conservancy an outright grant, the transaction with CMS had split into two separate sales, each for only part of the full value. Now the sale price was under $12 million and it could trigger Foster's right of first refusal.

Soon the top four CMS negotiators joined the fray. The call started badly and grew worse. Sharp witted and quick talking, Mike Stack had often clashed with CMS's legal counsel, David Barth. David's pace irked Mike. His focus on details seemed to create unnecessary delays. Each lawyer had grown more exasperated as the weeks went on. Now David lashed back. He would not compromise his company in anything risky. He would not budge. Under Mike's renewed pressure, David refused to let the land go.

Glen and I holed up in my office. We could not exercise the option. After months of searching the title, this last-minute blot could jeopardize everything we had worked for. The day dragged to an end, and with it our deadline. Outside it started to snow.

Glen sat propped on my desk, his left leg dangling down. Hour by hour, we hovered by the speakerphone, hoping to resurrect the project. Our attorneys railed at CMS and CMS fought back. I thought of the legions of Watervale families, farm families, and camp families and all their sacrifices. None of it would matter now. Around me the voices of the lawyers veered off legal matters and delved into personal jabs.

"Stop," I pleaded. "Stop!" But the assault continued. Somewhere in the tumult, I pressed the button that disconnected our attorneys' phone line.

Everyone was grumpy. Conservancy and CMS alike, we had all missed supper and wanted to be with our families. Glen was thinking about his mother. I was thinking about my newlywed husband. We had tickets that evening to see the *Nutcracker* at Interlochen.

"Sorry," I told Rick during a break between battle calls. "Go on without me."

"Do what you need to do," he said. "We'll go another time."

Glen and I said good night near 9 p.m. There had been no resolution, but there was a glimmer of hope—CMS Energy had agreed to extend the deadline to noon the next day.

Meanwhile, CMS Energy's Mary Anne Marr was trying to patch things up. The Conservancy and Mott Foundation needed clean title, but Calvin Foster's right of first refusal still lingered on the final title work. She called the northern Michigan title agency just before the next day's noon deadline. "Take it off," she said. If the title agency dropped reference to Foster's claim, the title would be clean.

"I can't remove it," said the title agent. "That right of first refusal is out there on the public record."

"But it doesn't apply," she answered. "It only applies if the purchase price is less than $12 million."

"Why doesn't it apply?" asked the agent. "You split the purchase price. The sale prices are for $13.15 million and $4.85 million."

Title insurance guarantees that a piece of property really does belong to the owner and that entity has the right to sell it. Removing the right of first refusal from the title was a huge risk: Foster had a history of litigation. The title agent appealed to the state counsel.

The deadline inched closer.

According to our contract with CMS, if the Conservancy did not properly exercise the option by the deadline, the deal was off, as if it had never been. If we missed the deadline, we would have no claim to the property.

Noon came with no agreement. CMS Energy set a new deadline of 1 p.m. Then 2, then 3. Glen and I stayed locked up in my office, pacing like caged wild animals. We cajoled, brainstormed, fought, and cried. The clock ticked past 3 o'clock, and with it the final deadline.

No deal. No new deadline. Legally, we didn't have a foot to stand on. We had millions of dollars pledged but no longer any claim to the dunes.

16 Heartbreak Hill

> The greatest threat to our planet is the belief
> that someone else will save it.
>
> —Robert Swan

December 2003–December 2005

A week later I stood in the bank parking lot at 6 a.m. The December day was still draped in darkness, and would be for another two hours. Beside me, Rick held my hand, his mittened paw in mine. We'd been married seven months, and I was still savoring the simple fact that someone was standing by me, supporting my work. Snow came driving down, swirling around my legs and my stash of dune documents.

We'd fixed the glitch. The terror of losing Arcadia still lingered, but we had cleared that hurdle. CMS Energy signed a letter indemnifying the title company, and the title company had removed Foster's claim from the paperwork. It was decided that the Conservancy's split purchase could be viewed as simply a matter of financing— the deal would be considered as all one sale of $18 million.

This day was closing day: December 19, 2003. Glen and I were carpooling to Flint with our banker and title agent. The banker was a loan officer. Despite all our fundraising, much of the money was in five-year pledges, so we still had to take on a multimillion-dollar loan. I said goodbye to Rick and slipped into the dark car.

Closing was to take place at the Mott headquarters on Saginaw Street. Soon we would greet Lois and the rest of the Mott gang, shake hands with the CMS Energy crew: Joe Tomasik with his solemn grey moustache, Bruce Rasher with his warm smile, and cautious David Barth. We would gather around a conference table and pass papers to sign.

"How did this project begin, Glen?" asked Larry, our banker, from the front seat.

Glen told tales as we drove steadily through the snow, three hours and 200 miles to Flint.

"We oughta write a book, right, Heather?" boomed Glen.

But my mind was far away, thinking about the future. Deep inside me a tiny speck of a child was growing, just two weeks on the path of life. I stared out the window as the pale December dawn finally touched the sky.

It was official. The Conservancy finally owned Arcadia Dunes. The closing day story landed on page 7 of the local *Benzie County Record Patriot* next to an article about butternut fruitcakes. People were focused on the holidays: only five more shopping days left until Christmas.

The extended Chown family gathered downstate in Ann Arbor. Though frail, his mother sat up and ate Yorkshire pudding and listened to Glen and his brother take turns playing carols at the piano.

In the winter days ahead Glen focused on curing his mother. He peppered oncology specialists with questions and stood by her side during endless appointments. *She's going to make it*, he told himself. *She's got to rally. This isn't the end.*

But by spring his mother had sunk into a coma-like existence. Hospice arrived. Glen's five siblings convened from all directions. The whole family of eight was together once more. It was April, one of lower Michigan's dreariest times. A season when the snow had lifted but the flattened earth had not regained its color. Mud season. There was still a month before new flowers would press through the caked crust. Through this bleak season, Glen raged with the passion of his love. "We can try something else!" he cried. "There's got to be something we can do!"

His wife stared at him in disbelief. She knew Glen. She knew there were times when he would never back down. He was accustomed to safeguarding land with his entire soul; he met each conservation challenge with a never-say-die attitude. He was not accustomed to failure.

But change was coming to his family, and even his fierce love could not prevent it.

Glen's mother slipped away on April 15, the same day Glen's hero, Abraham Lincoln, had died. Glen returned to his office at the Conservancy engulfed in sorrow. He drank mint tea from a thermos at his desk. He tried to concentrate on the fundraising task ahead, but his eyes looked shattered. As he drove home from work, he listened to music of Greg Brown:

> I only know
> I miss you so much
> I only know
> I miss you

There was more work to be done, but Glen had no heart for it. He slogged forward.

Even though the Conservancy owned Arcadia Dunes, the Coastal Campaign was far from over. We were burdened with $10 million in new debt and still needed to raise nearly $12 million more. Bills came spilling across the transom, including the latest attorney bill, which totaled $79,000. We were on track with our cash-flow projections, but the pressure was still on. We had entered the public phase now. The race was no longer a sprint; we were in the midst of a marathon. Instead of three months, we were facing two years of raising the remaining money.

The Conservancy slipped into a new mode of fundraising, a world of mailing appeal letters and cultivating gifts of every size, from $1 to $1 million. We were ready to welcome the little gifts now. We tried everything, from snowy Ski & Spree events on Baldy to warm barn parties with Zydeco music. Down in Manistee County, the Lions Club hosted an event with chicken cordon bleu and perky potatoes. And people responded. Conservancy mailings beat out the fundraising odds, sometimes so overwhelmingly that we wondered if people would believe the return statistics.

Everywhere it was time for celebration and thanksgiving. At Green Point Dunes we celebrated paying off our land contract early with champagne toasts on the beach with the Ranke family. Christine staged a "Coastal Campaign Gala" party complete with dance-band music by Harry Goldson. To major dune donors, we gave care packages of Gerard's bread and local jam. Then we thanked everyone again the next year with pies from the Grand Traverse Pie Company: quintessential cherry pies and lakeshore berry pies.

Back in his office, Glen strategized through his grief. Progress was phenomenal, but responsibilities were piling up, too, and the enormous burden of managing the land was already beginning to shake the stewardship branch. Conservancy staff had burgeoned to twenty people during the campaign. Health benefits, retirement accounts, extra computers, mileage checks, and salaries were all adding up, and the budget was looking like $1.7 million for next year. What if the Trust Fund money didn't materialize? What if the campaign goal turned out to be too small?

Glen set his eyes on a final grant from the Kresge Foundation. Kresge was known as the "finisher" in the nonprofit world. The foundation specialized in aiding momentum at the end of a campaign with ambitious challenge grants. As Glen well knew, sometimes the *last* dollars were also the hardest dollars to raise. Deep in his heart, Glen worried about the Conservancy. Was it stable enough to fulfill its obligations to the land? This property was huge—could the Conservancy effectively manage a piece as big as a state park? Another dollop of money might prove to be the difference between failure and success.

The Kresge Foundation offered the Conservancy a challenge grant to wrap up our Coastal Campaign. At stake: a $950,000 gift from Kresge if the Conservancy could bring in another $2.85 million of new private money in one year. Existing pledges did not count, only brand-new donations or increased pledges.

For a nonprofit that had just gathered $5 million from private pledges in a mere three months, *a year* to raise roughly half that amount could seem luxurious. Yet I watched uneasily. The task seemed daunting. Our obvious supporters had already stretched and bestowed so much. The Conservancy would have to work extra hard to find the remaining funds, and my colleagues looked drained.

The Conservancy inched its way toward the goal. Christine sent out grant request after request. Glen circled back to people who'd already made stretch gifts. "Could you extend your pledge for a couple of years?"

Another December approached. It was two years after buying the Arcadia land and the deadline for the Kresge challenge. The Conservancy had scraped together more than $2 million, but it was not enough to meet the challenge. "We don't have any more rabbits to pull out of the hat!" cried Glen.

Still he refused to give up, and convinced Kresge to extend the deadline by a month. With just days to go, Glen turned to his board: could it raise the remaining challenge money in a week?

"Glen is very convincing," remarked Betsy Dole, the new board chair. "Glen could sell you a refrigerator if you lived in Alaska in an igloo."

Betsy was a staunch believer in land conservation. She picked up the phone in her basement office and called nearly every Conservancy board member, all of whom agreed to a new five-year pledge on the spot. In one evening, she collected gifts ranging from $500 to $5,000. The collective gift was enough—even a few thousand *more* than enough—to meet the Kresge challenge goal.

The excited babble of voices in the Conservancy office made it sound like a call center. Celebratory phone calls rang out again as staff and board members announced: "As of 4 p.m. today, we have completed the public phase of the Coastal Campaign! Our numbers look fantastic! Thank you! We couldn't have done it without you."

Unbelievably, after not quite three years of intense fundraising, the Coastal Campaign was at an end. A Watervale guest asked to make the capstone gift. The total campaign brought in $35.4 million for the dunes, including more than $25 million from private donors. The campaign had been a huge success: 6,320 acres protected, close to 5,000 donors, and the campaign goal surpassed by nearly $5 million. What's more, the Conservancy had blossomed from a small-town land trust to a national conservation force.

I breathed a huge sigh of relief. Betsie Dunes, Green Point Dunes and Arcadia Dunes were saved. Dreaming impossible dreams had worked.

It seemed to be the end.

But the Conservancy's situation better paralleled the *Apollo*'s flight to the moon. After the amazing feat of the moon landing, the world cheered. But astronaut Michael Collins, alone in *Apollo*'s command module, knew that half the job still lay ahead. The team still had to get home safely. "The world reaction was: we did it!" Collins recalled. "We've done *part* of it."

We'd completed the part that got the cheers. Now we had to embrace a new side of saving Arcadia.

"How much longer will Benzie county's Dry Hill remain dry?" leads this headline story from December 1969 in the *Benzie County Patriot* (later the *Benzie County Record Patriot*). The story describes Derks and his mysterious purchases for the Viking Land Company and shows a sketch of the pumped storage facility built by Consumers Power in Ludington, MI. (Courtesy of *Benzie County Record Patriot*)

Bill White, president of the C. S. Mott Foundation, brings a bag of dune sand to the public announcement of the Arcadia Dunes project in Lansing, October 2003. From left to right: Bill White, Ken Whipple, CEO of CMS Energy, and Michigan Governor Jennifer Granholm. (Photo by Michael D-L Jordan / DLP)

The church at Putney Corners served as a gathering place during the Coastal Campaign for farmers to give input to the Conservancy. (Photo by Heather Shumaker)

Farmers and neighbors gather at the church at Putney Corners to learn about the Conservancy's early plans for Arcadia Dunes farmland. Brian Putney sits center, with red-brimmed hat. (Photo by Christine Arvidson)

Senator Carl Levin, center, examines a map of the Arcadia Dunes project during a site visit with Heather Shumaker, Dori Turner, and Glen Chown. (Photo by Christine Arvidson)

Glen Chown in action during the Coastal Campaign. (Photo by Bob Marshall)

Heather on Lake Mendota in Madison, Wisconsin, where she studied land trusts as an environmental studies graduate student. (Photo courtesy of Heather Shumaker)

Dori Turner, innkeeper at Watervale, plants yellow birch to aid forest restoration at the new Arcadia Dunes natural area. (Photo by Paula Dreeszen)

Conservancy staff Abby Gartland clears invasive garlic mustard from the land to allow native species to flourish. (Photo by Gary Howe)

Helen Taylor of the Nature Conservancy. As Michigan state director, Helen added a dynamic partnership and helped negotiate with CMS Energy. (Photo by Michael D-L Jordan / DLP)

The Inn at Watervale was originally built as part of a lumber town in 1892. Watervale has welcomed summer visitors for a hundred years, and is now recognized as the Watervale Historic District, a Michigan State Historic Site, and listed on the National Register of Historic Places. (Photo by Drew Smith)

Conservancy and CMS Energy representatives on closing day, December 2003, the day the Conservancy bought 6,000 acres at Arcadia Dunes. *From left to right*: Heather Shumaker, Bruce Rasher, Joe Tomasik, David Barth, and Glen Chown. (Photo by Michael D-L Jordan / DLP)

Glen Chown and CMS executive Joe Tomasik celebrate sealing the deal. (Photo by Michael D-L Jordan / DLP)

Negotiations could sometimes be fun. CMS director of real estate Bruce Rasher met his match with Heather and requested this photo be taken. (Photo by Michael D-L Jordan / DLP)

Heather as a new land protection specialist at the Conservancy's office on Third Street in Traverse City. (Photo by Ann Rigney)

Volunteers discover an old car body on a clean-up day. Multiple dumps were found and removed as part of restoration efforts at Arcadia Dunes thanks to a growing network of volunteers. (Photo by Paula Dreeszen)

Volunteers collect seeds to improve grassland habitat at the Grassland Preserve. (Photo by Angie Lucas)

Local farmers help hay the fields at the Grassland Preserve. Haying is used as a management tool and takes place after grassland birds have nested. (Photo by Angie Lucas)

Volunteer Paula Dreeszen monitors the status of invasive plants at Arcadia Dunes. (Photo courtesy of GTRLC)

A volunteer shoulders a baby's breath plant removed from Old Baldy. Baby's breath is an invasive species that poses a serious threat to the fragile dune habitat. Its deep tap root (up to 12 feet) makes it challenging to remove. (Photo by Paula Dreeszen)

Birders gather for a field trip at Arcadia Dunes. During bird blitzes they frequently find and record 2,000 individual birds representing 90 different species. (Photo by Angie Lucas)

A visitor joyously runs down Old Baldy, a cherished tradition for generations of families. (Photo by Heather Shumaker)

A trail through the trillium invites visitors to explore Arcadia Dunes. More than fifteen miles of sustainably-designed trails wind through the nature preserve. (Photo by Paula Dreeszen)

New orchard trees are being planted at Arcadia Dunes as farmers reclaim farmland lost to them more than forty years ago. (Photo by Heather Shumaker)

Part IV

More
Beginnings
2005-2009

17 Commencement

We set out to save land, but, in the end,
we build community, preserve beauty
and instill hope.

—Land Trust Alliance

Traverse City and Arcadia, Michigan
2005–2006

It wasn't the end, it was the beginning. Just as college graduation is aptly called commencement, we were entering a new era. Commencement of a lifetime—no, of multiple lifetimes—of stewardship. Land protection work is never done; the reward for success is constant vigilance. Now that the Conservancy owned the land, we had to manage it, keep our supporters informed and engaged, and interact with our new neighbors. Our new reality was stewardship: stewardship of the land, stewardship of people.

This new role was not obvious at first. We'd thought we were striving to protect rare shoreline, forests, and farmland. But the Coastal Campaign was mostly a campaign about community. This was the first time the Conservancy had attempted to own a parcel of land that covered a landscape. What we did impacted our neighbors' homes, kids, pastimes, and livelihoods. We were moving into a new neighborhood.

The Coastal Campaign had been exhausting, but the campaign had blessed us with laser focus to achieve one thing: raise a staggering amount of money. Now things got messy.

We quickly discovered that there was not just "one" community. Locals and neighbors were fractured into farmers and view seekers, hikers and mountain bikers, hunters and bird-watchers. There were horse people, dog people, snowmobile people and hang-gliding people. On top of that, there were organic farmers and nonorganic ones, people seeking solitude and people demanding paved access. As we weighed how best to open up 6,000 acres to the public, these factions splintered out.

In the town hall on White Owl Drive, crowds showed up to complain. I knew the scene well: folding metal chairs squeaking and scraping over the tiled linoleum, a facing line of township officials and plainspoken constituents wearing baseball caps and canvas work jackets. I watched as my coworkers came staggering back to the office, surprise and hurt often mixed in their eyes.

We had plans for the land, but it took time to explain our ideas, and time was something I didn't feel we had. My job was to resell the farmland parcels as quickly as possible. Our bank debt was looming, and its size made me quiver. We had to get moving, not only to fulfill our promise and our mission to put the agricultural land back into the hands of farmers, but also to keep ourselves solvent.

Wherever I went—stopping to chat to farmers along the roadside or fielding phone calls in the office—the litany of complaints intensified. Some people were afraid we would cut trees ("This area is supposed to be *preserved!*"), some afraid we would never cut one ("Are you going to let this all grow up? That's a critical air drainage for our orchard!").

"The farmland views are incredible," donors would tell me as I toured them around the back roads. "Where else can you drive for miles and see just farms and no buildings? It's so unique. We especially love the fall color or spring with the orchards in bloom."

An hour later I'd find myself listening to irate farmers responding hotly, "We are not in the business of providing views. We're not in business so you can drive by and see something pretty."

Bicycles became a point of tension in many directions. "These goddamn pedal pushers!" cried Brian Putney, standing next to his idling tractor on Joyfield Road. "They think they own the roads. I've got a tractor loaded with cherries and there's pedal pushers trying to pass me. I have to stop my work. They don't even think about whether I can see them. Are you going to bring more bicycles on the roads with this thing?"

Bikes caused trouble in the forest, too. Over the decades of CMS Energy's absentee ownership, a handful of Benzie County residents had constructed jumps and flagged trails for their mountain bikes. Now that we owned the land, their private trail was in jeopardy, and they were hopping mad. "The Conservancy's taking our land away from us!" they cried.

"Get this," said a farmer. "During deer hunting season, a guy in a brown and yellow coat comes by on a mountain bike. Is he crazy? Dressing like a deer in the middle of the woods!"

That great empty time when CMS ignored the property had created people who loved the land, but at the same time they'd begun to consider the land their own. We found the dunes and forest riddled with "social trails"—footpaths and bike paths that people had privately created. These paths ran this way and that, tracing routes where hundreds of individuals liked to go, but not following the land's contours. Now even more people were coming to visit the property and following these haphazard trails. Erosion was on the rise, especially in the sensitive dune area.

Clashes over visions for the land continued. Every fear was different, but equally heartfelt:

"What about horses? I always take my horse up here," or "Don't allow horses. They cause terrible erosion and mess up the trails."

"We've snowmobiled this area all our lives . . . we've always had access to hunt or mushroom here . . . the Conservancy's going to take it away," people cried.

Suddenly the world had flipped. We were no longer the heroes coming to save the land, we were the new landlord, and everyone had a complaint. People had trusted us to save the land from condominiums. Now they would have to trust us to manage it.

In the early shadows of dawn each day, Glen set out on his ritual run. He jogged down Whispering Trails, his two dogs, Laddie and Cherry, beside him. The dirt road was soft underfoot and there was very little traffic. It was good to feel the sudden rush of blood and the northern Michigan air race into his lungs, but once he got to work he couldn't sustain the energy.

At first it had been a relief to have a break. The Coastal Campaign was done. He'd sprinted full bore since the Conservancy's founding day, and now for the first time he got home regularly at 5:30 p.m. He had plenty of time to see the boys after school, walk the dogs, and help Becky with the laundry. He even had time to fix up the barn and feed their two horses, Liberty and Indian Paintbrush. So why did he feel so dejected?

Glen jogged past a neighbor's horse pasture, the Ocanas' apple orchard, and the Manigolds' cherries and vineyard. A red-shouldered hawk sailed above. He saw sunlight strike the painted Bear Paw quilt pattern on his own barn, illuminating the reds, orange, and cream.

He missed the Coastal Campaign, that was it. The intense focus had been oddly freeing. No distractions, no other problems, just clear the decks and concentrate on one goal.

Suddenly there were new, urgent needs everywhere clamoring for attention. The Chain of Lakes in Antrim County. What about a new nature preserve on Green Lake? Glacial Hills? Projects that had been waiting for the Coastal Campaign to end suddenly sprang to life even as Arcadia Dunes, as big as a state park, demanded continual time and resources.

Saving a landscape was so much more complex than it had seemed starting out. The focus had been on CMS and raising enormous sums of money fast. Now came the need to embark on years of careful stewardship. Arcadia needed dump cleanup, fire training, neighbor communication, and a forestry plan. The situation was like a marriage: after the brief moment of glory that was the wedding came day after day, year after year of devoted commitment and hard work.

The charge of adrenaline Glen always felt was slipping away. Sure, the Coastal Campaign days had been crazy, but also uplifting, miraculous, and focused. Now he was dealing with the aftermath, and the slew of meetings gave him a raging headache.

Glen wasn't the only one with a headache. During the Coastal Campaign, Glen had transformed me into the director of the Coastal Program, a position I was not sure I wanted. The original cash-flow plan called for hiring an outsider experienced in managing complex projects. I knew nothing about staff management, nothing about the practical side of land management and, most important, nothing about farming. The extent of my agricultural experience was a backyard garden with tomato plants. Now that negotiations and legal documents were shelved, I was the chief contact for Arcadia farmers and I had to grapple with the practical side of owning 6,000 acres.

Glen was sitting at the lunch table, napkins scattered, chairs askew, the remains of his meal pushed aside, the day he sprang the news on me about my new role. The rest of the staff had long vanished back to their work areas. I was sitting on a nearby filing cabinet swinging my legs as we talked, once again, about the behemoth that was Arcadia. "We were supposed to hire someone for this," I reminded Glen.

He looked back at me, and I realized finally that no outside savior was going to appear. The image of a competent, well-dressed project manager arriving from Pennsylvania, say, with hair brushed neatly to the right and a briefcase in hand, flickered for a last moment, then vanished.

"Who else but you, Heather?" he answered. I wonder if he heard my gulp.

It was true I knew the project details, but I wasn't sure about anything else. This stage was daunting. Much scarier than tapping on CMS's corporate glass windows, trying to attract attention. Taking care of a landscape looked tougher and more perplexing the longer I stared at it. That's what I was mostly doing, staring. Staring at maps pinned to my desk bulletin board, staring out the window at the skyline above the shopping carts, staring back again at the rose- and green-shaded maps, trying to unravel the challenges. A strong part of me longed to return to the simplicity of single land deals, chats with landowners, and options for protecting family land. Instead, I was faced with turning our landscape vision into on-the-ground reality.

In our fundraising pitches we had made grand promises: the dune and forest would be managed to the highest ecological standards, the farmland would continue as a living agricultural landscape. But how to do that? Everyone was looking to me to figure it out.

"When will the bids start?" asked a Benzie County farmer. "We need to get financing lined up."

"Who's going to get a chance to bid on Dry Hill?" asked another. "If you open it up to the wider public, it's going to kill the local fruit businesses."

We were at the Putney Corners church again, pressed into the social hall to start the process of figuring out future farm sales. As usual, I stood up front accompanied only by my maps glued on poster board. Everyone wanted answers, but all I had were more questions.

"I don't know," I said honestly. "Most of the details fall into the great unanswered questions category."

During the earliest fundraising days, the farmers had been wary but welcoming. They were willing to give us a chance but anxious to have plans pinned down as soon as possible. Everything we did up on the Arcadia land seriously impacted their businesses. Only speed and certainty could help them move forward.

I knew how eager farmers were to get the land sales going. Decades of uncertainty over the Arcadia land had left them in a tight position for business decisions. The pressure the farmers felt injected pressure into me. How could we speed this up? How could I figure it all out fast enough? I scheduled regular evening meetings at the church at Putney Corners to gain input and update locals. I wanted to bestow a sense of progress even if I didn't have answers. Everyone was getting older and I knew by now that newly planted fruit trees took ten years to mature before they turned a profit. My impatience merged with the farmers' impatience and filled the hall.

A week later I gave the same update at the Pleasanton Township hall, the restored one-room schoolhouse complete with its bell tower and white-painted clapboards. When I spoke of the urgency, a man in the back spoke up. He was wearing a red flannel checked shirt and introduced himself as Carl, a county commissioner for Manistee County. "Don't hurry," Carl advised. "Take your time. You should set on your decisions for a while, it won't hurt to hold the land for ten years. You have an opportunity that's possibly the greatest in the state. You don't have to rush into anything."

I nodded. He was granting me public permission to slow down. That's what the land needed. We would all age a year or two, but we needed to catch our breath and make good decisions. The choices we made now would last for lifetimes.

About thirty families depended on the Arcadia Dunes farmland through annual licenses when we bought it. I wanted to stop dealing in short-term one-year agreements, but it wasn't possible yet. Making another one-year agreement would mean more fields devoted to corn next year, but Carl was right, to make good long-term plans, we had to live with the short term a while longer. We desperately needed the planning time. I extended the annual farm agreements we'd inherited from CMS, and then we set about, once again, to learn more about the land and its people.

One of the top questions was taxes. Time and again, township board members had protested the great loss of tax revenue when we talked about owning the Consumers land. "If you take it off the tax rolls you'll ruin us!" township officials cried. "What about the schools, what about our kids?"

If the question wasn't coming during a regular Blaine Township Hall meeting, it was coming from Charlotte Putney, who'd been on the township board for thirty-five years, pegging me with questions in the dirt parking lot. Charlotte talked as fast as she drove her flashy black Neon down the rural roads, but the more she talked, the fewer answers I had.

"I don't know," I said. "Let's look into that."

It was quickly obvious that most township trustees had never met their counterparts a few miles over the county border. I introduced them.

We created the new Township Task Force: each township selected members, plus there were district representatives from Benzie and Manistee counties. Together we could sort out any local financial fallout.

The tax impact turned out to be a chimera. Once the members of the Township Task Force viewed the data, they saw that. Most of the taxes CMS Energy had been paying had gone to schools, not local government. When we eventually resold the farmland to private owners, tax revenue would be about the same for the townships and counties. I interviewed all five impacted school districts just to be sure, since the Arcadia project spread over many jurisdictions. The first school official said that the lost tax damage amounted to nothing, and every school official I spoke to echoed that refrain. The hardest hit was the Frankfort-Elberta school district, so I saved that phone call for last.

"It would be the equivalent of having one family with three kids move out of the district," the Frankfort-Elberta superintendent told me. His next comment put my mind completely at ease: "By the way, can we use the site for field trips?"

Finding a few answers gave me confidence in my role of Coastal Program director. I knew how to ask questions and seek out people who could answer them. Maybe that's all project management was: asking questions and making connections to keep things rolling forward. Seeking the right people to answer the school question had been obvious. But who could answer the rest?

For the farm acreage itself, I turned to the farmers. "Farmers" might sound like a unified group, but I knew now that Arcadia farmers were individual and opinionated. Friendly and knowledgeable, but subject to the usual share of small-town tensions. Still, there was nothing to do but dive in. I met with Putneys, Smeltzers, Evanses, and others. Families who displayed green centennial plaques in their yards, showing they'd farmed the area for a hundred years, and families who'd started farming more recently. I began to visit these houses, sitting at kitchen tables with Arcadia families, listening to stories. I trusted that if I listened and learned enough, we could sort out the right strategy.

Back at my desk, I stared at the shuffle of cars and grocery carts on the blacktop below. This very spot had been a forested hillside, back when the Conservancy office lodged on Third Street. We didn't usually have the chance to impact land-use decisions, but here I was with a grand opportunity in front of me. How to give this chance its due?

One of the pressing jobs ahead was to draft conservation restrictions on the Arcadia farmland. We were planning to sell thousands of farm acres back to farmers, but this land would still be protected. We'd shave off the development rights—no houses allowed—but keep the land available for farm activity, whether this meant clearing land or cultivating crops. I'd written many conservation easements before, but all my previous easements had been designed for natural lands. Wild-land easements were much more restrictive since they were trying to protect the ecological structure of the land as well as its scenic views. Of course, the Conservancy had dealt with plenty of farmland conservation easements in its history, but this was different. We'd be developing restrictions for multiple land parcels, impacting a whole landscape. Removing development rights would work—there were no houses on the Arcadia land now—but how would other restrictions hold up in the future? That was always the great untested question when it came to conservation easements. Foreseeing the unforeseeable.

What would happen if I opened up the process? It had worked once already. What if I invited a group of farmers to advise me, similar to the Township Task Force group I'd cobbled together to answer school tax questions? I'd gain insight, for sure, and my plan might gain legitimacy.

"We're going to need your help to draft a good set of restrictions," I said during home visits. "Who do you think would be good?" The same names kept coming up: Mike Evans, Bill Lentz, Larry Lindgren, and Brian Putney. I was grateful for the names they offered. These farmers were selected by their neighbors and peers. With their help we could figure things out.

A few days later, I sat in the conference room staring at the Conservancy's mission statement emblazoned in teal paint on the opposite wall. When we moved offices and gained a boardroom, everyone had thought it was a good idea to have the mission painted in unforgettably bold letters on the wall. Straying from our mission was always a danger for nonprofits; it even had a name: mission creep.

The mission clearly read: "To protect significant natural, scenic and farm lands, now and for all future generations." It didn't say anything about recreation as a goal. We had the chance to create an amazing new network of trails at Arcadia; should we do it? Or was recreation outside our mission?

That was the issue that puzzled and plagued me. It was one thing to improve old social trails—trails haphazardly formed over the years by human feet or deer hooves—but should the Conservancy be in the business of creating new ones? Our mission didn't say anything about it. We weren't a recreation group. But how often are you granted a landscape?

I couldn't shake the thought that here was a rare opportunity. A chance for a new network of hiking and cross-country ski trails—miles of them—trails that would lightly impact the landscape but deeply influence the people who visited. The idea of new trails arcing over the landscape called me. I felt we had to look into the possibility of recreational trails, even if the idea was ultimately discarded, so I hired a consultant from Trail Solutions, Scott, whose expertise was ecologically responsible, sustainable trails.

I envied Scott his job. He traveled the country walking gorgeous natural areas and laying out new trail routes. The work required hiking and imagination. I was a little put off by Trail Solutions' parent company, however, the International Mountain Biking Association. Fast-moving bikers didn't fit with my hiker's view of the world. How could you notice a red-eyed vireo or a wintergreen berry if you were whizzing by on a bike? Besides, bikes in the woods seemed to tear up the land.

"That's because most trails aren't designed well," explained Scott. He described how a sustainable trail fits into the contours of the land and needs minimal maintenance over time. A torn-up trail meant a poorly planned one. A good initial design and careful construction were key. I still didn't like bikes in the woods, but I knew many outdoor enthusiasts did. Arcadia couldn't remain my pet project; it was land for everyone. I was willing to give it a try.

Scott wandered the Arcadia land marking potential trails with his GPS. Altogether he flagged twelve miles of low-maintenance and ecologically sensitive trails. It looked promising on the new map I hung on my office wall, the potential path marked in blue and red lines. If only we could justify spending Conservancy resources on a recreation trail. Was it just a dream, or would I ever be able to hike it in real life?

Trail design was one of a suite of landscape studies we set in motion that year. The farmers were waiting for answers, biding their time with one-year leases again, but we were using our time well. We dived into investigations on the health and composition of forest stands, orchard air drainage paths, and places where aggressive nonnative species were taking over habitat. Some staff mapped out all the illegal garbage dump sites, marking small ones that were mostly paint cans and large ones that included old car bodies. Then there were boundary-marking plans, hunting plans, and plans for the dunes, grassland, and forest.

The forestry plan took center stage. We'd been saying the words "sustainable forestry" since the beginning when I'd first typed up our one-page dream to save Arcadia. It was time to live up to our ideals. Our goal was to restore the forest's mix of native species and make sure the forest stayed healthy. To save the forest, we might have to cut some trees.

The idea of cutting trees to save trees was hard for nature fans to understand. But chainsaws aren't the enemy—they're just one more tool for conservation. I knew this firsthand from my own chainsaw cutting days in Missouri. There I'd worked with the Nature Conservancy on prairie restoration. On fine days we burned prairies to encourage native plant growth, and on rainy days we sliced down invasive Scotch pines. The Arcadia land was similar in spots. It had stands of red pine plantations, planted to become power poles, and patches of old Christmas tree farms, the spruce and Scotch pine now grown too tall to fit in any holiday living room. The plan was to cut these over time and introduce hemlock, white pine, beech, and maple. Even in the more pristine forest areas the balance of species was off. Logging had targeted certain species like maple and black cherry, and it was up to us to restore diversity to the forest.

Hunting was another area where nature lovers often disagreed. There were all levels of hunting, some justified, some not, but I knew deer were a terror to Michigan's forests. The trouble was there were too many of them. A white-tailed deer is a lovely animal, fleet, alert, and wild. It gives most hearts a thrill as it leaps away, a flash of white tail against its tawny coat. But deer are mowing machines. They chew up forests, killing flowers and young trees indiscriminately. In graduate school, the wildlife ecology students held feasts to eat venison and encouraged hunting. In my field research work with biologists, I'd seen the damage deer do. We erected high fences in the forest to study what the forest floor would look like without deer chomping the plants. The fences had wide holes, allowing rabbits and other critters free access, but blocked deer. Inside the fences the vegetation grew tall. Saplings began to take root. The contrast between the deer ground and the non–deer ground was astonishing. It looked like the difference between the lush tropics and the sparse arctic. At Arcadia we wanted to encourage deer hunting to save our forest.

I chose a forester trusted by the Nature Conservancy to map the forests. We weren't after the typical forestry report. Our forester had to understand our deep ecological goals. If we harvested trees, it wouldn't be for short-term goals or profit. We were in this for the long haul, as long as the trees in the forest.

The grassland area was more perplexing. We'd never taken on large-scale habitat restoration before and we weren't even sure we could afford to own it all. It seemed smart to seek partners. The partner I'd always longed to combine forces with was right nearby, the Little River Band of Ottawa Indians. The tribe had, of course, the deepest reaches to this land of any locals, and their headquarters were in Manistee.

The Little River Band was impressive. Restored federal recognition as a tribe had come only in 1994, but already it had become a force in cutting-edge land conservation. Little River biologists were reintroducing native trumpeter swans, studying bear habitat, and pioneering a lake sturgeon release program in the Manistee River. The band was also actively buying back tribal lands along the river for hunting and land preservation. Thanks to the newly launched Little River casino, the Little River Band had funds to support its visionary work: from building affordable housing and exploring wind energy to amassing a fleet of hydrogen-fueled cars and introducing Native language lessons in Anishinaabemowin to local public schoolchildren.

Glen and I headed out to the grasslands to host the Little River Band one late August afternoon. The new *ogema*, or leader, strode out to meet us at Keillor Road. He arrived swinging his waist-long braids and six-foot-something figure. Was he six foot four? Whatever his height, I felt minute in comparison and had to crane my neck to peer up at him as we discussed land purchase and preservation. Members of the Tribal Council listened in nearby.

"One of our main interests is to buy back our historic land," the ogema said.

We'd looked at the maps together. Roughly half of the Arcadia project fell in the band's historic reservation area. Perhaps in a small way we could be part of righting past wrongs. We needed money and fewer management burdens. It might be possible to sell some of the farmland and grassland to the band, meeting its twin goals of cultural restoration and ecological restoration.

Since the Arcadia property was so big, we toured partly by car. Glen and the ogema rode together. I slipped in the backseat of one of the tribal councilors' cars. It was vintage. Of what vintage I wasn't sure, but the frame was broad and flat, like a 1970s boater. Two Tribal Council members got in the front. The seat springs caved in as I sat down.

"Hey, where do Indians go to buy a car?" the driver called out, turning around in his seat. He answered his own question, grinning at me. "eBay! Got this car on eBay. Hold on."

I braced myself as the car jounced off the road and over rutted fields, springs groaning.

We continued to meet with the Tribal Council over the next few months, exploring ideas, then parted ways amicably. The Little River Band placed its environmental focus further south, close to the river. We took on the entire responsibility of the grassland.

While I was enmeshed in this work, Christine and others agonized over a name for the newly preserved land. We were so used to calling this stretch of land "Consumers" that the corporate name lingered for years. Sometimes we called it CMS or Arcadia/CMS while searching for the right name. We asked the Mott Foundation to name it; the foundation shuttled the question back to us.

Finally we landed on the obvious choice: Arcadia Dunes: The C.S. Mott Nature Preserve. "Arcadia Dunes" was a perfect fit. The ancient Greek region of Arcadia was a remote, mountainous place, where the people supposedly lived in pastoral paradise, herding sheep and singing. Arcadia was the domain of goat-legged Pan, the god of the forest, who symbolized wildness. His courtiers were nymphs and dryads, the spirits of lakes, rivers, and trees. What better model to follow than a utopian vision of farming in harmony with nature?

Of course, there were no shepherds in Michigan's Arcadia. Some farmers raised beef cattle or pastured a few horses, and, of course, there was plenty of cherry farming. The steep terrain mimicked the mountains, though the Greeks surely did not have New World Great Lakes dune ridges in mind. But like the ancient namesake, the Arcadia region had largely sidestepped the modern world. Our Michigan version wasn't utopia, but Arcadia was a worthy name.

Just as we were settling into our new roles as owners of Arcadia Dunes, the tight team at the Conservancy began to reshape. A shared purpose binds talented people together, but collaboration is difficult to sustain. As Christine liked to quote: "The best people to run the revolution are not necessarily the best people to run the government."

The truth was we were human. Although we were committed to our jobs, there were other desires pushing into our lives. Christine had arrived in northern Michigan to nurse her ailing parents. She'd made it clear from the start that she would stay long enough to see her parents through their old age. Now her departure time was drawing near.

"You know I'll be moving back to North Carolina, Glen," Christine warned.

"When?!" Glen asked sharply.

"I'll let you know," said Christine. "But plan on it. We're putting our house up for sale this summer."

"Don't leave, Christine," said Glen. "We need you."

"You don't need me, Glen. You'll be fine."

Meanwhile, Glen was busy packing his own suitcase and brushing up on his high school Spanish. He was headed to Costa Rica with his family for a sabbatical. The boys were excited to see monkeys, quetzals, and toucans, and afterward Glen was planning a conservationist's pilgrimage to the western U.S. states. He was eager to pay homage to Teddy Roosevelt, see Yellowstone, and drink up the spirit of John Muir in Yosemite's wilderness.

I continued forward. As reports came in from foresters and biologists, the questions about what to do with the natural land simplified. We had a rough idea of where the best wild land was, and adjusted the boundary lines as we learned more: sometimes for access, so visitors could have a good trailhead, sometimes for biological reasons.

About this time, my coworker Brad approached me, map in hand. "You know, there's a part of the forest slated for resale here," he said. "Abby's been walking it. She thinks it should be part of the nature preserve, not sold to farmers. It's rich woods, full of mature trees and spring ephemerals. We've been calling it 'Abby's Woods.'"

Abby was a young plant biologist, ten years my junior. She'd grown up loving natural areas and learned plant identification from her ecologist father. When I first met her she'd been a Pop-Tart-eating college intern. Now she was grown up, married, and a key part of the Conservancy stewardship staff. Abby was one of those people who noticed wild orchids and cared about unusual sedges. If Abby thought we should add this 144-acre tract to the Conservancy-owned natural area, I was in full favor. I walked the land she'd pointed out and redrew the map again. Like Carl's black-and-white warbler habitat to the north, this woods was worth keeping. It also fit with our goals for the farmland. If we could own the land we *really* cared about, then it would be easier to let the farmers manage their land independently, free of micromanagement. Abby's Woods would stay.

I watched Christine make plans for departure. Step by step, she sold her house, found a new one close to her husband's family, and set herself up saving rivers with another nonprofit out east.

I waited for the stab in my heart to come, the one I usually felt when coworkers left for a new job. I typically felt a knot of abandonment twisted together with fear that things would fall apart. But this time the stab didn't come. Christine had played a pivotal role, but she was moving on. The loss wouldn't mean the end of what we'd worked for. After all, we were in the land business. Land and species measured life in geologic time. People were all ephemeral. We stopped in for a time and did our part to help lands like Arcadia, but the real test of land protection was to see if it could last. Far into the geologic future. Beyond Christine. Beyond Glen or me. Beyond us all.

18 Aftermath

What I stand for is what I stand on.

—Wendell Berry

Traverse City and Arcadia, Michigan
2006–2007

Dori's uncle Oscar sat looking out the west windows of his cottage and fumed. At age ninety-four, he used a lift chair now. From his station in the living room he could see the play of reflections on beech leaves, pine, and cedar boughs as Lake Michigan sparkled below. But although he loved the lake, today he hardly saw it. He sat heavily in his lift chair, his age-spotted hands curled on the armrests. Where was Glen? Where was the Conservancy? He'd donated the first-ever conservation easement while the Conservancy was still being hatched. He'd donated generously to the Coastal Campaign. Now they collected his pledge checks efficiently each year, but he never saw them.

Oscar wasn't the only donor who fretted. People had stretched and given generous gifts. In return they were used to feeling part of something grand. During the heady Coastal Campaign days they had been accustomed to receiving regular campaign updates, visits, phone calls, and cheerful postcards. Sure, it had emptied their pockets, but it had been fun. Now nothing. Silence.

Kate quietly panicked. Kate had joined the Conservancy just before the mayhem of the Coastal Campaign, an unusual time for fundraising, when money appeared to float in magically. She and her remaining fundraising colleagues had little experience with "typical" years. Now, with

Christine gone, Kate sat in her office squirming on the enormous exercise ball she used as a chair. The room was arranged following feng shui principles, complete with seafoam green walls and glass sculptures and mirrors placed strategically about her desk. Today, however, her room environment wasn't calming her. How could she meet the Conservancy's growing budget needs? What was the post-campaign plan?

Kate peered at the guide to capital campaigns that had always been spread open as a reference during the Coastal Campaign. She looked in the back chapters. Was there anything about what to do *after* the campaign? The book yielded no results, and neither did any others. They all ended when the campaign goal was met. She turned to the computer and searched online for clues. There was plenty of advice about feasibility studies and campaign mode, but after the goal was achieved, the campaign guidance stopped.

Kate picked up a pencil and scratched out a fundraising plan to meet the looming year-end budget. She wrote six bullet points, then stared at what she'd written. This penciled list was a far cry from the sophistication of the Coastal Campaign. She brought the handwritten plan to Glen and together they identified the next step: raise $850,000 before year-end in less than four months. The post-campaign Conservancy was like a child with an insatiable appetite. How could they keep up?

The truth was Arcadia was a burden. A joyous burden, like any newborn, but a burden just the same. The vast acreage and community needed continual care. As any new parent knows, you can't fully grasp beforehand how much having a child will shake up your world. Arcadia was doing the messy, necessary work of transformation.

As Oscar sat by his window, Kate drove to Toronto to learn from fundraising guru Bill Sturtevant. As she drove, Kate mulled over the Conservancy's position. Last year the organization had reached the operating budget, but just barely. It had taken some emergency phone calls to stave off red ink. But the budget was not her main worry. Every day she carried a gnawing fear, and she needed outside expert advice. At the conference, Kate signed up for a one-on-one slot with Bill Sturtevant.

"We finished a big campaign," Kate began. "Now we have thousands of donors we need to steward, but it's been more than a year since they've heard from us."

"A year?"

"Almost eighteen months by now," admitted Kate. It was hard to believe so much time had passed. Of course, everyone involved in the campaign had been exhausted, and then with Glen away, Christine gone, and gaps and changes in staff, it had been a challenge just to meet the operating budget to keep salaries and bills paid. Eighteen months had gone by in a flash.

"Those donors should have been getting contact from you every six weeks," Bill said. "You should be giving them regular updates. On every single action you take on that land."

"Every six weeks," said Kate, shaking her head. "Now what can we do?"

"Kate! How was Toronto?" Glen grinned and gave her a jovial slap on the back. They were standing in the green-speckled-carpeted hall outside Glen's office soon after her return.

Kate did not smile back. "Glen, we need to talk," she said. She slipped into his office and closed the door. "We really screwed up with the coastal donors," she said. She rattled off Bill's advice. Things were really bad. The Conservancy needed a fundraising plan right away.

"What would you give us, a B?" Glen asked, ever hopeful.

"No, Glen, a D," said Kate. "We get a D."

Glen stared at her in disbelief as tears suddenly welled up in his eyes.

The Conservancy was fifteen years old. Like any fifteen-year-old whose legs had shot up too fast, the rest of the body had some catching up to do. The Conservancy had hurtled forward with the invincibility of ado-lescence—now it was time to face up to adult responsibilities.

The future lay in balancing deals with careful stewardship. Stewardship of the land. Stewardship of donors. Stewardship of the nonprofit
itself. Easy to say. Difficult to accomplish.

After Toronto, Glen and Kate scrambled to recontact Coastal Campaign supporters as soon as possible. Kate delivered cherry pies and glass
plaques to special donors. Glen sent email after email, plus handwritten
letters, cards, and notes. They both called on people personally, including
multiple visits to Oscar's house. Dori wrote thank-you notes, and board
members made phone calls. Of course, all Arcadia's supporters had been
properly thanked initially, but Bill was right, the thanking couldn't stop.
Thousands of people had donated to the Coastal Campaign, and thanking people had to continue for the Conservancy to stay strong.

Glen knew what was at stake: all that he had strived for. Arcadia
Dunes plus twenty-five other nature preserves. The Conservancy had
been a deal-making machine. Why, we'd preserved nearly 30,000 acres.
Now the challenge was to endure. To be strong and resilient. To keep the
new friends we'd made through the Coastal Campaign and hopefully
gain lifelong supporters.

I understood what Glen was grappling with. Without a strong Conservancy, the land we'd so painstakingly protected would not really be
protected at all; it would be just a paper park. I'd studied paper parks in
graduate school and knew the consequences. A nature preserve might
look good on paper, but the actual habitat remained vulnerable without
careful management. This was sadly true for many national parks in developing countries, and it was also true at home. Our own Conservancy
nature preserve at Seven Bridges had suffered from illegal logging. We
all knew timber trespass was a real threat, and so were poaching, boundary encroachment, and illegal dumping. Calling a park protected just
because you owned it was the same as passing a law without money or
staff for enforcement. Land guardians had to be on the ground and ever
vigilant. But it took a staff member an hour just to drive to Arcadia to
remove a log that had blown down across a trail. How to be everywhere
when staff was already spread so thin?

The question of good stewardship was never far from Glen's mind, even when he worked at home around the yard that summer. The question followed him as he weeded the grapevines, stabbing the spade into the earth to uproot sumac. The sumac was threatening to choke out the sweet grapes. He had to keep on top of it. He flipped on the portable FM radio in the barn as he pitched hay to the horses. Tunes from Sting, James Taylor, Joni Mitchell, and the Rolling Stones enveloped him. Out by the fire pit he knocked the brush pile down to size, breaking up sticks and feeding them into the flames. Good hands work. Good thinking work. *I never have enough time. Everything takes so much time. What are we doing wrong? What should we be doing?*

Arcadia had been a dream, but now it was a reality, and the burden of caring for the land was intimately tied to the Conservancy's destiny.

A few months later I plopped down in a cushy armchair at the reconfig-ured Conservancy office. Beside me was a new item: a bubbling fish tank. I inspected the fish tank with some curiosity. It gave off a welcoming aura, but besides the bubbling water and pebbles lining the bottom, it was empty. "The fish will come later," a coworker told me.

That day I met Rolf, who joined the Conservancy as a volunteer coordinator. Rolf was a professional matchmaker who exuded quiet con-fidence. He matched volunteer skills and personalities with the right na-ture preserve or project, and already he was starting to discover people who wanted to devote their time to Arcadia. I listened, mesmerized, as Rolf painted his vision: a network of local, trained volunteers who could be the eyes and ears of the Conservancy. People who would continually deepen their relationship with nature.

It was so simple, really. It was the same answer that had surfaced during the final frenzied days of the Coastal Campaign in August. Share the burden. Open up care of the land to the community. Just as we'd shared our fundraising burden, now we would share the task of land management.

When I started working at the Conservancy, the nonprofit had no land stewardship staff. We all fit in a bit of trail weed whacking and boardwalk building in the midst of our regular jobs. Luckily we'd hired stewardship staff since then, and the number had grown to five: Chris, our first-ever stewardship staffer, and plant biologists like Abby. It was Abby and her volunteer crew I was coming to see today.

The air was cool so close to Lake Michigan. I was on my way home after a long field day, but I couldn't resist stopping to see the crowd that had turned out for one of Abby's first-ever garlic mustard–pulling work parties.

The first sound I heard was laughter. Then I saw the bob of Abby's blue knit hat as she bent over next to a trio of women rigged out in gardening hats and gloves. Behind the women another cluster of adults worked nearby. Someone had brought grandchildren, and the kids were alternately tugging at garlic mustard plants and hiding in the mass of green vegetation. Garlic mustard formed a formidable phalanx of thriving plants, all identical, all pushing out native forest species.

"We need to pull the garlic mustard." I remembered Abby's lone voice speaking up in the office conference room some months before. Garlic mustard was a known pest, but the idea of removing it from Arcadia seemed preposterous, especially with all the other demands before us. It was so dominant it seemed unstoppable.

"Pull it?" asked Glen.

"Impossible," someone said.

But Abby was undeterred. She'd researched methods used by the Nature Conservancy and learned it was possible to remove garlic mustard from an area. The plant had a two-year life cycle, so you had to be on top of it and make sure an area was fully cleared. Garlic mustard pulled easily. The idea was to get the taproot. She already pulled it wherever she walked, but to eradicate garlic mustard fully from Arcadia she'd need people power.

Now I had to smile. Abby's group had already made a sizeable dent in the flourishing stands of garlic mustard. Behind them were piles of uprooted plants waiting to be hauled off. With Rolf's support finding more volunteers, Abby's dream might not be so far fetched. Slowly, acre by acre, careful stewardship could transform Arcadia. I bent down and began pulling at the garlic mustard roots.

The fish tank was soon populated, filled with small, hardy tetras plus a bottom feeder that scoured the rocks. On the phone behind the tank, Rolf organized volunteers and encouraged neighbors to adopt nature preserves. "Friends" groups popped up in every county. Retirees cheerfully wielded weed whackers to keep hiking trails clear and plowed out trailhead parking lots. Now if a log fell across a hiking trail, a local volunteer rolled it to the side or cut an opening, saving Conservancy staff a half-day drive.

A year after Rolf arrived, 150 volunteers dotted the landscape, among them 35 people volunteering to care for coastal nature preserves like Green Point Dunes and Arcadia. Paula Dreeszen was one of them, a bird lover so passionate about the coast that she became a full-time volunteer for Arcadia, coordinating other volunteers.

I stood in awe of the growing new community. Coastal supporters who had donated money at first were beginning to turn into a loyal brigade of land volunteers. Paula and Rolf offered camaraderie. Belonging. Training in plant identification. Connection and meaning. They reminded people that family, friends, nature, and volunteering were what was important. "Turning toward family, toward community, toward life that's more sustainable," Rolf explained. That's what people were looking for: a return to the land.

Then a secret hope I'd been harboring gained momentum: trail building began. The Conservancy board agreed that establishing new nature trails would not be mission creep. While Abby was leading enthusiastic crews at her garlic mustard–pulling parties, Sarah led trained trail building volunteers. These were folks who enjoyed wielding Macleods and Pulaskis, the tools of trail building. Armed with lessons in how to bench cut and follow the land's natural contour lines, Sarah's team of trail builders created the first new sustainable trail at Arcadia: a loop that circled through a forest on the eastern part of the property, land locally known as Pete's Woods.

I marveled. Those blue and red lines on the maps I'd drawn with the trail expert were becoming reality. Foot by foot, volunteers were creating miles of new first-class nature trails. Ideas and dreams had come to life. We weren't just creating community from the people who'd always lived near Arcadia, we were expanding that community. I watched as the people who built the trail then volunteered again and signed up to be trail ambassadors. It was nothing short of magnificent.

"Sustainability!" Glen cried. He pounded his fist on his office table. The grey-topped circular table took the blow without a shake. *It's used to it,* I thought. Glen's eyes were sparkling and he was in the jovial, passionate mood he'd been in during the early days of the Conservancy, the days when the little round, brown table on Third Street had shaken and quaked with each pounce of Glen's fist. "The Coastal Campaign transformed us!" he cried. "Look, it's not just about the 6,000 acres. The true test of success of this campaign is what it does going forward. It's about what we do next!"

Glen outlined the new sustainability vision. We could handle Arcadia's vastness now, thanks to the influx of volunteers. To reach sustainability with our donors we had to nudge people to care about the Conservancy's full mission. Not just Arcadia. Not just the forest and shoreline near their house. Somehow that same passion for local land had to spread to *all* dunes, all forests, all wetlands and shorelines. To the northern Great Lakes landscape.

"Arcadia was our moon shot!" Glen said. "A project like that is once in a lifetime." He paused, boring his eyes straight into mine and nodding vigorously, willing me to agree with him. I nodded back. I knew what he meant. Arcadia had to be a springboard for more land conservation. We had to transform this burst of goodwill from dune lovers into long-term passion. It was one thing to donate a once-in-a-lifetime gift to save a special spot on the Great Lakes. It was quite another to carry that commitment to broader land conservation.

How do you transfer love to a broader need? A new project emerged to test this goal: Arcadia Marsh.

Located just two miles south of Arcadia Dunes in the coastal village of Arcadia, the marsh might as well have been on a different planet for all the attention it got. To most people, Arcadia Marsh was an unremarkable stretch of water by state highway M-22, soggy edged and lined with cattails. People zipped by in their cars heading north to Frankfort or south to Manistee, barely noting the flat marsh landscape or its inhabitants. After all, goldeneye ducks and common moorhens look about the same as mallard ducks at forty-five miles per hour. Yet Arcadia Marsh was something remarkable—a Great Lakes coastal wetland. Something rare, full of life, and disappearing fast.

Arcadia Marsh looked like a wasteland. Muck dominated. For much of the year, the marsh was a study in brown, from squelchy mud to withered reeds and grass. Compared to the dunes, the view was underwhelming, but Arcadia Marsh was a misunderstood prize.

"This is the sexiest project we have," my coworkers deadpanned.

Great Lakes coastal marshes like these were rare and teeming with biological productivity—nearly as much as a tropical rainforest. The marsh offered a sheltered nursery area for native fish like northern pike. Migratory salmon spawned here—steelhead, coho, and Chinook. The creek supported brown trout. Rare birds like merlins, black-crowned night herons, northern harriers, marsh wrens, black terns, short-eared owls, and least bitterns all lived in the marsh or stopped there on their migratory journeys. The marsh was damaged by weeds, ditches, and roads, but Arcadia Marsh survived as one of the last few Great Lakes coastal estuaries in Michigan.

Arcadia Marsh was a test. Could we sway dune lovers to embrace something new—something flat, brown, and apparently boring? If people could learn to love Arcadia Marsh as well as Arcadia Dunes, we would have achieved a new level of sustainability and community.

19 The Church at Putney Corners

Go to the people
Live with them
Learn from them
Love them.

Start with what they know
Build with what they have
But with the best leaders
When the work is done
The task accomplished
The people will say
"We have done this ourselves!"

—Lao Tzu, 700 BCE

Traverse City and Benzie County, Michigan 2006

Through all this, I was studying farm maps. During the main fundraising and landscape planning stages, the farmers' questions had had to stay on the back burner, but now it was time to dig into the details. How would sales of farmland work? Who would get to bid on the land? What about taxes? Would this project hurt local schools? How would we set prices? Who would go first?

The task before us—creating a fair process to resell farmland—brought to mind a cautionary folktale. An old man walks his donkey to market along with a little boy. The first person he meets cries, "Poor child! Forcing him to walk all that way! He should ride on the donkey." The man lets the child ride, but the next person says, "For shame! Forcing the old man to walk while the child rides." So the boy dismounts and the old man climbs up. The next passerby derides him for over-loading the poor donkey. Finally, the man carries the donkey on his *own* back, tangles the traces on the bridge posts, and they all fall into the river and drown.

I kept this story in mind throughout the months of farmland planning that followed. The Conservancy could collect ideas, but we could not satisfy everyone. We had to stick to our mission. We had to listen, we had to respect people, but ultimately it was up to us to do what we thought was right.

I knew local families relied on Arcadia's Dry Hill land, but the home visits brought this into focus. Some families used the property peripherally as extra acreage to grow feed corn as a cash crop. Some farmers were ready to retire. Others, like the Putneys and Evanses, centered much of their farm operation on the former CMS land. With farmsteads nearby and hundreds of acres at stake, these farmers were vulnerable. If they lost the Dry Hill land, it would be difficult to afford to buy other fruit land. In fact, even driving more than five miles away might make new orchards too expensive. Good fruit land was too far and too pricey.

I had no idea how to divide up 3,500 acres to resell to farmers, but I knew a couple of things: (1) the process must be fair, and (2) we had to stick to our mission. Our mission for the eastern 3,500 acres was to keep the land in active farming and forestry. I also knew I needed help. Input from the local farmers was wonderful, but I also needed dependable input from the Conservancy side. Our staff was swamped. Coworkers came to Arcadia Dunes meetings only sporadically because they were pursuing other projects.

"I need help," I said to Glen. "I need good people to brainstorm with."

"What do you need?" asked Glen.

"Some of the board," I said. "A group of good thinkers who can really concentrate on this with me."

"Pick the people you want," said Glen.

The new Arcadia ad hoc group contained Ed Bradford, Lew Coulter, Tom Palmer, and Jim MacInnes. All bright, calm, and creative thinkers. Ed knew Manistee County and local fruit production, Lew harvested cherries himself and could be counted on for a steady head, Tom was relatively new to the board but was good at cutting through the chaff and sticking to the mission. Jim had been involved in my hire years ago. Although he was not on the board any longer, he understood process, business, and long-range planning to fulfill visions.

We began holding evening meetings after Conservancy staff had gone home for the day. Over turkey gobbler sandwiches, we brainstormed together week after week.

Should farmers get preference? Should we be swayed by sentiment, such as the case of the man who wanted to buy back his grandfather's farm? Should we maximize money so the Conservancy could buy other lands?

"Stick to the mission," urged Tom. "We have to go back to our mission here."

The Arcadia land lay in Michigan's Fruit Belt. Should we favor orchard farming? Should we push for organic farming? Should we structure the process to favor locals?

"Fruit is what's unique about our farmland here," said Ed. "Our process can't hurt the local fruit economy."

"The locals can't be shut out of it," agreed Lew. "They can't compete with bigger guys, even on Old Mission or Leelanau County. Give the locals a chance to go first."

"Playing God could hurt the local economy," added Ed. "We can't get into social engineering. Make the land available for farming, but don't dictate the type of farming."

How could we define local? What if willing buyers owned important conservation land in another part of the county—would we want to accept noncash value? Should current license holders get kicked off the parcel they had been farming for years?

"Set up a fair process, and the farmers will sort it out," said Ed. "There's going to be horse trading."

How could we favor fruit farming without dictating how to farm? What about buildings? If our mission included saving scenic views, what would farm buildings do to the landscape?

"We have got to craft things so it makes sense to people who have to live with it," said Tom. "How well will the conservation easement survive through time? It's got to be practical."

And overall, we faced the big question: which land should we not sell at all but keep in the Conservancy's ownership?

"Do what the land tells you," insisted Jim MacInnes.

The question of which parcels to sell in what configurations would come clear once we got to know the land better. Once again I followed Jim's advice and studied the land, integrating all our landscape studies—the forest inventory, trail layout, grasslands, mineral study, and a new farmland inventory with an emphasis on fruit land.

The former county extension agent mapped good farmland, marking air drainage pathways and prime fruit land. Everyone who lived in northern lower Michigan knew the region was known for its excellent fruit sites, but some land was better than others. The best fruit land combined well-drained loamy soils with proximity to the Great Lake. The big lake moderated temperatures on the coastal and peninsular sites, and within this Fruit Belt, each land parcel varied. The best sites had high elevation and good airflow to avoid killer frosts. I tucked this new landscape knowledge beside my background in forest ecology. To do this job right I'd have to consider fruit sites plus infrastructure needs like farm stands, irrigation, fencing, and cooling pads.

By the end of a year, we'd mulled over the questions enough to have produced answers. Sustainable agriculture included the economy, the community, and the environment. If our goal was to identify unique farmland and keep it in active agriculture, then that pointed to supporting fruit land and doing our best not to hurt the local economy. We would hold a bid process but invite local farmers to bid in a special early round. "Locals" would be current license holders no matter where they lived, plus farmers who had at least half of their operation based in Benzie and Manistee counties. Farmers with active licenses could match the winning offer on their leased land. Any land that did not sell during the first round of bids would be open to the general public.

As for the land the Conservancy would keep, we would own all the highest-quality forest and dune land plus a buffer around a marvelous new trail system. Trails did belong as part of our mission at Arcadia. This was something I was most proud of. The design included more than twelve miles of new trails, still unbuilt, but located with satellite precision on the map.

As for the land we would resell, we had to give the new owners flexibility. If we cared *so much* that we were not prepared to have the land cleared, cut, or rearranged for farming's sake, then we should set that land aside as a nature preserve. And as for dictating farming practices, organic farming might come of age on its own, but we would let the market make that change.

Then, of course, we had to create a document that would be strong enough to protect the farmland we were selling. The Conservancy had written scores of conservation easements by this point, but farmland preservation easements were always tricky. How do you craft words that will protect land and views but will be flexible enough to move through the ages? Farming practices change. Farming with draft horses gave way to diesel tractors in a few decades. Now farmers use GPS to help lay out their crops. State and federal rules change. How could we begin to lock in rules to follow? I followed the advisory group's guidelines and created a draft document. Then I brought our vision to the staff.

The Conservancy now had a staff of twenty. Except for an intern or two, every staff member reported directly to Glen. I was "director" of the Coastal Program only by title. I came to learn that being director meant assuming all the responsibilities but none of the decision-making power.

After seven months of meetings and studies, the picture had become clear. I knew how the farm sales should proceed at Arcadia Dunes. We would do what the land told us, stick to our mission, and not play God. I showed the draft conservation easement to an overflowing team meeting.

Everyone was there, including a new intern who had started two weeks before. Bit by bit, the carefully constructed conservation terms began to fall apart.

You can't allow fences! You need approval before cutting any trees. You can't let farmers have small buildings. They need to check with us before putting in an electric line. No, they can't divide the land into two parcels. Even the intern chimed in: "You can't allow hoop houses. I've seen them. Those things are ugly."

Item after item got struck down. New rules were imposed, new language added for micromanagement. I had never written a farmland conservation easement before—my specialty was natural habitats—but I knew that if the Conservancy truly meant to follow its mission of promoting active agriculture on the back 3,500 acres, then it would have to ease up and allow people a little elbow room to actually farm. If the land was so exceptional that it could not be farmed at all, then it should be managed as natural habitat or included directly in the nature preserve.

I watched the destruction of the plans, stunned. The staff had just turned the farmland preservation terms inside out. I knew the farmers now. I knew what would break the deal for them. This concoction of rules was headed for an explosion.

I called Tom Palmer, the board vice chair. "Tom? I need you to come to a meeting with the farmers. The staff has me pinned to the wall." Tom had the air of a kindly doctor. He'd be the perfect one for this meeting. He listened well and carried an aura of calm authority about him.

Then I sighed as I sent out advance copies to Mike, Bill, Larry, and Brian, the four local farmers who had agreed to advise us. This was a group I had cobbled together to give us feedback on the conservation easement.

Tom Palmer and I shared the forty-mile drive to Putney Corners. Tucked in the backseat was my colleague Brad. I tried to include Brad in all my meetings. He kept a cool head and was able to change his mind when given new perspectives. He had more farm dirt on his work boots than I did, having helped out on the family farm in Ohio. But most of all,

I was keeping an eye on the future. Someday I would leave. I didn't know when, but I knew it was coming. Brad was my chosen successor, though I hadn't mentioned my plans to him, and I aimed to have the farmers build trust in both of us.

The explosion ignited as soon as the farmers walked in. Mike Evans arrived clutching the draft papers. He did not say hello. His lips stayed firmly pressed together as he took his seat on a metal folding chair. His face was pickled red with anger. Bill Lentz sat down quietly and played with the end of his handlebar moustache. Across from him sat Larry Lindgren, a towering fellow with broad shoulders and a bronze beard. He was also silent.

Brian Putney arrived last. He plunged into the room, producing a framed aerial photo, one that I recognized normally hung on Elaine's kitchen wall. "This here's our home farm," he said.

The photo had been taken several years back. He showed us the changes. How different cherry farming was then and now. "How do you expect us to work with this?" he asked, shaking the draft papers. "We can't do anything!"

"This document is nothing like what we had been talking about with you!" said Mike.

Then Larry spoke up, his deep voice rumbling. He was a corn farmer who presently leased land on Dry Hill, but he was not planning to buy any land. His presence on the committee was for the benefit of the community, not himself. "You just want this to be a place where people can drive by and think it looks nice," he said. "A place where people who gave you money can go on a Sunday drive. You don't want it to be for farming."

"You only really care about the dunes," accused Mike. "You never really wanted the farmland at all. We knew that all along."

Farming is dynamic, they all said. You've got to let it change with the times. You say you want to sell this land to farmers. We can't buy this. No one here would want it with restrictions like that. No one.

"Show us the problems," I said.

"You know what to do, Heather," Tom said on the drive home. "What the farmers are saying fits right in with how our Arcadia committee sees things. You know how to rewrite the easement now."

"Yes, we've got a clear mandate."

The next morning I simplified the farm conservation easements. Our main focus needed to remain keeping the land clear of houses and other buildings. That in itself would do so much for nearby habitat. As a conservation group, it was tempting to stick in additional restrictions to preserve pretty views and require owners to seek permission before cutting any bush or branch, but it wasn't sensible. A landscape wasn't a park, it was a vibrant, living, changing part of the planet. The farmland would be part of this tapestry of working lands and natural areas.

The mantra "Do what the land tells you" echoed in my mind. Except now it was "Do what the land and farmers tell you."

This directive would have surprised me when I first started at the Conservancy, yet now it made perfect sense. We'd promised the eastern Arcadia land would be for farming, active sustainable farming, and we needed to listen to both the land and the people.

The Blaine Christian Church was packed a few weeks later. Two and a half years after the first gathering of anxious neighbors, local families filled the church social hall again. I surveyed the faces. The same plaid shirts, jeans, baseball caps, and work boots crowd, but this time I knew the people who wore them. I'd sat with many of them at their kitchen tables, walked with them on their land, and eaten apples they'd given me fresh from the trees. Collectively, they had offered hours from their evenings, workdays, and family time to figure out details of the plan with me. They had explained their business constraints and in turn listened receptively to the Conservancy's constraints.

Scattered among the room were Conservancy board members. Tom Palmer was there, and Lew Coulter, Ed Bradford, and Bob Marshall. I spotted Arcadia locals like Brad Hopwood. All the farm leaseholders came. As at the first church meeting, the mood was charged with anxiety.

The unspoken concern was no longer: Who are these people? Can we trust them? It was now: We trusted them. Did they listen?

I unveiled the farmland reselling plan. What land the Conservancy would keep and why. How the bids would work and why the locals would go first. I outlined the restriction terms and the reasons. Here and there someone asked a quiet question. When I finished the room was still. I looked at the faces I knew so well. They had relaxed.

From his spot in the back, Bob Marshall gazed around the room and summed up the changed mood in his mind. *By golly,* he thought. *There isn't a single person with any criticism. All the things the Conservancy said in the first place that they were going to do is coming true. They really meant it. It's really going to be all that they said.*

Within twenty minutes, people scraped the grey metal chairs back and folded them against the wall. They shook our hands. They laughed and chatted with neighbors. It was as if Dry Hill itself had let out a tremendous sigh. After thirty-six and a half years, farmers were returning to Arcadia's Dry Hill farmland.

20 Letting Go

Every new beginning comes from
some other beginning's end.

—Seneca

Traverse City and Arcadia Dunes, Michigan 2006

That spring I lingered as I hiked the forest ridges at Arcadia. The loggers' cuts had removed some large black cherries that I still missed, but the forest itself was thriving. I bent to examine the white flying pants of the Dutchman's breeches springing up at the roots of a beech. Above my head, the tree leaves were at the early stage, almost budding out: green tufts visible but still swaddled up, giving the spring wildflowers a fleeting chance to soak up the sunlight. Spring ephemerals, that's what these wild, pioneering woodland flowers are called. Some people cooed over the first sight of tulip and daffodil spears poking through their lawns, but I marked spring by the arrival of spring beauty, Dutchman's breeches, trout lily, and their companions. Soon the tree leaves would burst out, blocking direct sunlight to the forest floor. Then the time allotted to spring ephemerals would be over.

The leaves had been at this same tightly bundled stage three years ago. Three years ago when we'd been preparing for the land's purchase. Three years ago when I'd hiked the dunes on my wedding day and secretly whispered to myself, *We're going to protect you, we're going to protect you.* Arcadia's story had interwoven into my life for eight years, but I wondered at my place in its future.

I was feeling ephemeral myself. My soul ached daily as I dropped my son, Alexander, at daycare. No longer did I come to work with single-minded passion for land conservation. My heart was split in two—between Arcadia and Alexander.

These thoughts were never far from my mind as I bicycled along the bay, pulling Alexander in a bike trailer behind me. At Clinch Park the bike path curved around a statue set in a flowerbed. The statue showed a parent with a bronze arm reaching out in a protective gesture. Ahead of the parent wobbled a child mounted on a bicycle. No training wheels. In this bronze version, the child will never crash and skin her knee, but you can sense the parent's mixed anguish and joy over this new stage of independence. The sculpture is entitled *Time to Let Go.*

Alexander wasn't old enough to even pedal a tricycle yet, but I could relate to the joy and anguish of stepping back. It was time for me to let go of Arcadia.

The master-planning and deal-making days were over. I had played a part, but this was a new era. The landscape needed so much attention, from habitat restoration to volunteer coordination. Now there would be years—hopefully centuries—of watchful care. It was time for the leaves to bud out and the early flowers to fade away.

I scanned the months ahead, eyeing the date I would resign. There was no good time to leave, but staff had a clear direction of what to do next, the stewardship team was skilled, and volunteers had formed a new protective web. In June the first round of farm bids would go out. I bent my mind to the task of tying up loose ends and working myself out of a job.

As I prepared the farmland bid packets, I slipped Brad's business card in the folder instead of mine. It would be exciting to be there for the grand transfer of land, but the farmers needed a new point person now, someone they could rely on. They didn't need me.

"But Heather . . ." began Glen when I told him.

"I'm replaceable," I answered.

We all had to be. Whether we were a new young black cherry establishing itself in the rich loam or a new person discovering the joy of helping a forest landscape, we had to continually replace each other. Here in Arcadia, and everywhere, we had to protect land we cherished, then trust enough to let it go. A forest isn't stagnant. It might look the same year after year, but a healthy forest is dynamic, a changing, living system. We humans who loved the land had to be the same. Coming and going. Nurturing new skills and appreciation in each wave of people, then stepping back and creating a gap of sunlight in the forest for a new tree to grow.

I spent that spring sorting through files and organizing Arcadia Dunes materials into project binders for my successors. My work hours dropped to three-quarters time, and every Friday I stayed home with Alexander. It was time to let the rest of the community care for the land. That's what would make it strong, in fact, that's what would *truly* protect Arcadia: a vast network of people who deeply loved the land and would care for it, season by season, generation by generation. That's what had saved Arcadia Dunes in the first place and that's what it would always need.

In May I prepared a farewell letter and read it aloud to the board and staff. We had come a long way together in eight years.

> When I arrived, there was a small staff of six. We operated by the skin of our teeth out of the Third Street house. We had no fundraising staff, no stewardship staff, and we stored direct mail in the bathtub.
>
> I know the land is in good hands. Thank you especially to the fundraising team who accomplished the impossible to save the dunes. Before starting this job, I wondered how grand it must feel to stand on a piece of land I helped save. It is grand, but it's also humbling, and the view is magnificent wherever you stand.

Afterward, the men shook my hand and congratulated me. "Good for you," they said. "You're doing the absolute best thing you can do for your family. You won't regret it. We'll miss you, but it's the right thing to do."

The women warned against the move. "You won't like it," they cautioned, "being at home with a baby. I hope you know what you're doing."

The women were wrong. Even after the excitement of Arcadia Dunes and years of professional land saving, I savored my new life. Measured days filled with reading, playing, and bicycling around town with Alexander. I was still a Lorax, but now I was a Lorax taking care of a child and pursuing a long-suppressed dream: being a writer.

I had just settled into my new mother-writer life when Glen proposed a get-together. He was perched in his office swivel chair tapping out emails when I arrived. As always, his front bangs were brushed to the right, and his metal watchband slid over his wrist bone, scraping across the table as he moved. Glen scooted his chair over to me and poured a mug of herbal tea to go with his take-out tacos.

"You want to be a writer?" he asked. "Someone needs to write the story of the Coastal Campaign. We need to share it with the world. Our mistakes, our boldness, our success. What a story!"

The next thing I knew Glen was proposing that I write a book about saving Arcadia.

"I'm too close to it, Glen," I protested. "I need some distance first. Let's wait a year or two."

"Great, we'll get a grant," said Glen.

It seemed my involvement in the Arcadia story was not over yet.

"We got it all figured out!" exclaimed Brian Putney. He was on the phone with Brad after the unveiling of the farm sale plan. It was June 2006, and the first bidding round for Arcadia's Dry Hill farmland was open for local farmers.

I was home with my young son, immersed in the world of board books with stiff cardboard pages and wooden blocks scattered over the living room floor. Alexander was gleefully into the dumping stage. When Brad called to give me an update my mind shifted. I could see the familiar Arcadia map again, and images of the farmers' faces floated in my mind when Brad mentioned their names. I knew the Arcadia farmland sales by heart. On the block were 1,300 acres labeled as parcels A, B, G, H, K, L, N, O, S, and T.

Brad filled me in as the bids rolled in. I listened, rapt. It was unfolding just as I'd hoped. There was horse trading, as the advisory group had predicted. The Arcadia farmers had hashed out between themselves who would bid for each parcel of land. I felt my heart glow as I heard the results of each sale, and the glow kept expanding.

Charlotte Putney bought back her home farm—120 acres where she and her husband, Ken, had first started out as a married couple, nearly fifty years ago. Putney Beef or Fruit, Brian's family's operation, bought a total of 263 acres. Larry Lathwell, a corn grower, and some others bid on the land they'd been licensing, but then flipped the land immediately to local fruit growers. Calvin Lutz, a large farmer from Manistee, bought several parcels, 436 acres in all, for orchards and Christmas trees.

Mike and Mark Evans of Evans Brothers Orchards bought 266 acres near their home orchard on Joyfield Road. This news especially pleased me. The Evans brothers were among the most eager to get trees planted, and I wasn't surprised to hear they already had 4,000 young apple trees on order with the nursery.

"We've been ordering a new batch of trees each year since 2004," Mike said. "Just to be ready. Just in case the deal with the Conservancy came through." Each year they'd been selling these extra tree orders to other farmers. But not this year. This year young Jonagolds, Empires, and Idareds would go in the ground at Arcadia come spring.

Our farm sales had only just begun—there would be another round of land parcels up for sale next year—but already the land transfer was stretching beyond Arcadia to impact local business. From Brad and others I learned that the Smeltzer family fruit-processing plant nearby on Joyfield Road was also looking to the future. When all the new trees on Dry Hill started coming into production, they'd have to add a new line to handle the additional fruit coming off the Arcadia land.

21 Heart and Soul

It's better to shoot for the moon and hit a star
than aim for the gatepost and miss.

—Favorite saying of Vera Kraft Noble

Arcadia Dunes, Michigan
2009

There's hope on Dry Hill once more. When I drive up the ridge past Putney Corners, up the Arcadia Dunes backlands, I see vast changes. The fields of ancient, wizened trunks are gone. Ever since the farm sales, Evans Brothers Orchards, Snyder Farm, and others have been pulling out old trees and planting neat rows of thin saplings.

The grant Glen talked about to write a book was approved, and here I am back on the Arcadia land again, this time as a writer and storyteller. I interview my old colleagues, sit at more farm kitchens, and drive the roads again, the roads Gerald Derks had traveled so long ago. It's been three years since I left the Conservancy. Before me a new story about Arcadia unfolds, and I'm witness to its joy.

Mike and Mark Evans have big plans. Besides the 4,000 apple trees they planted the first year, Evans Brothers Orchards planted 3,400 trees this spring, and they've got 6,000 apple and cherry trees on order with the nursery.

"By the time those cherry trees I just planted start being productive, I'm going to be sixty," Mike says. "We look so long term, it's crazy to the rest of the world. It's hard for farmers to retire because they're so interested to see the next thing. It's the trees down the road you're excited about."

The old trees Mike and his brother pulled were seventy to seventy-four years old, long past prime for an apple tree. They're trying out a new apple variety called SweeTango and experimenting with wine grapes.

Down the road in a literal sense, Calvin Lutz tends Douglas fir seedlings on 200 acres of his Arcadia land. A Christmas tree farmer, he also grows cherries and apples. He took out stands of overgrown Scotch pine that had languished for decades, and added new fruit trees there. Calvin's Snyder Farm is a big operation, and I'm delighted because it fits well with the Nature Conservancy's original list of preferred agriculture for Arcadia. Christmas trees are the most compatible type of farming the Conservancy could hope for next to its forestland. Calvin is putting in a lot of fir trees and also starting to farm some organic fruit.

Of course I have to stop to see how Elaine Putney is getting on. Elaine is sixty-one and walks with a shuffling step, but her grandkids keep her active. There's a slide and playset out back and a sign staked in the yard proclaiming, "Grandchildren at play." She beams as she talks about Elizabeth, Brian's oldest. Elizabeth, thirteen, showed a steer for the first time at the Manistee County Fair. Her animal weighed in at 1,300 pounds and won reserve champion. The Putney grandchildren also raised a feeder calf and five pigs for the fair. Ten-year-old Lauren's was 300 pounds, and all the grandkids got more than $2 per pound for their pigs. "Of course, they did their homework," Elaine explains. "They worked with the animals since New Year's and made appointments with potential buyers ahead of time. That's how you do it. Then the buyers are in the audience at show time and the kids make a nice deal."

This summer the two oldest girls, Elizabeth and Katelyn, worked the cherry harvest. Elizabeth was on the tractor and cherry shaker, and Katelyn checked the water level and temperature at the cooling pad with Uncle Frank. The next generation of Putneys is on the land.

Talk turns back as well as forward. Elaine's life is much the same. She still uses her grandmother's boiler for canning beans, corn, tomatoes, pears, and peaches, and she still misses Dave. She looks up at the framed wedding picture, then turns to me and tells me about his final days. "When he got sick near the end, we had to travel downstate to see specialists." Elaine suggested they "do something special" and take a trip somewhere.

"No, Mother," answered Dave. "I just want to go home to the farm."

Their home farm on Taylor Road, where Elaine once washed clothes with a wringer Maytag washer, will be up for sale next year in the Conservancy's next round of farm sale bidding. Her son Brian plans to buy it.

Brian Putney and his partners assemble in their shop, around the corner a handful of miles from his mother's house. Brian is in his forties now and has flecks of grey in his dark brown hair. He stands six foot four, the same height as his father. Beside him, also wearing Carhartt vests and baseball caps, are his cousin Adam and uncle Frank. The shop smells of motor oil, and faintly of manure. Six rows of deer antlers hang mounted from the rafters. The barn is next door, and the sound of lowing cattle comes through the splatter of rain on the roof.

The Putneys put in 3,000 trees this spring, concentrating on cherries and dwarf apples on trellises. The Arcadia cornfields they used to till are turning into orchards again. Last year they planted 4,000 cherry trees and 1,000 Honeycrisp, plus Jonagolds and other apples.

They talk about the price of apples for the juice market. The Chinese market is swamping apple farmers, and the price is down to a nickel per pound. But the real reason they're here is to talk to Brad Gerlach, the Conservancy's current Arcadia Dunes staffer, about the Grassland Preserve.

The first bout of grassland restoration was small, focused on a single hayfield. When the Conservancy added a mix of natives like little bluestem and Indiangrass, the new plants came in, but slowly. Now restoration efforts are expanding to a second field, one the Putney family had been farming in corn for years. This ninety-acre parcel was clear of weeds and full of nitrogen when the Conservancy spread its seed mix. Brad describes how the big bluestem and other grasses are coming in gloriously.

Brian nods. "You gotta take care of your dirt," he tells Brad.

Brian talks to Brad about every two weeks. Arcadia has made them partners. Brian mows fields for the Conservancy on the Grassland Preserve, and he offered use of his spraying building when the Conservancy's restoration needed herbicides. Mowing keeps the trees out and allows the grassland plants to thrive. Brian times his mowing around the birds' schedule so the grassland sparrows and bobolinks can nest safely.

I drive down Keillor Road and park at the edge of the Dry Hill Grassland Preserve, which stands at the southern end of the farmland area. As I step onto the open fields, I remember the dry, crunching, tentative steps I took when first evaluating the area with Carl Freeman. That day, a decade ago, he convinced me to consider grassland habitat, not just forest, farm, and dunes. Now I see why.

The area has been transformed. Ten years ago it looked like weedy wasteland. Few species. Cracked earth. Brown bracts of invasive spotted knapweed as far as the eye could see. Back then cornfields were encroaching, and short-grass nesting birds often failed to raise their young because hay mowing disrupted their nests. The future did not look bright.

Now the Grassland Preserve is one of the Conservancy's proudest achievements. Abby and her colleagues started small and began intensive restoration on the hayfield. The goal was to knock out spotted knapweed, that common roadside plant with its pretty purple tufty flower, and encourage native grassland plants to thrive. They cleared the area with mowers and herbicides and then seeded it. Seeds of June grass, Indiangrass, and big and little bluestem. Seeds of horsemint, coneflower, and coreopsis from the Michigan Wildflower Farm. Seeds of hope.

Now I stand and witness the power of restoration. Those first seeds on the forty-seven-acre hayfield have blossomed. The Grassland Preserve is 460 acres, with much of that habitat restored. The stewardship team improved methods, recruited volunteers, and moved on to new restoration tools. Several staff took fire training, since fire is a natural and necessary ingredient for grasslands, and then they conducted prescribed burns. At first the scorched, blackened land always looks dead, but fire clears out persistent vegetation and awakens native plants hiding dormant in the earth. The seedbed is a powerful time capsule. Buried in the soil layers, it contains germs of plants waiting for the right conditions to sprout.

Recently, with local input and advice from a prairie specialist, the Conservancy has started to plant Canada wild rye on the Grassland Preserve. Rye adds nitrogen to the soil, acting as a green manure, and it will also help fight the weed problem. Since rye attacks other plants through chemical warfare, the Conservancy won't have to use as much herbicide when the time comes to plant a new mix of native grasses. Already you can see results from the fire and the rye. Besides the planted bluestem, native plants like pearly everlasting are starting to sprout up, emerging after years from the seedbed.

Birders gather along Keillor Road, part of an Audubon Society field trip, to see what might be living in the restored Grassland Preserve. They spot sandhill cranes, northern harriers, orange-crowned warblers, and nine species of grassland sparrows. The talk is that soon the grassland might host a short-eared owl's nest.

I leave the grassland area, but not before I hear the news that Arcadia's grassland has even attracted international attention. A young biologist from the Bahamas was here last summer to study Arcadia Dunes. Her trip was sponsored by the Nature Conservancy, which sent her north to gain insight into managing nesting habitat for declining bird species. This, perhaps, is the most important link of all. Migratory songbirds, like warblers, have always linked Michigan with the tropics, and now people stewarding the land are starting to connect, too.

From the open grasslands I drive west to the forested interior. Here, in another corner of Arcadia Dunes, the Conservancy's forestry staffer is planning the next round of timber harvest. Vic waves and holds out the maps. This part is thrilling to see: logging in service of the forest itself. Another vision coming to life.

Vic is engaged in sustainable forestry at the highest level. Not just trying to log with a light hand, the way CMS Energy's forester had done, but logging with different goals than profit and board feet in mind. Typical logging targets the most valuable species, trees like cherry and maple that fetch good prices on the market. This leaves a lopsided set of species. Typical cuts also favor straight trees and remove ones that are crooked or disfigured. But crooked, broken, and dead trees provide habitat for forest life, from porcupine dens to insect supplies for pileated woodpeckers.

Logging on the preserve has a different goal: biodiversity and forest restoration. Logging takes place in winter when thick snow cover protects the land, but planning starts now. At times Vic and his forestry team thin maple and beech and then plant hundreds of hemlock seedlings, reintroducing the native mix. They leave some logs lying on the forest floor as nurse logs and shelter.

Vic shows me improvements to the red pine stands. The red pine plantations are a special focus. These blocks of trees are a common sight in Michigan: rows of red pines, planted in soldier-straight lines. The ground is barren under these plantations, and it's easy to visualize the utility poles these skinny, straight trees will become. The Conservancy's forest plan will restore these plantations to true forest by cutting some red pine and mixing in white pine, cherry, basswood, ash, and oak. A naturally grown red pine is a majestic tree. Someday, I know, people will be able to see those natural red pines at the old plantation sites on Arcadia Dunes.

"Here we are restoring prairie, all these trails, the farmland truly being farmed. It's so immense. It's wondrous," says Dori. She's joined me on the front porch of Watervale, plunked down on one if the inn's iconic green wicker porch swings. "I just feel truly humbled by the whole thing."

Dori fills me in about Arcadia Marsh. What we'd always hoped for has happened. Folks are beginning to understand that they must stand up for wild land, whether it comes attached to a pretty view or not. More and more people understand the overall importance of coastal habitat and interest is even spilling into muddy, misunderstood Arcadia Marsh.

Folks miles up the coast from Crystal Downs are donating, plus folks from Traverse City. Arcadia Dunes is showing it's not only a one-time wonder. It's a spark for more. Land is local, but hearts and minds can expand.

Dori turned seventy a few years ago, but she still heads into the kitchen early to make the breakfast coffeecake and start the bread to rising. She hikes to Baldy once a year, though the dune descent is hard on her knees, so she often walks the Conservancy's new trails. At other times you can find her along the roadside cutting bouquets of hot-pink sweet peas or back at the Watervale Inn arranging flowers for the tables. She shares the job of running Watervale with her daughter, Jennie.

Dori spends more of her time in the garden now. Besides Watervale's kitchen herb garden, with plots of basil, dill, oregano, parsley, sage, and thyme right outside the kitchen door, there is also a new coastal garden honoring Watervale donors. Nestled among the flowers are rounded stones, each carved with a message: "God's Glorious Coastline!" "Baldy and Beach Forever," "The Best Week of the Year," "The Magic Place," "A Joy Forever." Dori's own message says: "Shoot for the Moon."

There isn't a day that goes by that Dori does not look out her window and pause in amazement. "It's astonishing. The Coastal Campaign changed everything," she says. "It pulled the whole coast together, it's absolutely wondrous. Blaine Township is a miracle."

A conservation easement protects a mile of Watervale's coast, another conservation easement protects the forestland, and Dori's historic preservation easement protects the old inn and its cottages. Watervale is safe, ensconced in its aura of yesteryear. It's wrapped up by Arcadia Dunes on one side and Green Point Dunes nearby on the other.

Dori's mother died in 2005 at the tail end of the Coastal Campaign. She lived to know Arcadia Dunes was safe, and her garden rock inscription reads simply "Heart & Soul."

A month later it's no time for wicker swings. Ice pellets bombard a group of volunteers who cheerfully show up for a workday in part of the Arcadia forest. It's October and the weather is edging into northern Michigan's winter. Paula Dreeszen leads the group of almost twenty.

Paula herself is a volunteer. She lives locally and commits more than thirty hours a week to Arcadia Dunes. Paula delights in her volunteer job. She hikes the trails in every season, finds new favorite views, and learns more about native plants like yew and trout lily. Paula stretches out her "o's" Wisconsin style. As she talks, you can hear her northern Midwest roots shining through, especially when she invokes childhood hikes to Baldy. "I used to pretend I was on the moon and the big blowouts were craters," she says. "I've been coming here since 1959, ever since I was a baby, and my dad before me."

Today's volunteers hail from Interlochen, Lake Ann, Bear Lake, Platte Lake, and Arcadia, with a good number from the Arcadia Lions Club. Last night they gathered at Sally and Patrick Manke's house over cider and Paula's spicy Wisconsin pumpkin cookies. This morning the coast flings ice pellets, but everyone is dressed in rain gear, and the group good-naturedly sorts glass, cans, old tires, and license plates. Soon they'll move on to the Lions Club for a lunch of coffee, Coney dogs, and chili, but for now they drag a couple of car doors out of the vegetation and sort their finds into old apple bins Brian Putney dropped off.

The landscape of Arcadia is in good hands. Multiple hands.

I think back to a party where dune supporters gathered east of Arcadia Dunes at Misty Acres farm. Our host that summer evening was Naomi Borwell, the same staunch Conservancy supporter who'd hosted our schooner sail along the dunes. It was an evening of singing and celebration. Glen and his brother took turns at the piano playing and singing show tunes. "Nothing comes from nothing," Glen sang. "Nothing ever could, so somewhere in my youth or childhood, I must have done something good."

Dori was there from Watervale, along with Ruth, the nonagenarian Queen of Arcadia, and other villagers. Becky Chown's eyes sparkled as she sang. Nearby David Reese from Crystal Downs belted out a strong baritone. They sang *Hello Dolly," "Edelweiss,"* and then a tune for Green Point Dunes: *The hills are alive with the sound of music!*

As the last summer sun set, the group gathered closer and the melody shifted to a Louis Armstrong classic:

I see trees of green

. . . .

I see skies of blue

. . . .

And I think to myself, what a wonderful world,
Yes, I think to myself, what a wonderful world.

Epilogue
2015

A society grows great when its people
plant trees under whose shade they shall never sit.

—Greek proverb

Abby's Woods, Arcadia Dunes
2015

The story of Arcadia Dunes does not end, but we must leave it somewhere. For each of us, that's a different spot in time.

Abby's Woods was dedicated on a blustery, cold spring day. I arrived at the edge of the forest along with scores of others, my children bundled in rubber boots and mittens. To keep out the wind, the Conservancy had erected a white event tent. Origami cranes hung from the tent poles.

When someone who loves sedges and scarlet tanagers dies, the loss echoes into the natural world. When someone dies young, at age thirty-five, leaving behind a husband and two young children, the loss is incalculable. We lost Abby in January, when a new year was just beginning. Abby, who had been with us since a teenager, Abby, who stuck up for plants, Abby, who managed to find graciousness in the face of brain cancer.

After the dedication, we hiked the trails. Abby had gone, but Abby's Woods was bursting into life. Not the same spring flowers that had bloomed last year, but new individuals of the same species, claiming their spot on the planet. They were flourishing because of Abby's work to banish garlic mustard and give them space to breathe and grow. This is what stewardship and land protection "in perpetuity" means. We can't hold land for ourselves. A landscape must be protected over time as well as space. We must teach others so the land will flourish after we are gone.

Abby had a short time on earth. But in terms of the earth, we're all short-timers. Thirty years. Sixty years. Even ninety years. The days seem long, but it's all so fleeting. We're never here long enough to share time with the trillium and care for the wild. We must care when we can.

Rick is up ahead with the children. It's another spring. The air stirs with the pungent tang of wild leeks and the forest floor is such a carpet of trillium that you have to peer past the nodding heads to spot the other early bloomers: yellow bellflower, the mottled leaves of trout lily, squirrel corn, Dutchman's breeches, and here and there the lingering white and pink stripes of spring beauty.

May always draws me to Arcadia. We pack the children into the car and follow the familiar roads, turning at Putney Corners and winding up the crest of Dry Hill. There's nowhere I'd rather be on Mother's Day. First I carried my children slung in baby carriers as I tromped the trails around the Chestnut Loop or Pete's Woods. These days they dash about.

"There's a jack!" Six-year-old Luke has spied the purple spadix of a jack-in-the-pulpit. He hops ahead to find the next jack and keeps busy at this until he discovers the charms of bloodroot, a plant that seeps reddish juice through its veins. Soon the still air is pierced with giggles and fake cries of agony. My kids have smeared bloodroot on their arms and faces and are staggering about as wounded knights.

All around me, trillium heads nod. Hundreds of white petals in a flank of quiet witness. The children have found sticks now, and are balancing on logs. Logs, the unsung heroes of the forest. There's nothing I like better than to see a nurse log stretched out, cradling a young white pine or oak in its rich, crumbling column of decay. Logs give life and shelter to fungus, salamanders, and white-footed mice, but they also create valuable playgrounds. Each time a child scrambles up on a log and tries to balance, the world is gaining a new advocate for the wild. Logs create Loraxes.

Glen Chown, my fellow Lorax, continues as executive director of the Conservancy. His boys are growing up, the oldest heading out of high school, and Glen nurtures their love of nature through Boy Scouts, camping trips, and hikes to nearby nature preserves. He's proud to say

Arcadia Marsh is now a Conservancy-owned nature preserve, almost 300 acres in size. Next year he'll celebrate twenty-five years of land saving with the Conservancy.

Glen still partners with Helen Taylor, state director of the Nature Conservancy. Her big Upper Peninsula project protects much of the watershed of the Two Hearted River, which lies east of the landscape Ernest Hemingway extolled and is a model for sustainable forestry. Helen vacations at Watervale every summer with her family, and as they walk the dunes, she teaches her children to uproot invasive species.

Ken Whipple, CMS chief executive, had so much fun dabbling in land preservation with the Arcadia Dunes project that he accepted Helen's invitation and became a member of the Nature Conservancy's corporate advisory committee. Whipple continued on the Nature Conservancy's corporate advisor team for many years, even after he retired from CMS.

I think back to the gathering at Naomi Borwell's house, when the air filled with singing. That evening was the last of its kind. Naomi died the following May, leaving her 600-acre estate, Misty Acres, to the Conservancy in her will. It's now a nature preserve and education center.

As I walk the paths, beside young trees quietly growing, I realize the wild lands and farmlands are not the only place where change has arrived. Traverse City has transformed, too, since I first arrived with my ponytail and without my suitcase. The school district added the Martin Luther King Jr. holiday for the first time in 2010. Hundreds of volunteers renovated the historic State Theater, which now brings in films and live broadcasts from sports to opera. There's new vibrancy, as if the town itself has grown up and realizes it's the kind of community that supports books, art, music, film festivals, and local food. The kind of place that makes room for saving Arcadia.

"Saving Arcadia was one of the better things we've ever done," Conservancy friend Nancy Marshall told me. "It was a significant event in our lives. When I think of my life, it was right up there." Her husband currently chairs the Conservancy's board.

On Dry Hill, the Putney family has increased its holdings to 500 acres. Elaine Putney's son, Brian, bought the family homestead land in

2010. Brian is in regular touch with the Conservancy and continues to help out with mowing and management on the Arcadia land.

As for Old Baldy itself, the dune is thriving. A volunteer bucket brigade restored an eroded sand dune. Pitcher's thistle plants drop their seeds in the wind. Visitors enjoy more than fifteen miles of new sustainably designed trails. There is a new lookout platform at the *Sound of Music* spot on Green Point Dunes, and at Betsie Dunes a summer Americorps crew weeds invading baby's breath plants. A bird blitz counted nearly 2,000 birds at Arcadia Dunes, including ninety distinct species. The grasshopper sparrow in the Grassland Preserve was among them.

As I hike the hemlock and pine trails with my family, the days of real estate dealing seem far away. I forget the sacrificial efforts. I forget the near misses and times of despair. The land itself envelops me and I feel humble.

The pileated woodpeckers drum and the porcupines den, unaware that this land dodged an alternate fate. I'm glad they're unaware. The cycles and seasons simply continued according to their rhythms while humans battled over Arcadia Dunes. The wild species will never know they might have been refugees, displaced and searching for a home, or that the nonmobile life—dune grass or great white pine—would have been flooded or crushed on-site. But we know. We remember. We who walk the trails and plant the fields.

Acknowledgments

I am grateful to the generous hearts of those who love the land and were willing to share their story. We are all better off for making room for places like Arcadia Dunes on this earth. Perhaps this tale of forest, farms, and sand dunes can inspire others to save their beloved places.

A special thanks to Glen Chown for his courage and enduring passion for conservation. Thanks go to Glen also for suggesting this book and sharing his life and inner thoughts in its pages. Heartfelt thanks to the entire Chown family for giving of themselves so deeply to the Conservancy.

To Dave Dempsey, fellow author and environmental spokesman, enormous thanks for acting as project advisor from Minnesota. My respect and thanks also to Tom Palmer and his sage head, and to Jennifer Jay, who stood by this book through difficult times, midwifing it with a steady eye across the years.

Deep thanks and gratitude go to Gail Imig, Rick Foster, and trustees of the W. K. Kellogg Foundation for providing funding for the initial research and writing of this book, and to the C. S. Mott Foundation for its visionary leadership and support of the Coastal Campaign.

Additional sincere thanks:

To the folks at CMS Energy who helped make the project a success: Bruce Rasher, Joe Tomasik, Ken Whipple, David Joos, Rodger Kershner, David Barth, and Mary Anne Marr. Also to the board and staff at the Michigan Natural Resources Trust Fund, especially those involved in 2003, who quietly make the world better each year by creating new parks, trails, and natural areas.

To the Dry Hill farming community, particularly Elaine Putney, Charlotte Putney, Brian Putney, Frank Putney, Mike Evans, and Mark Evans for providing interviews, answering my most basic questions, and welcoming me into their homes and farms.

Acknowledgments

To community leaders at Crystal Downs, most especially Chuck and Nancy Brickman, and David and Weezie Reese. Thank you for sharing your time and talents.

To families in the Watervale area who promoted conservation for many years, especially Dori Turner, Steve Kraft, and those whom we remember: Vera Kraft Noble, Oscar Kraft, and Dean Luedders. Also thanks to Keya Kraft for compiling local history about the Arcadia land.

Thanks go to the courageous and dedicated team that worked side by side to shoot for the moon and save Old Baldy. This list properly includes more than 5,000 names, but special mention goes to: Max Bazerman, Reg Bird, Naomi Borwell, Ed Bradford, Chuck and Nancy Brickman, George Burgoyne, Keith Charters, Rob Collier, Lew Coulter, Lois DeBacker, Dana Debel, Steve DeBrabander, Dave Dempsey, Betsy Dole, Rick Foster, Governor Jennifer Granholm, Wayne Kladder, Joe Kochanek, Jim MacInnes, Bob and Nancy Marshall, Chip May, Tom Palmer, Bill and Kathleen Parsons, David and Weezie Reese, Mike Stack, Helen Taylor, Dori Turner, Judy Twigg, Tom Twigg, Bill and Claire White, and the communities of Blaine Township, Pleasanton Township, Arcadia Township, Crystal Downs, Watervale, and Camp Arcadia. You understand life's true values.

And, of course, thanks to my colleagues, the staff and board of the Grand Traverse Regional Land Conservancy, *every one of them,* but especially those who lived at the heart of the Coastal Campaign. Your names are forever inscribed in the dune sands. Special mention to the legions of dedicated volunteers who continue to love and sustain Arcadia Dunes. Eternal thanks to Helen Taylor and staff and supporters of the Nature Conservancy. Your expertise and good work create many Arcadias.

Special thanks to the photographers who offered their talents for the cause of conservation and allowed their work to be included in this book: Christine Arvidson, Paula Dreeszen, John Ester, Carl Freeman, Jim Gibson, Gary Howe, Michael D-L Jordan, Jim Lindner, Angie Lucas, Bob Marshall, and Drew Smith. Thanks also to the *Benzie County Record Patriot* and the *Traverse City Record-Eagle* for allowing excerpts from their articles to be printed.

Acknowledgments

Gratitude to my writing group, the Powerfingers, who give shape to my chapters and scenes and never fail to offer insightful ideas and heartfelt encouragement: Mardi Link, Cari Noga, Anne-Marie Oomen, and Teresa Scollon. Thank you for seeing me through another book. Thanks to my agent, Joëlle Delbourgo, and the book's first editors, Laurie Scheer and Zane Kathryne Schwaiger, who believed in the book early on, and Robin DuBlanc, who polished it. Thanks especially to editor Kathryn Wildfong and the dedicated team at Wayne State University Press, who immediately saw this book about Arcadia as part of the Midwest's story.

Finally, thanks to my parents, who introduced me to the joys of wilderness through years of childhood hikes and camping trips. And to my own family: to my husband, Rick, for keeping supper warm during the long hours of the Coastal Campaign, and to my children, Alexander and Luke, for sharing me during the book's writing and research.

List of Characters

Consumers Power / CMS Energy

Gerald Derks—mysterious stranger who buys land on behalf of Consumers Power

Bill Parfet—board member of CMS Energy

Bill McCormick—CEO, 1985–2002

Rodger Kershner—senior vice president and general counsel at CMS and negotiator on Arcadia project

Ken Whipple—new board chair and CEO in 2002

David Barth—corporate attorney

Joe Tomasik—vice president and negotiator on Arcadia project

Bruce Rasher—director of real estate and negotiator on Arcadia project

Mary Anne Marr—real estate staff

Fritz Duda—developer from Texas who partners with CMS and wants to buy Arcadia Dunes

Arcadia Farmers and Neighbors

Elaine and Dave Putney—orchard farmers on Dry Hill

Brian Putney—son of Elaine and Dave, Dry Hill farmer

Charlotte and Ken Putney—orchard farmers on Dry Hill

Carl Freeman—local bird-watcher, artist, and dragonfly expert

Brad Hopwood—Arcadia resident and ever-watchful Conservancy friend

Mike and Mark Evans—brothers and orchard farmers on Dry Hill

Larry Lindgren—Dry Hill farmer and member of Arcadia farmland committee

Bill Lentz—Dry Hill farmer and member of Arcadia farmland committee

Calvin Lutz—Dry Hill farmer who purchased land during the resale

Watervale Inn

Dori Turner—third-generation innkeeper

Vera Kraft Noble—Dori's mother, and innkeeper before her

Oscar Kraft—the man who bought Watervale when it was an abandoned lumber town and transformed it into cottages for summer visitors

Oscar Kraft—Dori's uncle, a nephew of Oscar Kraft

Steve Kraft—Dori's cousin involved in initial efforts to protect Arcadia Dunes

Dean Luedders—Watervale neighbor involved in initial efforts to protect Arcadia Dunes

Grand Traverse Regional Land Conservancy

Glen Chown—founder and director of the Conservancy, a nonprofit land trust based in Traverse City

Rob Collier—director of Rotary Charities in Traverse City who recruits Glen

Heather Shumaker—land protection specialist

Jim MacInnes—board member, owner of Crystal Mountain resort

Christine Arvidson—Conservancy staff who helps with Coastal Campaign fundraising

Reg Bird—board member, introduces Bill White to Arcadia Dunes

Tom Palmer—board member, works closely with Heather on Arcadia Dunes

Kate Pearson—fundraising staff

Brad Gerlach—land protection specialist

Abby Mahan Gartland—stewardship staff, namesake of Abby's Woods

Rolf von Walthausen—volunteer coordinator

Paula Dreeszen—volunteer at Arcadia Dunes

The Nature Conservancy

Helen Taylor—state director for Michigan

Dave Ewert—senior scientist, Great Lakes program

Max Bazerman—friend of Helen's, negotiation teacher from Harvard Business School and volunteer for the Nature Conservancy

Mott Foundation

Bill White—president of C. S. Mott Foundation

Lois DeBacker—grant-making staff for the foundation

Mike Stack—real estate attorney assigned to Arcadia project

Joe Kochanek—real estate attorney assigned to Arcadia project

Michigan Government

Jennifer Granholm—Michigan governor, 2003–2011

Keith Charters—chair of Natural Resources Commission, long-term member of Michigan Natural Resources Trust Fund board

George Burgoyne—deputy director of Michigan Department of Natural Resources

Rodney Stokes—director of Michigan Department of Natural Resources

Steve Arwood—member of Michigan Natural Resources Trust Fund board

Bob Garner—member of Michigan Natural Resources Trust Fund board

Dave Dempsey—member of Michigan Natural Resources Trust Fund board

Sam Washington—member of Michigan Natural Resources Trust Fund board

Arcadia Dunes Supporters

Chuck and Nancy Brickman—Coastal Campaign supporters, Crystal Downs

David and Weezie Reese—Coastal Campaign supporters, Crystal Downs

Naomi Borwell—long-term Conservancy supporter, host of schooner tour of Arcadia Dunes

Gerard Grabowski—bread baker and Pleasanton Township planner

Ruth Starke Burkhead—lifelong Arcadia resident

Nancy and Bob Marshall—Arcadia residents

Chip May—director of Camp Arcadia, Lutheran summer camp on Lake Michigan

Kathleen and Bill Parsons—lifelong Camp Arcadia campers

3,500-2,000 years ago	Perched dune forms near Arcadia
1860s	European settlement in Arcadia area
1969-1971	Consumers Power Company buys land from farmers
1973	Pumped storage power plant in Ludington opens
1986	Ludington fish-kill lawsuit begins
1988–1989	Early attempts to create nature preserve at Arcadia Dunes
1991	Grand Traverse Regional Land Conservancy forms
1999 (December)	Arcadia land conservation project begins

Timeline of Arcadia Dunes

2000 (July)	First meeting with board member of CMS Energy
2000 (September)	First negotiations with CMS executives
2001 (January)	Six-month Stand Still Agreement with CMS signed
2002 (May)	Bill McCormick resigns; CMS trading scandal
2003 (March)	Gov. Granholm meets with CMS executives; negotiations resume
2003 (May)	Conservancy signs option to buy Arcadia Dunes land
2003 (Summer)	Conservancy and friends raise $5+ million
2003–2005	Coastal Campaign exceeds $30.6 million goal for three dune properties
2006	Farmers buy back land at Arcadia Dunes

Main Sources

Prologue and Part I
Personal Communication

Putney, Charlotte. Interview with author, June 19, 2009.

Putney, Elaine. Interviews with author, September 11, September 29, 2009.

Turner, Dori. Interviews with author, October 9, 2008, October 2, 2009.

Other Primary Sources

Benzie and Manistee Counties. Public title records. Register of Deeds office.

CMS Energy. Records of private correspondence from Arcadia land purchase.

Couvreur, Robert, Michigan Natural Resources Trust Fund. Letter to Dean Luedders, rejecting application #N89-284, Old Baldy, with Dean's notes, August 17, 1989.

Kraft, Keya, compiler. CMS Arcadia property history, 2003.

Luedders, Dean. Letter to Tom Woiwode, director of the Nature Conservancy in Michigan, February 11, 1989.

———. Memo of transcribed phone conversation to Dick Erhardt, Consumers Power, March 10, 1989.

———. Personal history of Dry Hill, June 2003.

Turner, Dori. Letter to Donn Waage, National Fish and Wildlife Foundation, August 22, 2005.

Watervale Preservation Society. Memo of meeting minutes, September 4, 1988.

Wells, Jim, botanist with Cranbrook Institute of Science. Letter to Dori Turner, August 1, 1988.

Published Sources

Albert, Dennis A. *Borne of the Wind: An Introduction to the Ecology of Michigan's Sand Dunes.* Lansing: Michigan Natural Features Inventory, 2000.

"Blaine Land Buying Creates Mystery." *Benzie County Patriot,* December 25, 1969.

CMS Energy Corporation history. In *International Directory of Company Histories,* vol. 14. Chicago: St. James Press, 1996.

"Consumers Mum on Plan for 5,800 Acres." *Traverse City Record-Eagle,* June 18, 1988.

"Consumers Sells 5,700 Acres to Sister Company." *Traverse City Record-Eagle,* September 24, 1989.

Dempsey, Dave. *Ruin and Recovery.* Ann Arbor: University of Michigan Press, 2001.

Howard, John H. *The History of Herring Lake.* Boston: Christopher Publishing, 1929.

McCormick, Bill. Interview by David K. Allison, National Museum of American History, Smithsonian Institute, June 18, 1997, updated September 2002.

Turner, Dori, and Jim Arnold. *Watervale: The Diamond Years, 1917–1992.* Arcadia, MI: self-published, 1992.

"Utilities Settle Fish Killing Case." *Traverse City Record-Eagle,* October 5, 1994.

Part II

Personal Communication

Arvidson, Christine. Interview with author, January 28, 2009.

Bird, Reg. Interviews with author, November 13, 2008, September 8, 2009.

Chown, Glen. Interviews with author, July 8, July 15, July 29, 2008, May 19, September 9, 2009.

Chown, Rebecca. Interview with author, July 16, 2009.

DeBacker, Lois. Interview with author, January 2, 2009.

Grabowski, Gerard. Interview with author, January 13, 2009.

Moon, Lynne. Interview with author, September 29, 2009.

Ratliff, Ty. Interview with author, February 23, 2010.

Reese, David. Interview with author, January 12, July 21, 2009.

Taylor, Helen. Interviews with author, November 18, November 25, 2008, September 3, 2009, May 16, 2016.

Other Primary Sources
Grand Traverse Regional Land Conservancy. Project files.

Published Sources
"Chief of CMS Energy Says He Is Resigning." *New York Times,* May 24, 2002, C1.

"CMS Energy Admits to Bogus Power Trades." *Los Angeles Times,* May 16, 2002.

"CMS Quits Speculative Energy Trades." *Detroit News,* June 27, 2002.

"CMS to Move, Tighten Belt to Save $50 million." *Detroit Free Press,* July 10, 2002, 1.

Part III
Personal Communication

Anderson, Erin. Interviews with author, October 29, December 1, 2008.

Arvidson, Christine. Interviews with author, January 28, September 21, 2009, August 13, 2010.

Bird, Reg. Interview with author, November 13, 2008.

Brickman, Chuck. Interview with author, August 4, 2009.

Brickman, Chuck, and Nancy Brickman. Interviews with author, December 15, 2008, July 21, 2009.

Chown, Glen. Interviews with author, June 25, July 10, 2008, January 6, May 19, September 8, September 9, 2009.

Chown, Rebecca. Interview with author, July 16, 2009.

DeBacker, Lois. Interview with author, January 2, 2009.

Dempsey, Dave. Interview with author, November 25, 2008.

Dole, Betsy. Interview with author, December 12, 2008.

Evans, Mike. Interview with author, December 18, 2008.

Grabowski, Gerard. Interview with author, January 13, 2009.

Harvey, Kurt. Interview with author, June 19, 2009.

Jass, Stephanie. Interview with author, June 19, 2009.

Lambert, Chris. Interview with author, October 7, 2009.

Marshall, Bob, and Nancy Marshall. Interview with author, June 19, 2009.

May, Chip. Interview with author, June 19, 2009.

McGue, Christie. Interview with author, July 16, 2008.

Moon, Lynne. Interview with author, September 29, 2009.

Parsons, Bill, and Kathleen Parsons. Interview with author, September 3, 2009.

Pearson, Kate. Interviews with author, October 29, December 1, 2008, May 19, October 19, 2009.

Putney, Brian. Interview with author, December 3, 2008.

Reese, David. Interviews with author, January 12, July 21, 2009.

Stack, Mike. Interview with author, September 8, 2009.

Taylor, Helen. Interview with author, November 18, 2008.

Turner, Dori. Interviews with author, October 14, 2008, November 20, 2009.

Yetter, Birgit. Interview with author, December 11, 2008.

Other Primary Sources

Arvidson, Christine. Grand Traverse Regional Land Conservancy Coastal Campaign project file.

Granholm, Jennifer. Video of governor's press conference. Michigan Historical Center, Lansing, October 13, 2003.

Michigan Natural Resources Trust Fund. Minutes of Board of Trustees meeting. Clarion Hotel, Lansing, October 15, December 10, 2003.

Published Sources

"Arcadia Land Purchase Is Conservancy's Gem." *Traverse City Record-Eagle,* October 22, 2003.

"CMS Sells Lake Michigan Land." *Detroit News,* October 12, 2003, D1.

"Deal Saves Arcadia Dunes." *Jackson Citizen Patriot,* October 13, 2003, 1.

"Deal Would Preserve Dune Area Forever." *Flint Journal*, October 13, 2003, 1.

"30.6 Million Deal Preserves Dunes." *Grand Rapids Press*, October 13, 2003, 1.

Part IV
Personal Communication

Anderson, Erin. Interviews with author, October 29, December 1, 2008.

Bradford, Ed. Interview with author, January 30, 2009.

Brown, Katie. Interview with author, July 17, 2009.

Chown, Glen. Interviews with author, July 10, July 29, 2008, May 19, September 8, September 14, December 9, 2009.

Dreeszen, Paula. Interview with author, November 1, 2009.

Evans, Mike. Interview with author, December 18, 2008.

Gartland, Abby Mahan. Interview with author, September 18, 2013.

Gerlach, Brad. Interviews with author, June 19, December 11, 2008, August 27, October 16, 2009, September 17, 2013.

Jay, Jennifer. Interviews with author, January 6, December 3, 2009, January 26, 2010.

Kraft, Steve. Interviews with author, February 22, March 15, 2010.

Lane, Vic. Interview with author, February 3, 2010.

Lucas, Angie. Interview with author, September 17, 2013.

Marshall, Bob, and Nancy Marshall. Interview with author, June 19, 2009.

McGue, Christie. Interview with author, December 16, 2008.

Naperala, Sarah. Interviews with author, July 8, 2008, September 23, 2013.

Olds, Megan. Interviews with author, July 8, 2008, January 6, 2009, February 2, 2010.

Palmer, Tom. Interviews with author, January 15, September 17, 2009.

Pearson, Kate. Interviews with author, July 8, October 29, December 1, 2008, May 19, July 21, 2009, January 26, 2010.

Putney, Brian. Interviews with author, October 14, December 3, 2008.

Putney, Charlotte. Interview with author, June 19, 2009.

Putney, Elaine. Interviews with author, September 11, September 29, 2009.

Sullivan, Chris. Interviews with author, January 26, 2010, September 17, 2013.

Taylor, Helen. Interview with author, November 25, 2008.

Turner, Dori. Interview with author, November 20, 2009.

von Walthausen, Rolf. Interview with author, July 8, 2008.

Wolf, Dan. Interview with author, January 15, 2009.

Other Primary Sources

Grand Traverse Regional Land Conservancy project files.

About the Author

Heather Shumaker has worked in land conservation for two decades and was coastal program director for protecting Arcadia Dunes. She has a master of science degree in land resources from the University of Wisconsin–Madison and is a national speaker and author of *It's OK Not to Share* and *It's OK to Go Up the Slide*. She lives in northern Michigan with her family.

Photo by John Robert Williams